The Panama Canal and Caribbean Cruise Companion

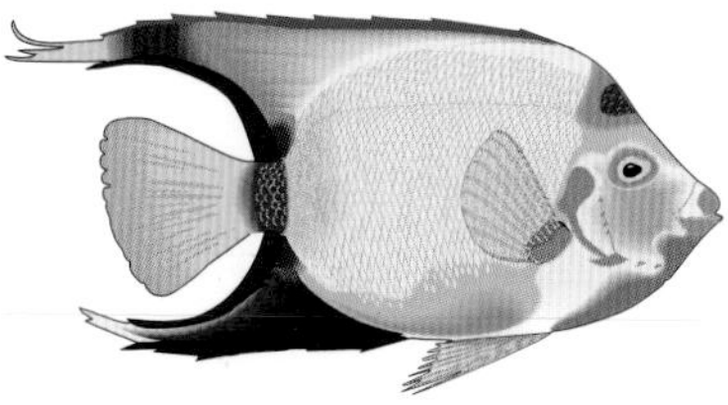

The Panama Canal and Caribbean Cruise Companion

By Joe Upton

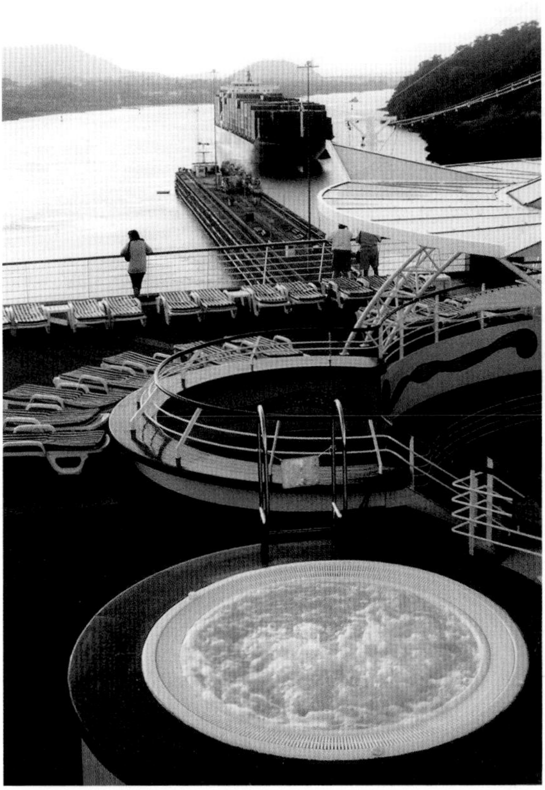

A Princess Cruises Companion Book

The maps in this book are not to be used for navigation.

2004 Edition

Coastal Publishing, Inc.
15166 Skogen Lane, Bainbridge Island, WA. 98110

Maps by Joe Upton
Design by Martha Brouwer

Photographs by Joe Upton unless noted with the following abbreviations:
DV - Digital Vision, Inc.
PG - Photogear
LC - Library of Congress
NA - National Archives & Records Administration
SFM - San Francisco Maritime Museum
SHERMAN - Gerald Fitgerald Sherman

ISBN 0-9645682-6-8

Printed in China

For

Mary Lou, Matthew,

and Katherine Anne,

explorers all.

CONTENTS

Section I: Panama: Building the Great Canal 11

Section II: The Thorny Path: A Family Journey 112

Section III: The Ports: 211

Ft. Lauderdale 212
The Bahamas 215
Princess Cays 218
Turks and Caicos Islands 220
Puerto Rico 222
Culebra and Vieques 226
US Virgin Islands 227
British Virgin Islands 234
Saint Martin/Sint Maarten 240
Anguilla 244
Saint Barthélemy 246
Saint Kitts and Nevis 250
Antigua 254
Dominica 262
Barbados 266
Saint Lucia 270
St. Vincent 274
Granada 278
Aruba 282
Curaçao 286
Cartagena, Colombia 290
Grand Cayman 294
Cozumel 300
Costa Maya 306
Belize 308

Other Sections:
Virgin Islands Scrapbook 232
Under the Sea 258
The Mayan Riviera 298
Exploring Mayan Ruins 304

Above: snorkelers at Dominica.

Opposite page: native craft vendors at Colón, Panama.

Cozumel, Mexico. Notice the remarkable clarity of the water. There are many ways to experience underwater life here–glass bottom style boats, real submarines like the Atlantis, scuba gear or just a plain old mask and snorkel.

To the Princess Traveler

In the spring of 2003, I overheard a conversation on a cruise ship as we were leaving Belize City. "You go ashore?" said one passenger. "Yeah," came the answer, "not much there."

I was stunned. My wife and I had taken a dive excursion out to one of the many reefs that are that country's most remarkable feature. We took the tender ashore to the new visitor center on the waterfront. There were several ships anchored off the shallow port, and the visitor center where the tenders from the ship landed was busy. It was crowded with people getting ready to explore on one or another of the many available excursions.

Forty-five minutes later we were flying in a Caravan–a large single engine plane that carries 18 people–over the amazingly clear waters of Belize. Here was the longest continuous coral reef of anywhere in the Caribbean and our little group marveled at what passed below us. The shapes of large rays were clearly visible moving slowly over the bottom. We passed over tiny islands barely larger than a quarter acre lot with all you'd need to live there–a small shack and a beach to pull your boat up on.

We landed at a small landing strip and a guy from the dive shop met us and showed us the path through the sand streets of a sleepy village to the beach. Thirty minutes later we were motoring over the turquoise waters. We anchored near a cut in the coral reef, and the first thing we saw when we jumped in was an eagle ray that must have been four feet across rooting violently at the sea floor in an effort to find crabs to eat. It was an amazing sight. Another ten minutes in the boat took us to Shark and Ray Alley, a spot where fishermen used to clean their catches at a tiny island. A hurricane had washed the island totally away, but the sharks and rays kept coming. Now it was a Marine Park, and a couple dozen other snorkelers were there, paddling or sitting in the boats watching the scene.

We could clearly see the dark shapes of the big rays as they moved among the swimmers and snorkelers. When we jumped in, a powerful sight was waiting–three big rays, as interested in us as we were with them. They moved among us, and our dive master stroked and played with them. As big as the eagle ray, and perhaps a hundred pounds or more, they'd pass just inches away from us, swimming with slow undulations of their powerful wings. Lurking in the distance were the shadowy shapes of the sharks, but we were content to have them keep their distance.

Back on the ship our daughter told us of her day–she'd gone with a friend on a bus to a place where you walked 45 minutes through the jungle carrying an inner tube, then put on a miner's style headlamp to tube down a river that disappeared into a cave. Sometimes it was almost totally dark except for their headlamp beams shining out on the odd rock formations. And in other places a shaft of sunlight would penetrate through a crack in the cave's roof, and beam down into the clear water.

In Barbados, a few years earlier, I'd come on the *Sun Princess*. Our excursion was just a half dozen of us in a rattling old van, bouncing over the back roads, as our guide filled us with tales of local history, all in the rich West Indian version of the King's English.

In Dominica on the same cruise, I went on an excursion with just eight others. At an exquisite small fishing village, we got into kayaks and paddled along the shore. After a couple of hours, we beached the kayaks, and swam out to the dive boat to snorkel a place where volcanic gases were bubbling up out of the bottom, and the water was filled with brilliantly colored small fish. It was an incredible day.

Big ship or small, a trip among these islands is an exciting opportunity to explore off the beaten path.

Don't miss any of it!

Your mapmaker at Lemeseur Bay, US Virgin Islands, 1999.

Almost a mile long, four years in the building, these locks are one of the largest manmade structures in the world.

Pacific lock gates under construction, 1913.
NA 185-G-0538

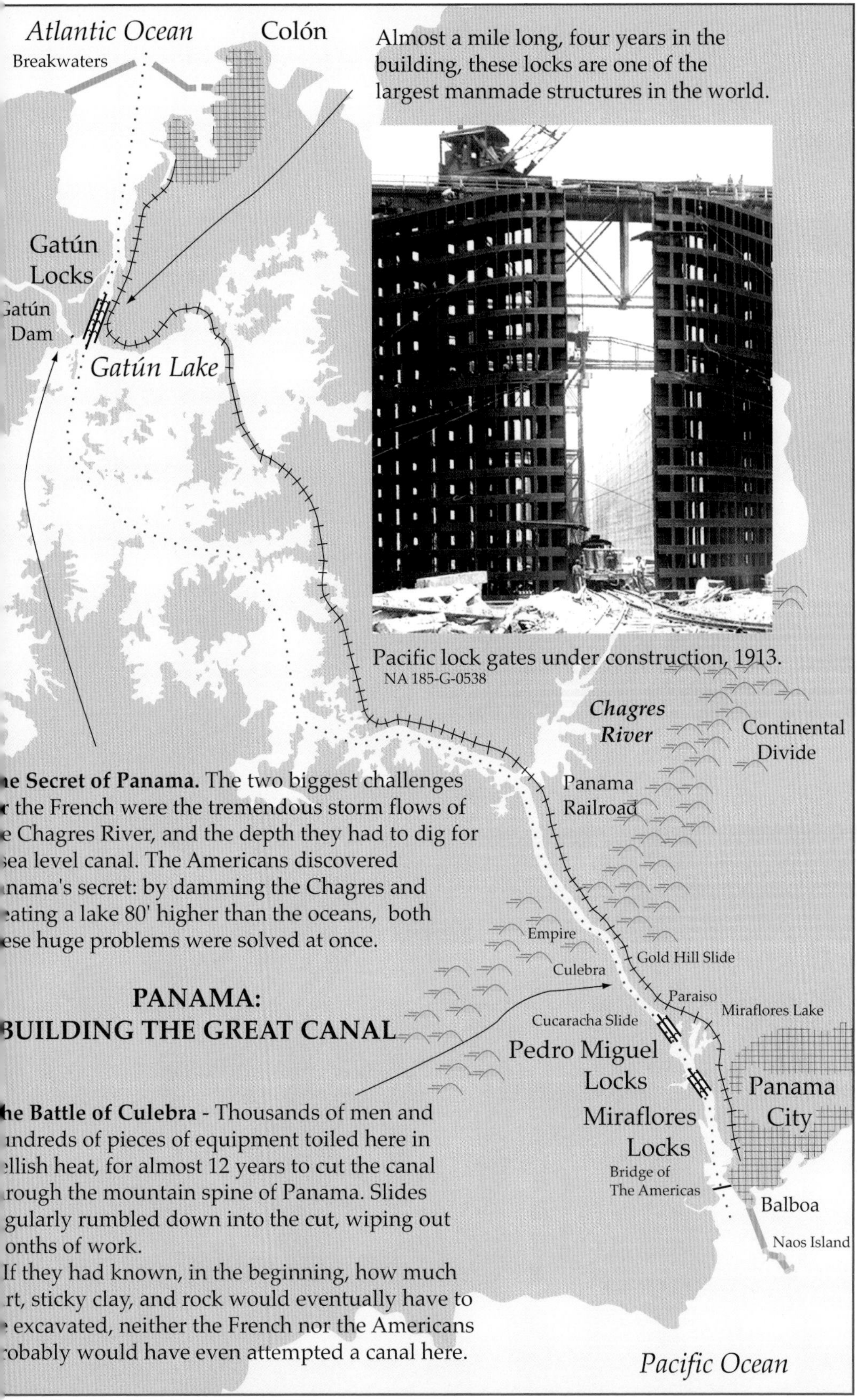

ıe Secret of Panama. The two biggest challenges ɾ the French were the tremendous storm flows of e Chagres River, and the depth they had to dig for sea level canal. The Americans discovered ınama's secret: by damming the Chagres and ɛating a lake 80' higher than the oceans, both ese huge problems were solved at once.

PANAMA:
ƁUILDING THE GREAT CANAL

ɦe Battle of Culebra - Thousands of men and ındreds of pieces of equipment toiled here in ɛllish heat, for almost 12 years to cut the canal ırough the mountain spine of Panama. Slides gularly rumbled down into the cut, wiping out onths of work.

If they had known, in the beginning, how much ɾrt, sticky clay, and rock would eventually have to ɛ excavated, neither the French nor the Americans ɾobably would have even attempted a canal here.

A CANAL FOR THE NEW MILLEN
MIRAFLORES

Cape Horn deck view, any day in April.The ship is the *Passat*, a 365-foot steel hulled, four-masted ship with steel masts, yards, and wire rigging. These ships were built to take whatever the Horn could throw at them. Yet each year, vessels like her went missing in the vicinity of that feared Cape. SFM

Left. *Sun Princess* in Miraflores Locks, around 7 a.m., with two big Panamax class container ships locking in beside her.

BEFORE THE PANAMA CANAL

AROUND THE HORN

THE WHEEL IS NOW ABOMINABLY HEAVY: the boys strain there manfully, three of them now. Hail and rain and snow lash at us alternately; the sea smokes with its fury. Seas over the length of her, the great hull plunging and trembling, now and then with the shock of the seas. A bad night: well, the wind should begin soon to go down.

Still the gale increased in madder and madder squalls; it had not blown itself out. It was only beginning. Now it screamed and roared against the rigging and the straining sails.

...Then came the squall which almost robbed us of our morning, of all future mornings. With awful suddenness there came a mighty squall which made all its predecessors seem like doldrum airs. The helm would not go up, not for the combined striving of four boys and the mate: green water smashed along the length of her. Now the sea held her down, now it had her!

– Alan Villiers, *The Grain Race*

"Cape Stiff," the old timers liked to call it, that stone sentinel at the very southern tip of South America. The latitude was nicknamed the "Roaring Forties," for the strength of the wind and the size of the seas.

The prevailing winds were from the west and so the greatest challenges were for ships bound out from Europe for South

Square riggers moored in San Francisco Bay, circa 1900. Most of these ships had to make the dreaded passage around Cape Horn from the east coast.
Although passengers could travel across the USA in just eight days following the joining of the Union Pacific and Central Pacific Railroad Lines at Promontory Point in Utah in 1869, much freight was still carried by sail into the first decade of the 20th century. A continual challenge for captains and ship owners was to keep their crews after they arrived in California, where the climate was pleasant and the economy was booming. SFM

American or Pacific ports.

Square riggers sailed best with the wind from behind them, so to pass the dreaded cape meant days and sometimes weeks of tediously "wearing ship" - hauling the yards or long cross–pieces on the mast that held the sails around to face the other direction and then turning the ship approximately 120 degrees.

Many ships suffered the bitter experience of clawing their way very slowly upwind, and almost getting to the Cape itself, where they could run northeast up the coast of South America and into better weather. Then, just a few miles from that point where the crew could finally rest their cracked and swollen hands, a gale would come up, and blow the ship back, a hundred miles or more, and all the hard fought progress toward the Cape would be lost.

Ships would sometimes attempt to pass Cape Horn by a more southern route, hoping to find less contrary winds. But if they went too far, they would encounter another enemy: icebergs, broken off the vast glacial shelf of the Antarctic continent, and pushed north into the shipping lanes by the current.

Vessels that suffered damage in the struggle to round the Cape were far from any help. The nearest downwind harbor with any sort of good shelter lay 400 miles to the east in the Falkland Islands. A number of vessels found themselves so damaged by storms that running to the shelter of Port Stanley in the Falklands was their only chance at survival.

Going West to Get East

Of course, the early explorers didn't expect to find any impediment between Europe and Asia. When Columbus left Spain in August of 1492, with three ships and 88 men in an expedition financed by Queen Isabella, he was betting on a novel theory first advanced by the Greeks: that the Earth was round, and

A Difficult Passage:

Square rigger *Susanna*:
94 Days to round Cape Horn.
Aug. 25 - Nov. 25, 1905

Cape Horn roundings are usually calculated from latitude 50 east of the Horn to latitude 50 west of the Horn. The *Susanna* encountered fierce gales. A more normal rounding would be 2-3 weeks.

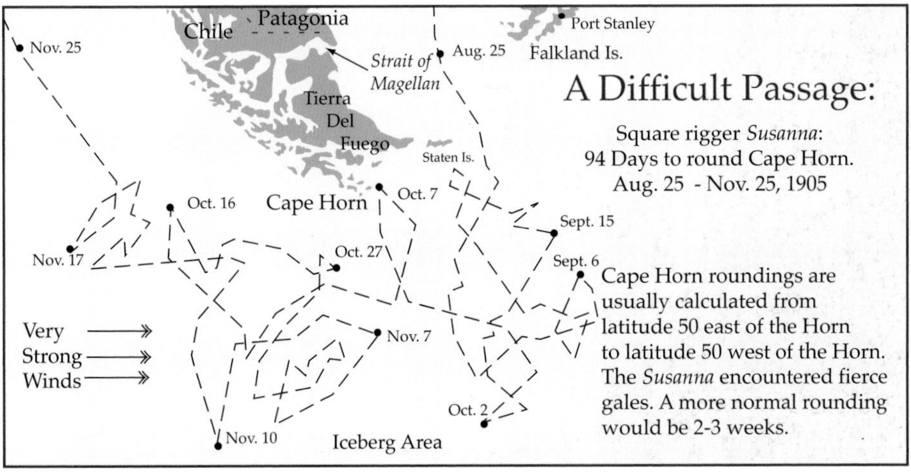

that therefore the Spice Islands of the East could be reached by traveling west.

Getting to the East Indies by the traditional route around Africa in the small ships of the day meant fighting against the prevailing winds for months. Westbound ships would have the advantage of traveling with the winds. And if, Columbus explained to the Queen, the East Indies could be found by traveling west, then Spain's trade and Isabella's wealth would expand greatly. Instead Columbus discovered what came to be called The New World–America, but not much gold or spices.

DISCOVERING THE PACIFIC OCEAN

By about 1511 or so, the geography of the Caribbean basin was beginning to come into focus for the Portuguese and Spanish explorers and two things were obvious: 1) if there were gold and spices–the main reason for coming in the first place–they hadn't yet been found, and 2) there was a large land mass, extending as far north and south as anyone had been able to determine, that was in the way of any progress further west toward the real "East Indies," if indeed they lay to the west at all.

On September 29, 1513, Spanish explorer Vasco Nuñez de Balboa landed a force of 190 Spaniards, supported by 1,000 natives, on the coast of Panama, about 120 miles east of the present Canal Zone, to explore, and to determine the truth of native stories that another body of water lay beyond the mountains.

By amazing good fortune, he had chosen to begin his exploration at one of the isthmus's narrowest spots.

He came face–to–face with the infamous Panamanian rain forest, and set out immediately to hack his way towards the west.

Twenty-five grueling days later, he was rewarded by a stunning sight–a vast body of water, stretching far away to the west. He named it the South Sea, and took possession of both it, and

Going around Cape Horn against the prevailing westerly gales could be a grueling experience. This is the approximate course track for the square rigger Susanna, which took 94 days to get around in 1905. Imagine what it must have been like to be on the crew on such a voyage. The narrow and very windy Strait of Magellan offers an alternate route, but almost all big sailing ships were hard to maneuver in narrow channels and so preferred the rough but open ocean.

Source: Alan Villiers, *The War with Cape Horn*, Scribner's, New York, 1971

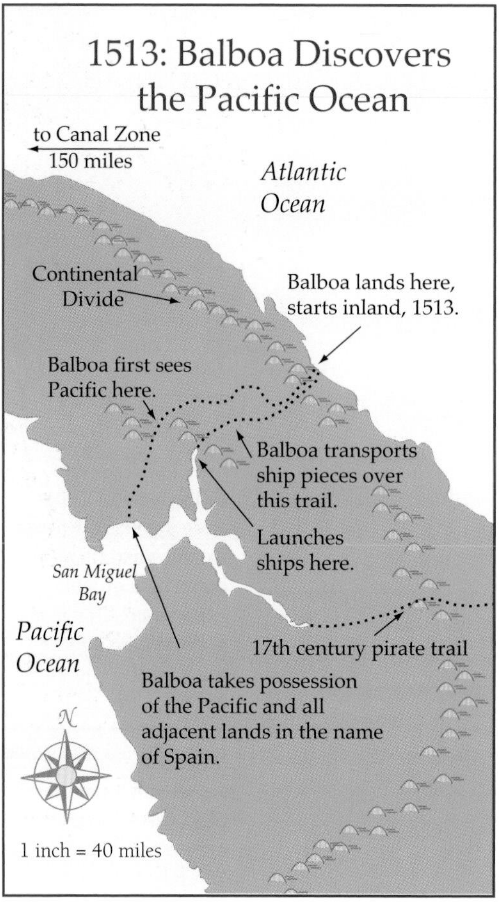
1513: Balboa Discovers the Pacific Ocean
to Canal Zone
150 miles
Atlantic Ocean
Continental Divide
Balboa lands here, starts inland, 1513.
Balboa first sees Pacific here.
Balboa transports ship pieces over this trail.
Launches ships here.
San Miguel Bay
Pacific Ocean
17th century pirate trail
Balboa takes possession of the Pacific and all adjacent lands in the name of Spain.
N
1 inch = 40 miles

A stunning discovery: following up on native stories of a large body of water beyond the hills, Spanish entrepreneur Balboa hacked his way with tremendous difficulty to the top of the mountains and discovered the Pacific Ocean. It took him almost four weeks to reach a place where he could see the water, but the discovery led to a whole new era of exploration.

all the shores that it washed, on September 29, 1513.

Balboa, who had begun that expedition as a stowaway only to become its leader, was nothing if not strong willed. Understanding that sailing on the Pacific would be an immense achievement for Spain, he organized an expedition five years later in 1518 to carry the pieces to construct two small ships across the isthmus. Following an old trail about five miles south of his previous track, he was able to find a route from the Caribbean to the head of tidewater of a long narrow bay that was only 32 miles away. Considering that today's Canal route from Caribbean to Pacific is also around 32 miles long, it was a substantial achievement.

The search for a passage around or through North America was to consume European nations for much of the next 250 years–only when English Captain George Vancouver made his definitive four year voyage of exploration along the northwest coast of America, was the attractive idea of a safe existing Atlantic to Pacific passage finally abandoned.

The 8,000 miles of potential distance saving (as opposed to a New York - California passage around Cape Horn) was a powerful stimulus to search for a route somewhere through Central America. As the geography of the region became more known, Nicaragua began to present itself as an alternative to a canal that crossed the difficult jungle and mountain terrain of Panama.

The attractive features of Nicaragua were a lake and river system that would seem to allow vessels to enter from the Atlantic, and with a little judicious dredging, to get to a point where they were only separated from the Pacific by a narrow neck of land and what seemed to be a low range of hills.

It was obvious, however, that either route involved a lot of plain old digging–the excavation of immense amounts of dirt and rock. In the 1700's such digging was done by picks and shovels and the dirt moved by horses and wagons.

The jungle primeval with black-crowned night heron. As much as anything, it was the thickness of the jungle and the force and the persistence of the Panamanian rains that daunted canal planners.

The amount of dirt that could be moved by such human and animal powered systems was tiny compared to the vast amounts that had to be excavated in even the most optimistic of canal scenarios. And so until the Industrial Revolution that swept across much of the western world in the 1800's, canal digging languished.

Steam Power Brings New Possibilities

The development of the modern steam engine and labor saving machinery associated with it totally transformed the industrial landscape in the 1800's.

By the 1820's steam-powered river boats were beginning to be seen on United States rivers, and the steam-powered locomotives allowed the development of railroads beginning in the 1840's. By then, steam was powering most new factories as well.

But the application of steam power to trains and ships did more than move folks and cargo around; it expanded their horizons as well. As steam engines changed the nature of work, the whole concept of what man could do naturally changed as well.

Panama and the California Gold Rush

The event creating the most interest in a possible canal was the discovery of gold, on the American River in California, in January of 1848. Over the next 15 years the population of California would jump from 15,000 to over 300,000 as almost 500 million dollars of gold was taken from the hills.

If you lived on the East Coast, and wanted to get to

Steam engine component at abandoned quarry. The rapid development of steam-powered machinery in the 1800's completely changed the industrial landscape. Huge excavation projects that would have been impossible in 1800 were quite achievable, just 75 years later.

California in 1849, you had basically three choices: by sea, by land, or a combination of both. The land route was the most challenging–you traveled by rail and steamboat to St. Joseph, Missouri, where you began the 2,000 mile trek, by foot or horseback, to California.

The most popular land route had to cross both the Rockies and the Sierra Nevada in California. As the Donner party discovered in 1847, deep snows can make crossing the high passes impossible: of their group of 87, only 47 survived, and some of those only did so by eating the flesh of those who had succumbed to the cold.

For these reasons, going by sea was much more attractive, until you looked at the route: around dreaded Cape Horn, and then doglegging way into the western Pacific to get the best winds to get to California–a total of some 13,300 miles.

Enter the entrepreneurs. As in many gold rushes a surer path to riches was often found in providing a service for the prospectors. To serve the California-bound hordes starting in 1850, two different competing land routes were developed.

Cornelius Vanderbilt, taking advantage of Nicaragua's river and lake system, established a route in 1851. Passengers traveled by steam or clipper ship to San Juan del Norte, where the San Juan River emptied into the Caribbean. Boarding a smaller steamer, passengers would travel as far as the rapids, where after a short overland portion, they would board another smaller steamer that took them to Lake Nicaragua, where they would disembark at a place just 11 miles from the Pacific Ocean. With exotic birds and

Volcanoes in Lake Managua, Nicaragua. Central America in the 1800's was the site of a lot of volcanic activity. Despite a lot of interest in a canal route across Nicaragua, it was the worry about possible volcanic activity that probably swayed opinions in the end.

monkeys in the trees along your route, it was also a bit of an exotic experience for Americans unused to the lush life of the tropics.

Next was a mule ride over a low pass in the mountains and through the jungle down to the Pacific Ocean, where, if the would-be prospectors were lucky, ships would be waiting. Actually crossing Nicaragua might only take a day or two.

It was a lot easier than what could be an exceedingly rough and dangerous trip around Cape Horn.

The Panamanian route, developed by the Pacific Mail Line, was a lot more challenging, at least until the Panama Canal Railroad was completed in 1855. Though the route was a lot shorter than across Nicaragua, it was hacked through steamy jungle, and up and over a significantly higher pass than on the Nicaraguan route.

Early travelers along the Panama route would land at the settlement of Chagres, at the mouth of the river of the same name. Set on the edge of the thickest jungle, in 1849, it was little

It Makes It Sound So Easy

THE NEW AND INDEPENDENT LINE FOR CALIFORNIA VIA NICARAGUA

The steamship *Prometheus* will leave Pier No. 2, North River, on Monday, July 14th, for San Juan direct, connecting with the new and elegant steamship *Pacific,* Captain D.G. Bailey, to leave for San Juan del Sud on the 25th. Passengers will take a new iron steamer at San Juan, sent there for the purpose, and pass up the River and across Lake Nicaragua to Virgin Bay, and pass over a good road, 12 miles distant to the Pacific, where the steamship *Pacific* will be in readiness to receive them. Passengers may secure through tickets at No. 9 Battery Place.

Passengers by the line have the preference in crossing from ocean to ocean, by arrangement. All persons going to the East by the line should procure tickets for the *Gold Hunter* and *Prometheus.*

— *New York Courier and Enquirer,* circa 1851

Chagres, Panama, in 1848, probably looked a bit like this. To California–bound travelers from the East Coast, at the beginning of the Gold Rush, Chagres was where they disembarked from the ships and started their trek by mule across the isthmus to the Pacific.

more than a collection of thatched huts on the shore of an exceptionally muddy river.

Disembarking passengers would then mount mules for the challenging trek through the jungles and over the mountains to the Pacific Coast, not far from the present town of Colón.

If they were lucky, a steamer or sailing ship would be waiting to take them on the last stage of their journey–up the coast to San Francisco. If nothing else, the number of travelers that the California Gold Rush sent eagerly scrambling across Nicaragua and Panama heightened the interest at the highest levels in the possibility of a canal. The biggest challenge in those early days of canal interest was this: no one

First Gold Rush Passengers Cross Panama

When the 200 plus passengers disembarked from the small steamer *Falcon* at Chagres on January 7, 1849, they didn't have a map, or even a clear idea of where the Pacific Ocean lay.

But what this group of young gold-hungry Americans did have was enthusiasm, and a wild energy to get to the California gold fields in time to get in on a share of the riches. To the amazement of the Panamanian onlookers, the group took up their packs, arranged to rent the crude canoes made by hollowing out huge trees, and disappeared up the Chagres River.

Like other travelers before the construction of the Panama Railroad, they found deep muck that threatened to swallow their mules, dysentery to sap their strength, and the fetid Panama humidity and heat.

Somehow, the group found the trail, and eventually staggered out of the jungle into Panama City on the Pacific coast, but no one would recommend the journey to others.

In the 1850's most of the steam-powered vessels on the New York to Panama, and Panama to San Francisco runs were still paddle wheelers, powered by massive single or two-cylinder steam engines. Steam engine technology was progressing rapidly and by the end of the century, large multi-cylinder engines like this one were powering ships that used more efficient propellers.
SFM

really knew the geography of the isthmus well enough to be able to determine if a canal was even feasible, and if so, where would be the best place to construct it.

"An Effortless Walk From the Atlantic to the Pacific" – Was Cullen a Liar?

In 1850, the electrifying news of the discovery of a perfect canal route spread among the international community. Dr. Edward Cullen, a respected member of the Royal Geographical Society, declared he had found a route across Darien (roughly 120 miles east of the present canal) where he strolled easily from the Atlantic to the Pacific. Furthermore, he assured the eager public that the highest point on the route was no more than 150 feet above sea level.

Eager to capitalize on the exciting news, the United States sent a Navy ship, the *Cyane*, as part of an international expedition to investigate. When the *Cyane* reached Caledonia Bay, none of the ships of the other nations had yet arrived, and so Lieutenant Isaac Strain and 27 men rushed ashore with provisions for a few days and headed into the jungle. Dr. Cullen had reported that he marked the trail well and Strain expected to get to the Pacific and back before the other ships had arrived.

Forty-nine days later Strain staggered naked, starving, and bleeding from brush cuts into a native village near the Pacific Ocean. Rescuers who followed him back into the thick jungle found the survivors barely still alive. Of the 27 that had left the beach at Caledonia Bay in high hopes of a quick walk between

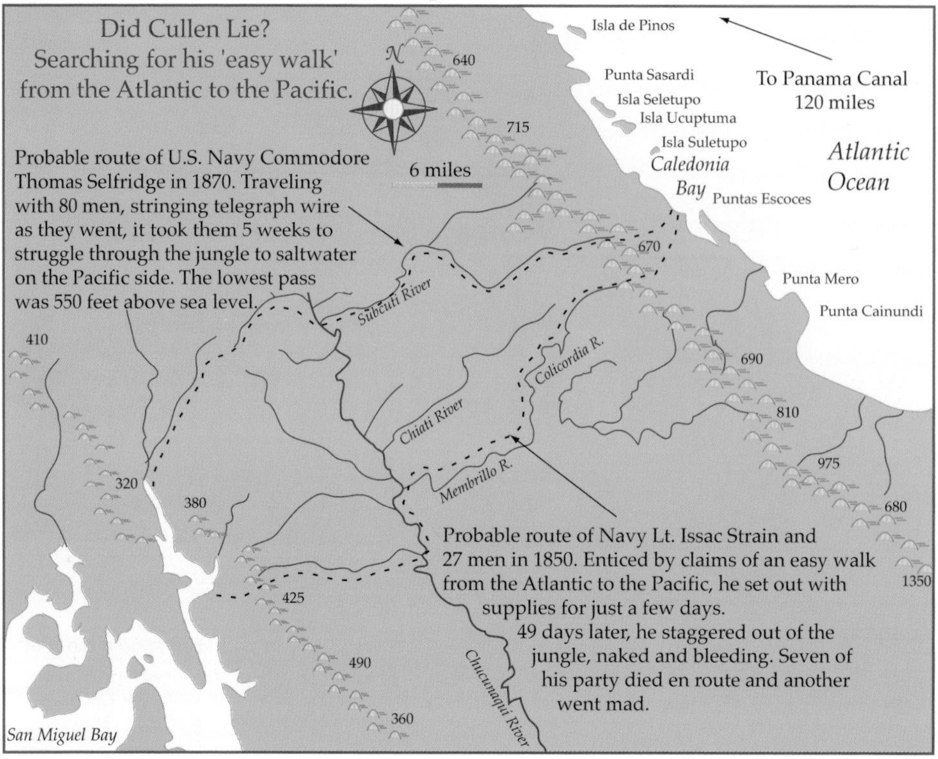
Did Cullen Lie?
Searching for his 'easy walk'
from the Atlantic to the Pacific.
N
6 miles
Isla de Pinos
Punta Sasardi
Isla Seletupo
Isla Ucuptuma
Isla Suletupo
Caledonia Bay
Puntas Escoces
To Panama Canal 120 miles
Atlantic Ocean
Punta Mero
Punta Cainundi
Probable route of U.S. Navy Commodore Thomas Selfridge in 1870. Traveling with 80 men, stringing telegraph wire as they went, it took them 5 weeks to struggle through the jungle to saltwater on the Pacific side. The lowest pass was 550 feet above sea level.
Subcuti River
Colicordia R.
Chiati River
Membrillo R.
Chucunaqui River
Probable route of Navy Lt. Issac Strain and 27 men in 1850. Enticed by claims of an easy walk from the Atlantic to the Pacific, he set out with supplies for just a few days.
49 days later, he staggered out of the jungle, naked and bleeding. Seven of his party died en route and another went mad.
San Miguel Bay
640
715
670
690
810
975
680
1350
410
320
380
425
490
360

The Caledonia Bay area was the site of an intense exploratory frenzy in 1850 and 1870, triggered by a claim that there was an easy path from the Atlantic to the Pacific.

the Oceans, only 20 were left alive. They reported conditions of travel so difficult as to make them wonder if Cullen had even stepped ashore at all.

Strain had lost almost half his body weight in the crossing, and died a few years later, just 36 years old, of complications from that journey. No one, he reported, should consider Darien as a possible route. It was simply impassible.

Cullen conveniently disappeared from the Panamanian scene, but not before insisting that Strain had simply taken the wrong route, that had he waited for Cullen to lead him, the way would be clear.

The sobering experience of Strain's expedition cooled the ardor of canal backers for a decade or two. Yet still, there lingered this doubt: what if Cullen had been right?

Meanwhile, as the thousands headed for California and its gold crowded onto the mule trails across Panama, it was quickly obvious that a railroad across the narrow isthmus of Panama could be a financial success.

The founder of the Pacific Mail Steamship Company, William Henry Aspinwall, quickly found investors, and began to work, constructing a single line railroad through some of the thickest jungle and deepest swamps that any railroad had ever crossed. But more than anything else it was

Would you go around Cape Horn in this? When the California gold rush sent thousands of prospectors scrambling to get passage from the East Coast to California, paddle wheelers like the *Ancon* were on regular around-the-horn routes. Most also stopped at Panama on the way north up the Pacific coast to fill any empty berths with San Francisco-bound travelers, who had crossed the isthmus by mule, or after 1855, by rail.
Author's collection

the heat and disease-laden climate of Panama that was the hardest obstacle to surmount.

Its backers had hoped the railroad could be built in three years or less; it took five. The first cost estimate had been 1.5 million dollars; the final tab was 8 million.

Yet despite the deaths, the delays, and the cost overruns, the single track Panama Road (with sidings where two trains could pass) was a financial success way beyond the hopes of the company founders.

For as word trickled back to the East Coast not only of the gold to be had in California, but also of the gentle climate and the fertile land and the opportunities for those who made the voyage, the numbers of trans–Panama travelers just kept climbing. In the decade after the railroad was completed in 1855, it carried over 375,000 passengers and delivered consistent profits to its owners and large dividends to shareholders.

However, instead of exciting enthusiasm for the logical next step of building a canal, the experience of building the railroad was a cautionary tale. Anyone who considered a con-

Working on the Railroad – How Many Died?

"A dead man for every tie," (there were approximately 70,000 ties along the Atlantic to Pacific route of the Panamanian Railroad) was the rumor that spread out of the squalid construction camps. Any reasonable analysis of the numbers shows this estimate to be hugely off, perhaps by a factor of 10.

But nothing can dispute the fact that for literally thousands of workers, the Panamanian jungles were a death trap. So many working so close together in hot jungle conditions, and living in squalid quarters, were a perfect environment for malaria and yellow fever to multiply rapidly. Asians, Irish, Caribbean negroes all suffered equally.

John Stephens, in charge of the line's construction, had traveled extensively through Central America before coming to Panama. But even he wasn't immune to the plagues that swept Panama, and he died of cholera in 1852.

The Panama Railroad, circa 1860. This railway was key to making the Panama Canal possible. The Canal closely followed the route of the tracks (which had to be moved as Gatún Lake was created), and then the rails served as the core infrastructure for moving dirt from the great cuts to the dumping areas. Drawing is of summit station, where "Old Joe Prince served warm beer and raw brandy at his 'groggery.' "
NA

struction project in Panama that would be many times more expensive and challenging than construction of the railroad had been had to consider the stark facts: as many as 10,000 deaths (no accurate number can ever be known) and a project that ran five times over budget.

Also, during the construction of the railroad, surveyors were able for the first time to accurately measure the height of the mountains that any canal across Panama would have to cross. The lowest pass that they had been able to find was at a place that was to become legend: Culebra. Here, they measured the height above sea level at some 275 feet. While canal building had been progressing rapidly in the US for much of the 1800's, most were still hand-dug shortcuts across relatively flat ground. The idea of a canal that must somehow surmount a height of 275 feet on top of the already challenging construction climate of Panama was incredibly sobering to anyone considering it.

It was obvious the next step towards a canal had to be a more rigorous search of all possible routes.

Still, doubts lingered. Perhaps Cullen had been right; maybe an easy and short route could be found.

Sixteen years after Strain and his party of 27 had stepped so hopefully into the jungles of Darien, another US Navy party, this time aided by surveyors, again came ashore at Caledonia Bay. The idea of an "easy" canal route (if there even could be such a thing, given the working conditions of Panama) was so attractive, that the US had decided to explore this area one more time.

This group came a lot better prepared. Hundreds of pairs of extra shoes and plenty of food were packed to survive the tropic

British and French warships at Port Said, the southern entrance to the Suez Canal, around 1882. Although small barge canals had been built in many places before 1870, the size of the Suez Canal excited nations about the possibilities of a similar canal across Central America.

Author's collection

heat and damp. Even telegraph wire and equipment were brought so that they could report their progress.

But the result was no more encouraging–the terrain, with its deep swamps and the lowest mountain pass at 550 feet, made it impossible to construct a canal.

The expedition reboarded the ships and sailed west, to the Gulf of San Blas, nearer to the location of the present canal.

Once again the surveyors were stymied by what they had experienced in Darien: swampy lowlands and steep mountains.

In the next few years, two more US expeditions would explore other possible locations on the Panamanian coast, but always without finding a canal route that would be possible with the earthmoving technology of the time.

The Suez Canal: A Misleading Prelude

During this period the first great canal venture in world history was taking place in Egypt. In 1854, an untrained but ambitious Frenchman named Ferdinand de Lesseps put together an organization to cut a channel though the Suez Desert and link the Red Sea with the Mediterranean.

What was remarkable was this–de Lesseps had little training, as engineer, financier, or administrator. But what he did have was an energy and enthusiasm that enabled him to successfully overcome challenges that would have defeated a lesser man.

Construction began in 1859 on a 100-mile-long canal that

When the Europeans and Americans arrived in Panama to begin exploration for a possible canal, civilization only existed in a few widely scattered towns. For the most part natives lived away from the cash economy, on subsistence agriculture and fishing.

had the advantage of connecting to several lakes along its route to lessen the amount of actual digging. As was to be the case in Panama, there were thousands of fatalities from the difficult working conditions. During the latter part of the canal construction, de Lesseps presided over a change in construction techniques that was to change earthmoving forever: machines instead of animals. The introduction of steam-powered earthmoving equipment opened up new horizons of what was possible.

The Suez Canal opened with great fanfare in 1869, and de Lesseps was hailed as a hero in France and Europe.

Intoxicated with his success in the Suez, it was only natural that he turn his energies to an Atlantic-Pacific canal. Yet de Lesseps' considerable success at Suez almost certainly caused him to substantially underestimate the challenges of a canal across Panama.

Suez was flat, dry, and most of all, accessible. Panama was exactly the opposite. And if de Lesseps had a character trait that wasn't to serve him well on the Panama Canal project, it was that his enthusiasm for any project in which he was involved could be so great as to blind him to bad news, or any news that didn't fit in with his vision.

Those Frenchmen who had invested in the Suez Canal Company were well rewarded, and when de Lesseps announced his interest in a canal at Panama, eager investors stepped forward to support it and him.

An expedition was assembled to investigate several sites in Panama, led by Lucien Wyse, in whom de Lesseps had great confidence.

In Panama, Wyse ran head-on into the wet and thick Panamanian jungle and came up with a totally unrealistic plan–a canal at Darien with a tunnel, possibly several miles long.

A tunnel of the dimensions proposed by Wyse was so far beyond any technology of the day that de Lesseps would have none of it. He sent the tired Wyse back to Panama to try again, but this time with specific instructions to look along the route of the Panama Railroad.

He furthermore insisted that the canal had to be at sea level, without locks.

Why? If there was a single decision that essentially doomed the huge and terribly costly French Panama Canal venture from its earliest days it was this one. It made no sense, and flew in the face of a very large body of information mainly collected by the Americans, but freely available. There were two truly huge obstacles along this route–the mountains at Culebra and the Chagres River.

Culebra, circa 1905. No one, French or American, was able to foresee the almost insurmountable challenge of cutting through the Panamanian mountains. And if they had, most probably they never would have started. NA 185 - G 0666

Culebra: Remember This Name

There was a place that was to haunt the canal builders, both French and American, that was to achieve legendary status to the tens of thousands who worked there. It was Culebra, or Snake, the pass through the mountains where a channel would have to be dug. The surveyors for the Panama Railroad had already determined that the lowest point at Culebra was some 275 feet above sea level. Assuming that the canal would have to be a minimum of 25 feet deep required an excavation of 300 feet. No canal had ever successfully cut through such a mountain pass. Furthermore, the experience of the builders of the railroad indicated that the soils in the Culebra area were mostly clay and apt to be unstable. If either the French, or later the Americans, had realized as they planned their project how much material would eventually have to be removed from Culebra, quite possibly they would have never started.

The mighty Chagres River drained most of the mountains and hills that stood in the way of the powerful "Northers" sweeping in off the Atlantic. When the rains came on heavy,

Clay, near Culebra. Ample evidence was available to indicate that digging a sea level canal through this kind of clay was probably impossible. If de Lesseps had availed himself of the large body of information on the geography and geology of Panama, and decided in the beginning to construct a canal with locks, he probably would have succeeded, albeit with a much narrower canal than what the US eventually built.

the thousands of square miles of slopes all exposed to the torrential rains shed torrents of solid water into the Chagres. When one party of American surveyors was working along its bank, the water rose so rapidly the men were forced out of their tents and into trees in the middle of the night. A canal route that paralleled the Panama Railroad would have to cross the Chagres several times. The Chagres River was another immense obstacle to the construction of a canal along de Lesseps' proposed route.

At de Lesseps' instruction, Wyse and his party set out once again for the heat of Panama, but it was clear Wyse had lost his stomach for the task. He assigned the task of studying the railroad route to his assistant, and traveled to remote Bogotá, Colombia, to negotiate with the Colombian government for rights to build a canal. (At this time, Panama was a province of Colombia.)

Wyse's assistant, Lieutenant Armand Réclus, spent a few days exploring the route along the Panama Railroad, took sick, and returned to France.

When Wyse and Réclus returned to Paris, they made their recommendation to de Lesseps: a sea level canal, with a tunnel through Culebra. They got the route right, but their plan for a tunnel was an admission that the challenges of cutting through the mountains at Culebra might be something that even the hero of Suez should take a second look at.

The Chagres River after heavy rains, circa 1944, almost washing over the bridge downstream of the Gatún Dam. When those legendary Panamanian rains came, the Chagres River could rise ten feet in an <u>hour</u>! The French canal route planned to cross the river several times, yet without fully appreciating the challenges of doing so.
NA

Last Chance to Get It Right: The International Congress of Canal Studies

To obtain legitimacy for his proposals, de Lesseps arranged for a conference in Paris, in May of 1879, to study all the facts, to listen to all the experts–or so it was hoped.

The Americans presented the results of their decades of research. Given the challenges of cutting through Culebra and dealing with the Chagres River, a series of locks was the only possible way to get across Panama, but a canal through Nicaragua was cheaper and much more feasible. Much of the Nicaraguan route would be up a river and across a lake, so that the actual digging would be only a bit more than in Panama, but in easier conditions. It was clear to all the listeners that the Americans had studied both routes extensively.

Wyse then made his presentation of the French plan. He proposed a sea level canal with a tunnel, along the route of the Panama Railroad. Yet to the engineers present, it was obvious almost immediately that the French plan was made without detailing how it would deal with huge challenges so specifically laid out by the American report.

Then that remarkable man, the silver-tongued Ferdinand de Lesseps, stood up and smoothly assured the delegates that by geography alone, Panama had to be the obvious choice. He acknowledged that there were challenges to be met, but that as the French had done at Suez, they could be surmounted.

When the votes were counted, de Lesseps had had his way. His skills as a promoter had turned the Congress into a sham, approving a route that was almost entirely at odds with the majority of the evidence presented.

The die was cast: de Lesseps and investors all over France were soon to be swept up into one of the greatest financial failures in European history.

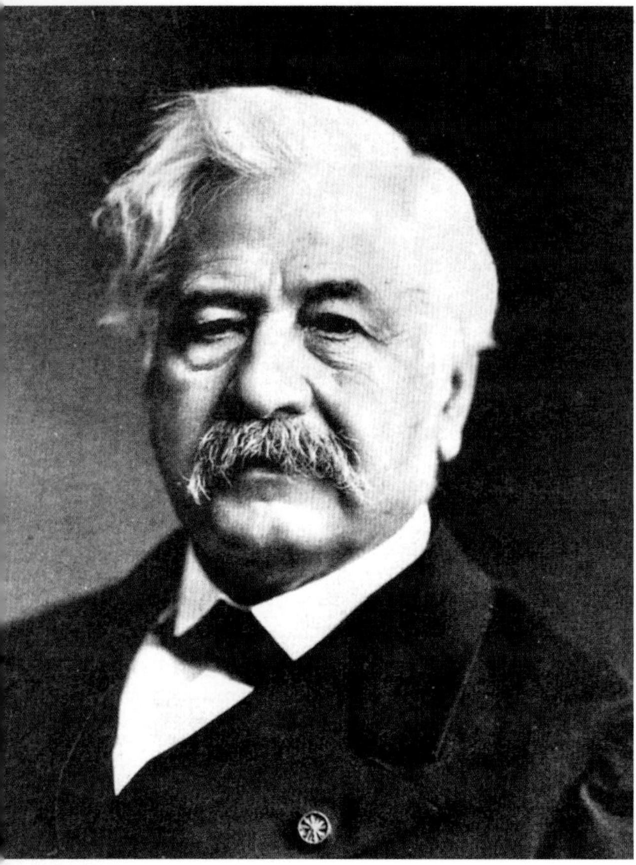

Ferdinand de Lesseps, around 1880. A true hero to the French people, his immense personal charisma wasn't enough to conquer the considerable challenges at Panama.

Culver Pictures, Inc.

FERDINAND DE LESSEPS – A GIANT FIGURE

David McCullough, whose excellent book *The Path Between The Seas*, is the definitive work on the Panama Canal, called his chapter about de Lesseps, "The Hero." McCullough noted that even if de Lesseps had never gone to Panama, his life would have stood out as, "one of the most extraordinary of the nineteenth century."

When the Congress to determine the best Panama Canal route was held, de Lesseps was almost 75 years old. At this age, most men in de Lesseps' position would have been content to rest on their considerable achievements.

It seemed that the power of seeing so many excited faces supporting what was, in essence, his vision was too much for him. At a climactic moment during the final vote, de Lesseps stood up and thrilled the eager audience by announcing that he himself would lead the French Canal venture.

As he had with the Suez project, de Lesseps' next move was to form a company with capital from a core group of rich friends. He then tried to sell enough stock to the French public to fund the huge project. Counting on his high personal popularity, de Lesseps began touring France to promote his canal stock.

THE ANSWER WAS THERE ALL ALONG: DE LÉPINAY'S PROPOSAL

Among all the ironies of the rise and fall of the French Panama venture, none is more cruel than this: that the proposal advanced by Frenchman Baron Goudin de Lépinay at the Congress could have led to a successful canal. He proposed a dam on the mighty Chagres River to create a lake to cover most of the canal route, then build a set of locks to help get over Culebra. No one listened.

Yet when the French effort failed, and the Americans stepped in, what they eventually created was very similar to what de Lépinay had proposed.

If only de Lesseps would have listened. . .

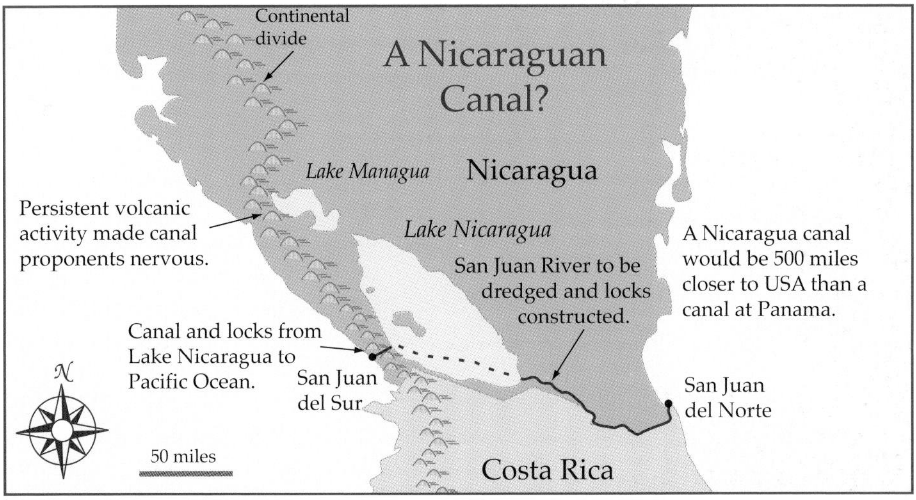
Continental divide
A Nicaraguan Canal?
Lake Managua
Nicaragua
Persistent volcanic activity made canal proponents nervous.
Lake Nicaragua
A Nicaragua canal would be 500 miles closer to USA than a canal at Panama.
San Juan River to be dredged and locks constructed.
Canal and locks from Lake Nicaragua to Pacific Ocean.
San Juan del Sur
San Juan del Norte
N
50 miles
Costa Rica

Would a canal at Nicaragua have been better? The Americans certainly thought so, and had studied Panama in far more detail than the French.

But Panama wasn't Suez, and the word, already on the street, was that this project presented so many challenges that its value as an investment was dubious.

Essentially, de Lesseps was trying to make an end run around the bankers by attempting to sell his shares directly to the public. The French bankers were influential enough to trump even de Lesseps' popularity and the initial stock offering raised so little money that the money was returned. Chagrined, de Lesseps turned to the banking community, who, now assured that they would get their slice of the pie, moved to make an effective stock offer.

But there was a darker side to the success of bank led stock sales. The critics who had so disparaged the chances of a success at Panama just a year and a half earlier, and made the initial stock offering a humiliating failure, had suddenly changed their tune for a single reason: they were bribed. If the canal at Panama had succeeded like Suez, where the stock both went up and paid handsome dividends, this manipulation of the public opinion would have gone unnoticed and unpunished.

Next, de Lesseps had to see Panama for himself. He set out on a five-month tour, both of the canal site and then to the United States to promote his vision.

The thing to remember about the French trip to Panama at the very end of 1879 is that by this time, the Americans had exhaustively surveyed possible canal routes both in Panama and Nicaragua. The French had not, yet were about to commit an immense amount of capital, human lives, and national pride to the venture. It would seem, then, that de Lesseps' visit would have been the perfect chance to explore the route in detail and most of all to compare the negative reports of the route paralleling the Panama Railroad with the reality of his own experience.

Instead, the Panama portion of the trip was more like one

continuous 19th century version of a photo op: a quick train ride across the Isthmus followed by several weeks of high profile social events back in Panama City.

The Chagres River Bridge: Didn't de Lesseps Notice?

Lesseps seems to have missed the single opportunity where the challenge of building a canal was writ large. This was at the bridge that crossed the Chagres River at Barbacoas. Here the entire party including de Lesseps' young wife and children had to get out of the gaily decorated train and cross the 600-foot bridge on boards that had been hastily arranged after the bridge had been damaged by a flood. Did he even inquire how the river, at that moment flowing perhaps 40 feet below the level of the bridge, had damaged it? History doesn't relate, but had he done so, he would have heard a tale that should have been very sobering to anyone considering a work of such magnitude.

After a cold front swept in from the Atlantic with heavy rains, the river had risen over 40 feet in just three days. If de Lesseps had cared to ask, the railroad staff might have also told him that such floods were not uncommon. Had he sought this fact out, and thought about how exactly he and his engineering staff were going to tackle such a challenging problem, he might have been more open to different canal designs than a simple sea-to-sea ditch. He might have grasped the unique secret of Panama: that the mighty Chagres presented the opportunity to create a huge lake covering much of the Panama Canal route.

The locals might have told de Lesseps one additional thing as well: he was visiting in the dry season.

Upon his return to France after Panama and a barnstorming trip across the United States (where bankers and investors displayed little interest in investing in his project), de Lesseps was greeted in France like a conquering hero.

Thinking Sand, but This Wasn't Suez

After their success in the Suez, the Frenchmen who made estimates of the cost of the amount of material to be moved at Panama had a fatal blind spot. They assumed that the digging would be of the sort encountered in Suez–sandy. If anyone in either of Wyse's two exploratory trips to Panama had done some core sampling or simply dug a pit with a shovel along the proposed canal route, they would have realized that they were facing an entirely different enemy: sticky clay.

Not only did the clays of Panama have a particular quality, clinging tenaciously to hand and power shovels alike, but they were layered and unstable, easily sliding downhill when disturbed. If the French or the Americans had known in the planning stages of the project how much dirt would eventually have to be removed to create the canal, they might not have begun at all.

Sun Princess at Culebra - Consider this: the water level for the proposed French sea level canal at this point would have been more than 80 feet lower! Imagine the immense additional amounts of dirt that would have had to be excavated here.

1881: At Last the Work Begins

The first group of French engineers, mostly graduates of the well respected École Polytechnique, arrived in early 1881 and began setting up the classic mode of large construction projects. White engineers and supervisory personnel managed a mostly black and Asian labor force. Early laborers were local natives and blacks from Caribbean islands.

First was building housing, shops, and the dozens of ancillary buildings the huge project would need, and clearing a coast-to-coast path through the jungle along the approximate canal route.

France has a temperate climate, warmed by the Gulf Stream, with hot but generally dry summers, and dreary cold winters, with snow in the higher elevations. Some of the engineers who

Why Didn't de Lesseps Raise More Money?

The initial stock offering for the Canal was 60 million dollars (roughly 300 million francs), and was eagerly snapped up by mostly working class investors, hoping to get in on the ground floor of an investment as good as the Suez Canal had been. It was the perfect time to raise money – before the digging and the dying began, and the ominous reports began to trickle back from Panama.

So why didn't de Lesseps raise more? The latest cost estimate, which would also prove to be wildly optimistic, had the canal being built for around 135 million dollars. So even as he raised the first capital, de Lesseps knew that it was far below what he would need. Did he think investors would be scared away by too large an offering? Whatever his reasons, it was a crippling error in judgement. Though the project ahead was to prove immensely difficult, not raising enough capital in the very beginning, when the French public was bullish on the Canal and in a buying mood, would make raising money later more challenging.

came to Panama had experience in the tropical heat of Egypt, but that had been a dry heat. Nothing in their experience had prepared them for the wet of Panama.

In mid-winter, for three or four months, there was a drier season. But once the rains started, usually in late spring, Panama had a climate that was to challenge the French and later the Americans–tropical downpours that flooded suddenly from the skies, followed by sultry sunshine just a few minutes later.

And there was the humidity. Almost anything man or machine-made quickly rusted or molded. Furniture that had lasted for generations in France would come apart at the joints in Panama after just a few months. And worst of all, clothes never really dried well. For poor laborers with few changes, the sweat-soaked clothes they wore in to dinner at night were the same ones they wore to breakfast and to work in the morning.

The jungle was incredibly thick, a wall of vegetation that was simply too thick to be effectively overcome. Even when a path was cut, the edges started growing back almost instantly, competing for the life-giving sunlight any cut in the jungle creates.

As laborers and carpenters constructed shops, houses and warehouses, another group started hacking away at the jungle, slashing away along the route the canal would follow. Opening up the jungle in this fashion allowed survey and core drilling crews to best plan the exact route.

It was grueling work. Clearing forest in the heat of the Panama jungles was rigorous beyond anything the French had ever experienced. There were no chain saws nor other machinery that could work effectively in the wet lowlands; the only way to attack the wall of green was with brute force and hand tools.

The heat, away from the cooling sea breeze on the imme-

Could Any Nation Have Built the Canal in the 1880's?

The popular impression of the early efforts to build the Canal might go something like this: "Well the French failed, and so the US had to come in and do the job right."

But the question needs to be asked, could any nation or group have completed a canal at Panama before 1900?

Technology, especially the application of steam power to earthmoving machinery, was advancing rapidly in the 1880's and 1890's. Some of the French equipment, especially their touted giant bucket steam shovels, was state of the art in 1880, but wasn't particularly effective in the wet clays of Panama, and would be totally eclipsed by the power of the huge 95-ton Bucyrus steam shovels that were to be the centerpiece of the US effort.

Also disease control took huge strides between 1881, when the first French work crews began arriving in Panama, and when the Americans took over in 1904.

Furthermore, before they started, the Americans had the advantage of studying the French experience to determine what had worked and what hadn't.

What would have been the outcome then if history had been different, and it had been the Americans who had first tried to dig at Panama? There are a lot of reasons to think that they might not have fared much better than the French.

Miraflores Locks, circa 2001. Despite new locomotives, better wiring and lighting, etc., the core mechanisms of the Canal are essentially those installed when it was built. That it has lasted so well is a tribute to its designers and builders.

diate coast, was ferocious. Poisonous snakes lurked, insects swarmed and bit, day and night. The footing was wet and treacherous. Whatever dreams the French engineers had had about building a canal like the straight and dusty Suez faded against the realities of the Panamanian jungle and climate.

And as the Americans who had built the Panamanian Railroad had discovered, the locals had little appetite for it, even at what were then high wages, $1- $1.50 a day. So a constant supply of laborers had to be recruited, imported, trained and housed. Natives from Jamaica and Barbados were used to a hot humid climate, and eager for work. But even these hardy workers found the intense heat and jungle working conditions at Panama difficult. Keeping a reliable work force was to be a nagging problem.

In essence, the French had to create everything from scratch at Panama. The construction of the Panama Railroad after the California Gold Rush had brought sleepy Panama into the 19th century, but the very modest shops and other facilities weren't close to being able to supply the needs of the growing international work force. Every shovel, every drill, every can of oil, kitchen table, chair, or stick of dynamite had to be imported, stocked, and tracked with paperwork.

Soon after arriving, the French purchased the Panama Railroad for the wildly inflated price of 20 million dollars.

Selling the stock (and bribing newspaper editors), paying the bankers, and brokers' fees had come to over 6 million dollars. So before the real work–the actual excavation of the millions of yards of material to create the Canal–had begun, de

Lesseps had already spent 26 million dollars out of the 60 million he had raised. It was not an auspicious start.

Drilling crews followed the men clearing the jungles. Working with the heavy steam drills of the time, they tediously drilled and brought earth samples to the surface to be cataloged and tested.

One thing was almost immediately clear–the Chagres River, so casually passed over when de Lesseps visited in 1880, was going to be a major problem. Much of the proposed Canal route was to follow its course–the line chosen by the initial survey crossed the Chagres at least 12 times, and that was in the dry season, when the river stayed in its banks. At the very least, the Chagres would have to be dammed and rerouted, another immense task.

And then, as it does almost every year in May, the rains came. Sweeping in off the Atlantic in great sheets, filling the rivers, overflowing the gutters, making life for the work force that was already difficult, that much harder.

The First Rainy Season: Yellow Fever

The rain brought something else–yellow fever. It had already taken its toll on the workers on the Panama Railroad, and although the French had downplayed its danger, they were aware that it was a challenge they might have to face.

In 1881, it was a killer; fatal for perhaps 50 percent of its victims, and a particularly nasty way to die. First came the fever, with occasional shivering fits, followed by headaches and unbearable pain, and a noticeable yellow coloration in the face. There was no effective treatment, and white Europeans seemed to be especially susceptible to the disease.

The French built an excellent hospital complex – better than many of the facilities in the US. Unfortunately doctors knew neither the treatment nor the causes of either yellow fever, or the other deadly disease of Panama at that time, malaria. Thus the well designed hospitals could only treat the symptoms, and the hospitals became nothing more than clean places to die.

At that time, malaria was endemic in tropical countries all around the world. It was somewhat less feared than yellow fever, because a bitter powder, quinine, was found to be effective as a preventive. Malaria symptoms included high fever and body-wracking chills. Next was a soaking sweat, and if you survived, a pervasive feeling of exhaustion and sometimes depression so severe as to cause suicide.

In 1880, the causes of these diseases were unknown, but suspected to somehow be related to the rotting vegetation that created the so-called noxious gases or miasma that Panama was known for.

Slashing the route of the Canal through the rain forest, at the Chagres RIver, near Gamboa, circa 1881. This river can rise 20 or 30 feet after a rainstorm and presented the only workable canal scenario: create a lake and use locks to get up and down from it. The French, unfortunately, didn't see this possibility until too late.

NA 185 R Vol 2, # 10

Unbeknownst to the French medical staff at Panama, some of the very same elements that gave the hospitals such an organized and orderly appearance also contributed substantially to the spread of both yellow fever and malaria.

Containers of standing water were common both inside the French hospitals at Panama and on their grounds. Each bed was set in containers of water so as to deter ants and other insects from climbing the legs. Extensive gardens surrounded the hospital buildings. All the plants grew from the hole in a doughnut shaped dish of water, again to keep ants and insects away.

Though well intended, the hundreds of little standing pools of water surrounding both patients and medical staff alike essentially ensured that all would have maximum exposure to the particular species of mosquito that would later be revealed as the carrier for these diseases. Stagnant pools of standing water were the perfect breeding environment for mosquitoes.

If only the French had known . . .

To US visitors, or American Panama Railroad staff (even after it was purchased by the French, many US workers worked on the railroad), it was the debauched French lifestyle that was the cause for so much disease. Particularly offensive to the somewhat prudish Americans was the high wine consumption, with many remarking about the sizes of the piles of old wine bottles around the towns where the French canal staff lived. In reality, given the difficulty of obtaining a totally clean water supply in Panama, wine was probably healthier to drink than Panamanian water.

1882: The Actual Digging Begins

The actual digging on the canal began on January 20, 1882. A swath had been cut through the jungle from Atlantic to Pacific; housing and facility construction was well underway; and at a place called Emperador, just north of the hill that was to become the great cut at Culebra, the work crews sunk their picks and shovels into the sticky Panamanian clay.

Initially progress was good on most fronts. It was the dry season. However, soon the French had to come to grips with what was to become one of the projects most challenging problems–getting rid of all that dirt, or spoil as it was called.

Compared to what the French faced at Panama, the Suez had been easy. There, they were digging sand, across dry and flat terrain. For the most part all they had to do was to dig the sand up and just get it far enough back from the cut so that it wouldn't slide back in. Most of the material excavated from the Suez was deposited within 100 yards of where it was dug from.

In Panama, except in a few places, such an approach was impossible. First of all, there was a lot more digging–the total excavated at Panama was many times what was moved at Suez. Second, much of what was removed was clay, and when it was exposed to the heavy rains of the wet season, it would want to flow downhill. Thirdly, because of the terrain, sometimes the clay had to be moved several miles from where it was excavated.

This meant that along with a mechanized system for digging up the clay, a sophisticated system also had to be developed to move the spoil to a dumping or disposal site. Where the cuts or excavation sites were near the water, trains took the spoil out on long docks and simply filled the bays, but the deeper cuts, like Culebra, required that immense amounts of dirt had to be disposed of in the jungle nearby.

Trains were the answer, moving lines of dirt-filled cars to disposal areas. As the French were to quickly learn, effective disposal had to be carefully planned. For as the heavy clay got piled higher and higher, and the rains came down, the clay would start moving downhill, taking anything that was in the way, including train and tracks, with it.

The French engineers at Panama were no slouches. France in 1880 was as modern as any country in the world, and besides their triumphs at Suez, the French had an impressive array of public works in place.

But in one sense the French experience at Suez was to cast a broad shadow over the effort at Panama. Many of the French who came to Panama had either worked at Suez, or been familiar with the methods that had succeeded there. They brought this baggage–what had worked at Suez should work at Panama.

Lonely graves in a lonely land — so many of the best engineers from France ended up like this, buried overlooking the Panama Canal. In David McCullough's ***Path Between The Seas***, there is a photo of five French engineers, and the caption notes that probably three out of the five died of yellow fever. It didn't take too long for the word to get back to France that Panama was a deathtrap.

NA 185G 872

As the effort expanded at Panama in 1882, as more workers and equipment arrived, it put a severe strain on the canal companies' organizational capabilities. Ships were arriving weekly with loads of equipment that had to be assembled and used efficiently.

It was clear that another of the challenges that had to be solved at Panama was logistics. The first project manager and then his successor resigned, along with the largest subcontractor. All were frustrated by the complexities of effectively organizing such a huge project and the particular challenges of Panama.

Reading between the lines, however, the management turnover indicated a broader problem. It was becoming evident after a year of digging that the challenge was much larger than anyone had first thought.

New blood, in the person of Jules Dingler, was recruited. He arrived in Panama in early 1883, determined to get a handle on the complex mess that the project had become.

Supremely organized, Dingler worked on the canal companies' first master plan, and shook up the French already on the job in Panama with his no-nonsense attitude. If you didn't produce, you were out.

His plan revealed for the first time the immensity of the job ahead. A huge 150-feet-high dam would be required to control the Chagres River, and he revised the angle of repose for the big cuts like Culebra.

This angle of repose was the point at which the cut slopes would be stable (i.e., not slide back down into the cut), and it represented for the first time a public acknowledgement of the extraordinary difficulties ahead.

For as the work had proceeded at Emperador, Culebra and the other big cuts through the big clay hills that stood across the canal route, it had become abundantly clear that the relatively steep angle that earth would remain stable at in France and Egypt simply wouldn't work at Panama. As the digging exposed the clay to the rains, the cuts would simply slough off and slide down into the cut as small landslides. Changing the excavation requirements to cut a flatter and more stable slope also meant removing a lot more dirt.

Dingler's new estimate was that 120,000,000 cubic meters would have to be removed. The estimate on which the cost and completion date had been figured was 75,000,000 cubic meters. This 60 percent increase in the excavation estimate obviously would mean that the project would take a lot longer and be a lot more expensive. Yet, back in Paris, when de Lesseps learned of the new figures, he made little mention of it, insisting that the project was on budget and on schedule.

1883: Full Speed Ahead

Meanwhile, some of the really big equipment that had been especially designed and ordered for the canal began to arrive.

Entrepreneurial blood flowed through many Americans, and to San Francisco druggist H.B. Slaven, the French call for bids to dig at Panama (the French, as opposed to the Americans, subcontracted much of the actual digging out to different companies who had submitted bids) was a wonderful opportunity. When his bid and design were accepted, Slaven found a backer and ordered five huge floating dredges, 130 feet long by 30 feet wide, that looked as if they could have been designed by Jules Verne.

When they arrived at Panama after a harrowing trip, they were the talk of the town. With three steam engines, a 60–foot tower, an endless bucket train that did the actual dredging, high pressure water pumps to clean the mud off the buckets, and two long discharge booms, they were the epitome of the power the industrial revolution would bring to excavation.

And they worked! (Probably to the amazement of Slaven and his partners as well as the French.) In the soft dirt of Limon Bay, at the Atlantic end of the canal, they made good progress, moving themselves forward as they worked and repositioning themselves with the moveable spuds or long wood pilings that stuck through holes in their structure to moor them securely.

Not only did they work, but they worked day and night, and their noisy and obvious presence, essentially right in front of downtown Colón, was living proof that the canal was well underway.

By the end of 1883, the French operation at Panama was a

French steam shovel, circa 1882. The French earth moving equipment simply wasn't big enough to move the vast amount of clay and rock that had to be excavated in anything like the time frame that was planned. Compare this to the American Bucyrus steam shovels, seen on pages 55 and 81, that were the backbone of the US effort.

NA 185 G 2198

huge enterprise. Fourteen thousand workers toiled in the heat and rain; ships arrived each day, and the great noisy and steaming dredges worked right next to town. On both the Atlantic and the Pacific coasts were loud and very visible signs that at long last the excavation was progressing.

To those in charge, however, two persistent problems were growing more and more intractable.

The first was simply the digging–as the equipment worked its way deeper and deeper into the cuts, the problems of landslides and simply finding an efficient way to get rid of all the spoil, or dirt from the cuts, was getting worse.

When the canal was initially planned, French engineers assumed that cuts through the hills at Panama could be made with the hillsides at a 45-degree angle. The core of the problem was that the geology of Panama consisted of layers of clay on top of rock. The forces that had formed the hills and mountains that the canal had to cross had folded up this rock into steep slopes overlaid by the clay.

When it rained, the water seeped down through the clay, but stopped at the impervious rock, essentially lubricating the place where the clay and the rock met. Wherever the underlying rock sloped downhill, and the vegetation was stripped off the clay, it was just a matter of time before the clay would try to slip.

When the seasonal rains came, whole sections of these terraces would give way, sloughing off and sliding into the cut, sometimes taking trains, tracks and steam shovels down as well.

As the slope gave way, the only way to stabilize it from further slides was to cut it back–changing the angle. Of course, the problem with the big cuts through what were essentially

Entrance to old French sea level canal, on the west side of the channel, on the Atlantic Ocean side of the Gatún Locks. Seen today, it seems tiny compared to the very much wider American canal.

passes in the hills was that if you flattened the angle, you had to cut higher and higher in the hills, thus drastically increasing the amount of dirt to be excavated.

The French struggled with this problem as did the Americans after them. The thunder of landslides down into the big cuts was a constant feature of canal construction for decades. As French engineers had nightmares of slides, of months of work lost in a few long seconds, so did the Americans. The huge challenges of the big cuts, especially Culebra, became legend in the worldwide construction community. In the end, the amount of dirt excavated from Culebra alone was more than twice the first estimate for the entire canal!

With many construction projects there is a tendency for the work to go more smoothly over time, as the best approaches to problems are found. Not so at Panama with the digging. The deeper the cuts became, the more pressure the wet clay created on the open sides of the cuts, and the more they slid. The French engineers, arriving at Panama excited and full of hope, were quickly confronted with daily problems that were of a dimension larger than any they had ever dealt with before. Many became discouraged at the immensity of the task and the slow progress.

Another huge lurking issue was how to deal with the Chagres River. Just seven miles north of where the machines and crews struggled at Culebra, the Chagres, meek in the dry season, ferocious in the wet season, crossed the path of the Canal. Dingler's master plan had included damming the Chagres, but engineers hadn't yet determined the best way to do it.

Digging with picks and shovels, Culebra, circa 1881. The French mindset when they came to Panama was that it would be like Suez–easy digging in sand. What they found, sticky unstable clays was more than they had bargained for.

NA 185-R-2-16

As de Lesseps should have understood in 1879, when he and his party had to walk across the bridge, the Chagres wasn't just any river. When conditions were right and the trade winds pushed the big storms in off the Atlantic, all the northern slopes of the hills were solid running water that flowed down into the Chagres River. Any dam would have to be designed to hold an immense amount of water as well as safely spill the really big floods.

Had innovation been a strong feature of the curriculum at the big French engineering schools, the combination of these two huge issues at Panama–the immense river flows of the Chagres and the ever greater problems of digging at Culebra and other cuts–might have resulted in a commonsense solution. Damming the Chagres to create a lake, with locks on the Atlantic and Pacific sides, would have solved the two problems at once.

The geography along the route chosen by the French, paralleling the Panama Railroad, was almost unique of all the routes considered by both the Americans and the French. A large river wound through a basin bordered on either side by a range of low hills. Had the French fully grasped the implications of the geography and the rainfall at Panama, the history of the next few years might have been very different.

1884: Yellow Fever Strikes Dingler's Family

Sometimes, even in huge projects like this, small events can have a huge resonance, affecting the outcome of the whole. The

Smaller bucket excavator operating near Emperador, circa 1884. The big cut in the distance is Culebra. When the Americans took over the project, dozens of huge pieces of machinery and thousands of men would be working here.

NA 185-G-2040

striking down of Jules Dingler's children in the winter of 1883–84 by yellow fever was a sobering omen of the growing scourge that was wracking the canal.

Dingler brought out his adult son and daughter as well as the daughter's fiancé in the fall of 1883 when he returned from a consultation trip back to France. A few months later, the three new arrivals were all dead from the yellow scourge.

The news of the deaths hit France and particularly the community of professional engineers hard. France wasn't a huge country and the community of professional engineers was small. As the word came back of the deaths from yellow fever and malaria, the names were often well known to those who remained, and who themselves were considering work in Panama.

In France, while going to Panama was considered by some a patriotic act, the news of the deaths in the Dingler family had an immensely sobering effect in the French engineering community. Within weeks, the word was spreading–Panama was a deathtrap.

This grim news also had a serious effect on de Lesseps' ability to raise money to finance the project.

While the French engineering staff was dying by the dozens, each to be buried and mourned with poignant ceremony, the laborers that had been brought to work on the canal from Barbados, Jamaica, and a dozen other countries died by the hundreds, sometimes never to be mourned at all.

As in the construction of the Panama Railroad, the final toll of canal workers lost to disease during the French effort can

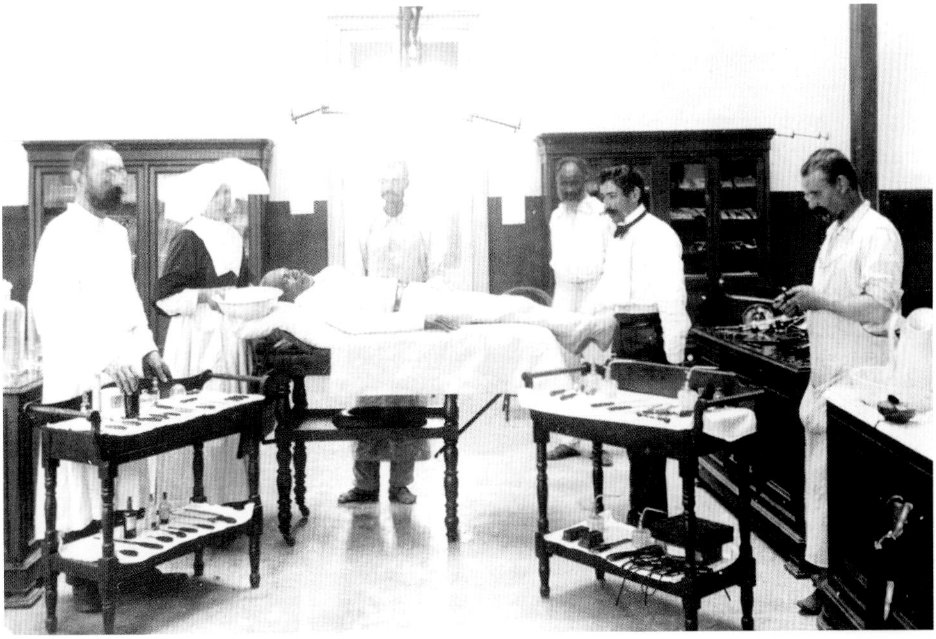

never be fully known. Many sick workers never went to the ample French hospitals and clinics. In the first place, you had to pay to go and the going rate was about what a worker earned in a day.

But the word had also gotten out–few people that entered the hospitals came out alive. It was reliably reported that during 1884 and 1885, mortality in the French hospitals at Panama was a horrifying 75 percent. Three out of every four that entered died.

Many dead laborers never saw a cemetery, their bodies reportedly dumped wherever it was convenient–by the side of the road, into the ditches and streams or just into the recently excavated stream of dirt that was being dumped into almost every convenient place near the great cuts.

It was tragic for the French who came to Panama to die, but their relative numbers were small. The true tragedy fell to the unnamed workers who came from their families in little hamlets and villages all around the Caribbean basin. Families were

French hospital in Panama, circa 1885. It was a great facility, but few patients left it alive. Because of all the containers of standing water, both inside and outside, it was a perfect breeding ground for the mosquitoes that carried yellow fever. Also, in that there was no cure for yellow fever at that time, the hospitals were just clean places to die.

NA 185-G-2231

Those Changing Excavation Numbers

The first rough estimate of the total earth to be removed for a French sea level canal was 45 million cubic meters. During de Lesseps' 1880 trip to Panama, his technical committee prudently raised that number to 75 million cubic meters. After the digging had begun and progress could be more accurately calculated, the estimate was further raised to 120 million cubic meters. The final total before any ships could pass from the Atlantic to the Pacific would be almost 200 million cubic meters. Of this total, almost half would be eventually excavated from the massive cut at Culebra.

Working quarters for West Indian laborers, circa 1910. Actually these were very nice compared to the jungle shacks where the majority of the natives from the Caribbean lived, both during the French and American eras. NA 1850-G-1595

left behind, dependent on their man to bring back the money so crucial for their meager needs. So many people, never hearing, never knowing.

Why was yellow fever, and to a lesser degree, malaria, so deadly at Panama in the 1880's? In the past, yellow fever had run its course in cycles, every two or three years. But when the huge labor immigration that was to support the canal construction really got ramped-up at Panama in the early 1880's, the level of sickness never seemed to lessen.

Probably it was the natural effect of just having so many people crowded together, for the most part in very poor living conditions.

As the numbers grew, so did the consensus: that disease was endemic at Panama. There was no apparent reliable indicator of who would get the disease, nor was there any clear understanding of either where it came from or how to treat it.

This was the true tragedy of Panama.

Yet, remarkably the work went on. Despite one estimate that at any time during the French Canal effort, a quarter of the workers were sick or dying from malaria or yellow fever, the machines were working and the dirt was flying.

In the winter of 1884 - 85, almost 20,000 workers were attacking the world's largest construction project. About 3,000 were white, mostly French, engineering and administrative personnel. The balance were laborers, mostly blacks from var-

That Elusive Angle of Repose

Both the French and the Americans had hoped to excavate at a steep angle, but the unstable clays of Panama required that the slopes be cut at a much flatter angle, requiring excavation vastly greater than planned.

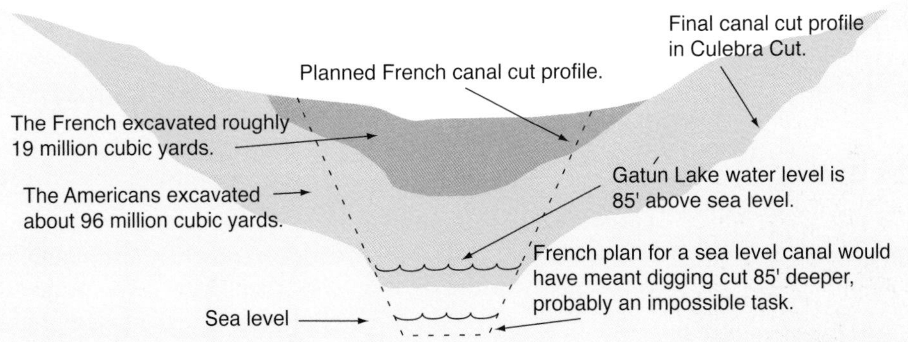
Final canal cut profile in Culebra Cut.
Planned French canal cut profile.
The French excavated roughly 19 million cubic yards.
The Americans excavated about 96 million cubic yards.
Gatun Lake water level is 85' above sea level.
French plan for a sea level canal would have meant digging cut 85' deeper, probably an impossible task.
Sea level

ious countries around the Caribbean basin.

While machines were at work in all the diggings, a substantial number of laborers were struggling away with pick, shovel, and wheelbarrow. For these folks especially, the work in the steaming tropics was truly brutal. For many natives, it did not take them long to realize that Panama was a deathtrap. Whatever their situation was where they had come from, after a few months in Panama, it was a lot more appealing than remaining in Panama and most probably dying. The result was predictable: many natives left as soon as they had enough money to bring a little home.

What would the planners have done if they had known it would end up like this before they started? The dynamics of cutting through the Continental Divide meant simply that the more you dug, the more there was to dig as the slides sloughed down into the excavation!

1885 – The Natives Get Restless

Though it was a part of Colombia, Panamanian politics had their own volatile, homegrown flavor. In the spring of 1885, a conservative was elected as President of Colombia and fighting broke out. Troops stationed in Panama headed to Cartagena, the Colombian capital, to help quell the uprising, allowing a Panamanian leader to take advantage of their absence and take over Panama City. The remaining troops in Colón quickly crossed the isthmus by train to retake Panama City, leaving Colón essentially defenseless.

The situation allowed Pedro Prestán, a Haitian native who resented whites, to seize Colón and burn much of the city, making perhaps 8,500 workers homeless, though fewer than 20 people died.

For Dingler, the Frenchman in charge of the canal effort, the fire and its aftermath may have been the straw that broke the camel's back. Two and a half years of struggling with the intractable problems of a plan that was flawed in its core elements and the grief of losing his entire family to yellow fever had taken its toll. In August of 1885 he resigned his post and returned to France. When he had arrived in Panama, he was truly one of France's best and brightest talents. His experiences in Panama had almost totally shattered him.

Paris: The Financial House of Cards Gets Shaky

By now experienced journalists from other countries besides France were reporting that the work at Panama was not going well. The core yardstick of progress–the amount of earth excavated–was way less than had been projected. Malaria and yellow fever killed workers in epidemic numbers and any projections of when the canal would be completed were nothing less than fiction. Crucially, the key engineering challenge at Panama, what to do with the Chagres River, had not yet been solved even after five years.

To make things worse, in December of 1885 an especially violent storm ravaged the waterfront at Colón and sent an astounding, even by Panamanian standards, deluge of rain onto the northern slopes of the hills and mountains.

The Chagres River, as if to demonstrate once again its violent power, rose 25 feet in less than a day and flooded the diggings and Panama Railroad alike.

The news hit the French press, and along with the recent critical articles in British and American newspapers, served to exacerbate a deep seated doubt in the success of the venture at Panama.

The price of the Panama Canal Company stock plunged. To reassure worried investors, the grand old man, Ferdinand de Lesseps, then 80 years old, announced that he himself would go to Panama.

Here, once again, was an opportunity for de Lesseps to educate himself on the real progress that had been achieved at Panama, and to listen carefully to the engineers' appraisal of the chances of success of the plan that he had insisted so forcefully upon–the sea level canal.

If he received that information isn't clear. It is possible that no one wished to give the immensely popular de Lesseps the bad news. Yet he scheduled ample meetings with the French engineering staff. How could they not have said anything to him about the impossibility of the task before them?

Back in Paris, his message that while the challenge was far

Like something out of a Jules Verne novel, the big steam and smoke belching Slaven dredges were a dramatic sign that the work was progressing.
NA 185-R-0702

greater than at Suez, all was still well, was undercut by three different engineering reports.

Each carried different versions of the same conclusion: a sea level canal was impossible; however, a canal with locks would most likely succeed.

1886: If Only de Lesseps Would Have Listened

Here then was an opportunity, probably the last, that de Lesseps would have to modify his plan and still have a chance of successfully completing the canal. It was the spring of 1886, probably not too late to change course and still complete the project, if it was done quickly and forcefully. As in no other project, the economic future of hundreds of thousands of French citizens and the national pride was wrapped up in the effort to build the Panama Canal.

The stakes were so huge, the answer so obvious. So, why didn't de Lesseps see it?

Most probably just pride, his inability to acknowledge he had been wrong in his insistence on a sea level canal. The irony is that probably, for a few months that spring of 1886, there was a small window of opportunity that gave the French a chance of succeeding at Panama. That chance depended totally on de Lesseps, who was still lionized by so many French.

The only way it would work was for de Lesseps to publically pronounce that new evidence at Panama required that the canal design be modified to one with locks. He could then promote the canal company stock creditably and effectively among the working class of France that were the core of his financial support, and he would most likely raise enough capital to have a genuine chance at success. But he had to acknowledge that the new canal design had to have locks.

The French middle and working classes that had provided the money in the earlier bond sales were eager to believe in de Lesseps. Indeed, almost a half million workers, with families to support and little financial security, had put their meager earnings into the Canal bonds. More than anything, they very badly needed the project to succeed.

A detailed and novel plan by Philippe Bunau-Varilla, the energetic French engineer who had eventually taken over the head of operations at Panama after Dingler left, even gave de Lesseps an easy way to support a locks system.

The big Slaven floating dredges had proven so effective that Bunau-Varilla reasoned that they could also work at Culebra and the other big cuts if a system of locks and canals was created to bring them to Culebra from the Atlantic coast. The advantage was that the cut at Culebra would have to be made only about half as deep as already planned. This alone should have made it an extremely attractive alternative.

Furthermore, the locks would be made large enough to allow ships to pass, so that as soon as the work canal with the locks was constructed, ships would be able to use it. This would bring in desperately needed revenue as the sea level canal was being dredged slowly deeper and deeper. Here then, was an opportunity for de Lesseps to wriggle out of the box he had created for himself. He could support a locks canal as a way to best deal with the challenging conditions they had encountered, without having to admit that his original concept was wrong. The locks would be built, the big Slaven dredges moved in to start working in the big inland cuts through the continental divide, and as soon as a narrow channel was cut through the mountains, small ships could begin to transit the new canal, paying their way. Then over time, the idea of a sea level canal could be slowly and quietly dropped, as the channel was widened to accomodate larger ships.

Meanwhile, the finances of the company were unraveling. The cash flow needed to maintain the work at Panama was immense. The failure of de Lesseps to raise enough money for the project when the enthusiasm for it was so high was now coming back to haunt him. To keep the money flowing the company had been forced to sell bonds at higher and higher interest rates to

make them attractive to investors. Because of these rates and of the heavy costs of promoting the bond sales, the net cash yields were growing too small to keep the work going at Panama.

At the end of the Suez Canal project, when cash flow was tight and investors were tapped out, an innovative scheme called a lottery bond was developed. This required government approval. In essence the bonds were also lottery tickets, and regular drawings were held and cash prizes given out. The idea was to make the bonds more attractive to investors.

It had worked in Suez, and de Lesseps and the officers of the canal company lobbied government officials fiercely to approve it for Panama.

By the fall of 1887, de Lesseps could hold back the tide for a canal with locks no more and finally, in a letter to the stockholders, he announced that a new plan had been just developed for a canal with locks and that the famous Gustav Eiffel would build the great locks.

The plan would reduce the amount of dirt to be excavated by almost 50 percent, a savings that made the canal achievable.

But still the financing issues were sobering. By this time the French public had invested roughly a billion francs in Panama; now de Lesseps had to somehow convince them to invest half that amount again.

Only a lottery bond could provide a possible incentive for investors so late in the game. The members of the French Parliament were no fools, and many had no illusions about what was happening in Panama; but the sheer power of de Lesseps' supporters carried the day and the bill finally passed, in April of 1888.

Better view of French bucket excavator, circa 1887. Notice the line of ready dirt cars. One of the biggest challenges at Panama was getting rid of the huge amount of dirt in an efficient fashion. The concept of this machine was great – an endless stream of dirt flowing into the waiting train cars. But it had problems in hard clay and especially in rocks, and was totally outclassed by the enormous 95-ton Bucyrus steam shovels that the Americans used.

NA 185-G-1361

Last, Last Chance: The Lottery Bond Sale of 1888

The turning point, the last, last chance to possibly save the French canal effort, came in late November 1888, when the final batch of the so-called lottery bonds went on sale. Despite de Lesseps' pleas to the French public, earlier sales had been disappointing. The final offering had to be widely sold, or the necessary target wouldn't be met and the existing bond purchasers would have to be refunded and the Compagnie Universelle du Canal Interocéanique would be bankrupt.

It was a high stakes gamble of the highest degree and as the deadline approached, the rumors ebbed and flowed around the company offices. Hundreds of anxious investors waited for news of strong sales that would save their desperately important nest eggs. On the last day of the sale, de Lesseps announced that the sale had been a success, and the next morning a large excited crowd mobbed the company offices to cheer the canal.

But instead came bitter news: de Lesseps had been misled. The sale had failed to attract enough investors and the company, along with the savings and financial hopes of many, many French citizens, would soon disappear along with the reputations of many of its backers.

Aftermath: Scandal and Recrimination

The news hit hard and the disappointment was intense. In its inevitable backlash, the unsavory side of the Compagnie Universelle's dealings with the press and the government was revealed–millions of francs had been paid to influence journalists and politicians alike to promote the sale of the companies' bonds.

It was a scandal that shook France. Charles de Lesseps, the great man's son, was sent to jail for a short term. In reality,

Why Didn't de Lesseps Go to Panama Earlier?

One of the most curious questions about the French canal effort was why didn't de Lesseps visit the project between his first visit in 1879 before the digging had started and his 1886 trip when the project was in deep trouble?

During this entire period, de Lesseps enjoyed a wide and deep popularity among the French middle and working classes who were the core investors in the canal company. He must have known that the initial offering was far less than the funds required. The prudent thing would have been to conduct another stock offering during this time, before the bad news about progress at Panama became difficult to deny. Clearly, he must have heard the details of the challenges at Panama. Apparently, he never felt the need to visit in person, leaving almost all administrative work to others.

Had he visited the digging in, say, 1884 and talked to engineers on site, he may have discovered that it was becoming more and more obvious to those in Panama that construction of a sea level canal was impossible.

Culebra, circa 1911, during the American era. The French plan for a sea level canal would have meant that blasting and steam shovel and excavator crews would have had to dig another 80 feet below the level of the cut shown here. Would it have even been possible, given the technology available to them at the time? Also note in the photo that the top of the cut is already beginning to break off and slide.
NA

Charles' financial misdeeds were relatively minor and he was essentially pilloried as a scapegoat. The news deeply saddened his father, one of France's brightest lights for most of a century. Ferdinand de Lesseps faded from public view and died, a deeply saddened man, at his country estate in December of 1894. He was 89.

Both father and son deserved better than they got. Neither reaped any financial gain from the project. Ferdinand, especially, was a true hero, whose vision, even though flawed, ultimately facilitated the Panama Canal.

History wasn't kind to either de Lesseps or the French. The events in Panama and France led to the almost universal belief that the French effort had been nothing but a misguided boondoggle from start to finish. David McCullough reported in *The Path Between The Seas* that many Americans who worked in Pānama during the American era believed that de Lesseps had died insane, in an asylum.

In France, the wound to the national psyche was large. Already humiliated by the defeat of the French army and the capture of 80,000 troops at the Battle of Sedan in 1870, in addition to the subsequent capture of Paris and the loss of the rich provinces of Alsace and Lorraine to the Germans, the country needed a boost to national honor. It had swelled with the successful completion of the Suez Canal, but then collapsed after the effort at Panama ended in bankruptcy and scandal.

A kinder view would be more appropriate. Clearly, the French failed at Panama. Yet as the Americans would discover, the challenges in that rain-soaked, disease-ridden country were immense, almost beyond imagination. That the French had managed to achieve what they did, against all the odds that they faced, was a triumph by itself.

The tragedies are twofold. First is that this scandal clouded France's and the world's perception of the huge accomplishments that were achieved. But the larger tragedy still lingers, even after the Americans' success with their much better equipment, methodic approach to attacking disease, and the much deeper pockets of the American government.

And it is this: the French might have succeeded. Despite the disease, despite the Chagres River, despite the financial difficulties, failure was not the inevitable outcome of their huge enterprise. If the French engineers had grasped the unusual possibilities that the geography of Panama afforded. If they had been able to persuade de Lesseps to modify his dogged insistence on a sea level canal. If a new plan and appeal to investors had been made, say, in 1886, then history might have been very different.

A new company was formed in 1894 and work began again at Panama. But this was at a much smaller scale, in essence just doing enough work to keep active the concession that had been granted by the Colombian government. The larger goal was to hopefully sell the equipment, concession, and work already achieved to an organization better equipped to finish it. After the French experience, it was also obvious that only a very large nation, probably Russia or the US, had sufficient resources to finish the canal.

THE MAN AND THE MACHINE THAT MADE IT ALL HAPPEN. Teddy Roosevelt, at the controls of the "Machine That Built the Panama Canal," the 95-ton Bucyrus Erie. The unscheduled photo was taken when the President, on a train tour of the Canal, saw the big shovel and asked to have the train stopped and marched through the rain and the mud to sit in the seat and talk to the driver, a man named A.G. Grey. The President was thrilled to be there and that he had helped make it all happen.
NA

THE AMERICAN ERA: 1903–1914

MAKING THE DIRT FLY

This photo of President Teddy Roosevelt at the controls of the 95-ton Bucyrus steam shovel, shows clearly his interest in, and excitement with the Panama Canal project. Without the determination of this President and the sheer power of that remarkable steam shovel, which moved dirt many times faster than any French machine, it is unlikely that a canal at Panama would have ever been completed.

Would you walk over this bridge? On the Northern Pacific Railroad, circa 1880. As the French struggled in the mud of Panama, the railroads and the industrial revolution were bringing sweeping changes to America. The breadth and pace of these technological changes would place the Americans in a much better position to attempt the canal than the French, just 20 years earlier.
NA

Background: Changing the Face of America

Canal developments in Central America and Panama occurred during an accelerating pace of change that would dramatically reshape the face of America during the last half of the 19th century.

In 1850 almost 90 percent of the US population was classified as rural–living on farms and ranches and producing much of their own food. There was no electricity or telephones, and most transportation was by foot, horse, riverboat, and to a lesser degree, the rapidly developing railroads. Many families led extremely isolated lives with little information about events beyond their local communities.

One of the biggest changes had begun with the building of the first US railroads, beginning in the 1830's. The first trains were slow, undependable, dirty, and noisy, but on May 10, 1869, tracks from the Union Pacific and Central Pacific rail-

St. Louis waterfront, circa 1900. The Panama Canal project was just a logical extension of the transportation revolution that was sweeping the US at the turn of the century. These paddle wheel steamers just pushed their bows up to the muddy shore and lowered a gangplank.
NA

roads were joined at Promontory Point, Utah, creating a true transcontinental line. For the first time freight and passengers could travel easily from coast to coast.

Coal powered the trains and steamships and coal oil-fueled lanterns lit most of the country as well. But in 1858, an unemployed railroad ticket-taker, using a crude drilling rig, struck oil just 70 feet below the surface at Titusville, Pennsylvania. That first well yielded just 400 gallons a day, but this liquid fuel was to initiate a transportation revolution that would, within a few decades, begin to change the nature of US society.

Thomas Edison invented the light bulb in 1878, followed shortly thereafter by the first installations of central electrical generating plants in larger cities across the US. The change wrought by electric lighting cannot be overstated.

Imagine the wonder of the first users to have their houses wired for electricity, as they were able to live for the first time in rooms lit by more than occasional pools of dim light.

Communication changes were next. In 1876 Alexander Graham Bell spoke his famous words, "Mr. Watson, come here. I want you," and the modern telephone, as much a transformational invention as electric lighting, was born.

The Brooklyn Bridge was opened in 1882 to fanfare that excited the nation about the possibilities that technology and industry were creating for everyone.

The century that began with less than six million people living in the US ended with 76 million. It was an exciting time to be alive.

Teddy Roosevelt: A Man to Match the Times

In September of 1901, President William McKinley was assassinated and Teddy Roosevelt, known to some in Congress as "that damned cowboy" became President.

At 42 the youngest President to ever serve, "Teddy" was to the 1900's what Jack Kennedy was to the 1960's–young, energetic, visionary and exciting to be around.

Born to a wealthy New York family, Roosevelt was an avid outdoorsman even as a boy, and was elected to the New York state assembly shortly after graduating from Harvard. But after his wife died in childbirth, a distraught Roosevelt left politics to pursue the hard life of a rancher in what was then the Dakota Territories. For two years he worked long hours in the saddle, enjoying a fulfilling outdoor life. But after most of his cattle died during severe winter blizzards in 1885 - 86, he returned to New York, remarried and began raising a large family. Becoming active again in politics, Roosevelt was made assistant secretary of the Navy in the first McKinley administration.

Roosevelt had already become friends with Alfred Mahan, a passionate advocate of sea power and author of the very influential book *The Influence of Sea Power Upon History.*

A man of action to the very core, Roosevelt became impatient with McKinley's reluctance to go to war with Spain after the US battleship *Maine* was blown up in Havana harbor. When war was finally declared, Roosevelt quickly resigned his Navy post. He organized the First Volunteer Cavalry Regiment with a mixture of college athletes, Western cowboys and other men eager to fight the Spaniards. Roosevelt and his unit gained national fame as the "Rough Riders" after a particularly dramatic charge up San Juan Hill in Cuba.

The Spanish American War also served as a catalyst for Roosevelt's interest in a US–controlled canal somewhere across Central America. For when news of the explosion of the *Maine* was received in Washington, a critical battleship, the *Oregon*,

Why Did the U.S.S. Maine Blow Up?

When the US government sent the battleship *U.S.S. Maine* to protect Americans against rioting mobs in Cuba in late January of 1898, tensions between the United States and Spain were already high.

But when a devastating explosion destroyed the *Maine* and killed 260 American sailors on February 15, an outraged American public pushed the government closer to war.

At the time it was assumed that the explosion had been caused by a Spanish bomb or torpedo, but subsequent investigation revealed that the most likely cause was some sort of internal explosion that had nothing to do with Spanish forces.

Sea power: the battleship *U.S.S. Connecticut* at San Francisco, shortly after leading a fleet of 15 other battleships around Cape Horn from Virginia, a 12,000-mile trip. Painted brilliant white, they were known as The Great White Fleet. Teddy Roosevelt was a passionate advocate of sea power and keenly felt the need for a canal somewhere in Central America that would be controlled by the US.

SFM

was in San Francisco. She started steaming for the East Coast, but with no canal, it was 12,000 miles away.

Her voyage was followed by an eager nation. It took 67 days and the lesson wasn't lost on Roosevelt. He understood, better than most, the importance of sea power, and that in order to be a true two-ocean power, the United States had to have access to and control over a canal.

Roosevelt had also become President at an unusual juncture in US history. The new century had begun with a remarkable optimism in the US population. The debilitating depression that had gripped much of the country during the 1890's had finally given way to better times. The war with Spain had been short, dramatic, and victorious. The US had exerted its naval strength in two hemispheres–in the Philippines and in Cuba. The Republicans, Teddy Roosevelt's party, controlled Congress.

Taking advantage of the opportunity, Teddy quickly established himself as a congenial, but energetic and forceful President. Observers noted that he set a pace of activity never seen in the office before.

He didn't waste any time focusing on what he perceived as an essential piece of US military infrastructure–a canal. In his very first address to Congress, Roosevelt called a canal one of the single most important tasks ahead for the nation.

Nicaragua, Naturally?

When Roosevelt became President in the fall of 1901, no betting man would have put a nickel down on the chances of a US canal at Panama.

In a sense, the French experience had poisoned the attitude of many US policy-makers. Panama was seen as too hot, too disease-ridden, too rainy and too unstable, geologically as well as politically. Roosevelt had already revealed his preference for the Nicaraguan route in a letter to his friend, the naval historian Alfred Mahan four years before becoming President.

Nicaragua was closer, there would be less digging and there was the lake already in place. The river would have to be widened, deepened, and a short canal cut from the lake to the Pacific. Most of all, the jungle wasn't as thick as Panama and the dreaded problems of yellow fever and malaria probably would be less severe, or so the thinking went.

If there had been just a single lesson from the French experience at Panama, it might have been this: the financial and organizational challenges of an inter-ocean canal, be it at Panama, or somewhere else in Central America, were simply too large for any private company.

Players at High Stakes Poker

Given the evidence and the mood of the times, it seemed inevitable that the American effort would be at Nicaragua.

Perhaps the biggest reason for this was Senator John Taylor Morgan, chairman of the Senate Committee on Interoceanic Canals. Seventy-seven years old at the turn of the century, he was a Senator to be reckoned with. Morgan was from Alabama and saw a canal at Nicaragua as something that would reap major benefits to Alabama ports as they found themselves so close to a major world shipping route.

But Morgan and his pro-Nicaragua colleagues hadn't counted on the wily persistence of a particularly determined man, Philippe Bunau-Varilla.

He had taken over the management of the French effort when Charles Dingler had quit after the fire at Colón and deaths of his family. Bunau-Varilla had quickly grasped the depth of the problems ahead and been an early proponent of a canal with locks.

Short, balding, with jet-black hair and a pointed and waxed mustache, he had an intense manner and a fierce obsession: to get the canal built at Panama.

He was articulate, forceful, and spoke English well. But most of all he was incredibly *knowledgeable!* He had been an engineering student in France when the great de Lesseps arrived, fresh from Panama, to excite them all about the grand French destiny that was the canal.

At Panama, Bunau-Varilla quickly rose through the ranks to a division chief, eventually managing the entire French canal effort.

He was someone who could speak passionately and in detail about the difficulties of digging at Culebra, the challenges of damming the mighty Chagres River, which pieces of equipment were effective, what strategy had worked best. He grasped the implications of the unique geography of Panama, including that several dams in critical places would create a lake across much of the isthmus, and that much of the digging was already done (or so he believed).

When the US commission to study possible routes–the Isthmian Canal Commission–arrived in Paris in the summer of 1899, Bunau-Varilla sprang into action. Also known as the Walker Commission, this group of nine, headed by Rear Admiral John Walker, was to report to Congress on the feasibility of the different routes.

Entertaining the Commission with his charm, eloquence and wit, he persuaded Walker and other key members that Panama needed serious consideration.

The mysterious man who managed to change the will of a President and the Congress – Philippe Bunau-Varilla. Intimately familiar with every detail of Panama and the French effort, Bunau-Varilla pulled off an enormous coup by getting the US to purchase the French holdings in which he was also an investor.
LC

With great fanfare, the final report of the Walker Commission was delivered to Congress in November of 1901. As expected the Commission recommended Nicaragua. The irony was that a very strong case was made for Panama on its technical merits, but the high price (109 million dollars) that the French wanted for their Panama properties made that route unattractive.

While the US House of Representatives quickly passed a Nicaragua bill and sent it on to the Senate, things were heating up behind the scenes. First, due to Bunau-Varilla's efforts, the French dropped their price to 40 million dollars. Curiously, this was exactly what the Walker Commission had estimated they were worth. Then Teddy Roosevelt got directly involved, interviewing each member of the Commission privately.

The bombshell came on the 20th of January when the Walker Commission changed its mind. Led by George Morison, who had been intensely lobbied by Bunau-Varilla in France, the entire Commission voted to purchase the French holdings and finish the job.

Roosevelt's involvement had been pivotal, but also chancy. To support Panama when the most powerful men in the Senate plus the American public were all in favor of the Nicaraguan route put him in the uneasy position of possibly losing a major battle early in his Presidency.

A Panama bill, to buy the French holdings, negotiate rights from Colombia and build a canal, was introduced in the Senate and the battle was on.

Martinique Volcano Blows Up; Uneasy Senate Votes for Panama

Despite the positive slant on Panama in the Commission's report, the sentiment in the Senate was predominantly pro-Nicaragua. Bunau-Varilla, lobbying intensely behind the scenes for Panama, had tried to bring up the spectre of volcanic activity in Nicaragua threatening a canal there, but without much luck.

Then, as if on cue, Mt. Pelée on the Caribbean island of Martinique, after rumbling for a week, exploded on May 8, 1902. The eruption killed almost the entire population of nearby St. Pierre, some 30,000 souls. The only survivor was a criminal jailed in a dungeon with thick walls.

A week later, Momotombo in Nicaragua erupted as well, in flames and showers of lava bombs.

Bunau-Varilla knew how to take advantage of the situation. With the crucial Senate vote imminent, he arranged to have a Nicaraguan one-centavo stamp delivered to every senator. It was impossible to ignore the stamp's official message: it showed Momotombo in full eruption.

Three days later the Senate voted, 42 to 34, for Panama.

Colombia Rejects Treaty

Of course, there was still the sticky issue of dealing with Colombia, through whose territory any Panama Canal would have to pass. In 1902, Bogotá was the most remote capital in South America, and desperately broke after a two-year-long civil war.

While Bogotá had given Washington assurances of wanting to work towards a US canal, it rejected a treaty after months of incredibly tedious work by a series of diplomats.

It was no secret that Teddy Roosevelt had little patience with the lengthy treaty negotiations or respect for the politicians in Bogotá.

What followed, between the rejection of the treaty on August 12, 1903, and the Panamanian Revolution in November, was a plot straight out of a spy novel.

Bunau-Varilla, conspirators from Panama, as well as various US government officials, had meeting after meeting in New York and Washington, trying to iron out all the details of a coup. Intrigue and secrecy were the watchwords of the day, but it all hinged on Colombia not sending heavy reinforcements to guard their most valuable possession, a half-dug canal.

Though approached several times by conspirators wanting to secure US involvement, President Roosevelt played his cards very close to the chest, not committing the US to any action that was not sanctioned by its existing treaty with Colombia concerning US interest in the Panama Railroad.

Once again, Philippe Bunau-Varilla showed himself to be incredibly resourceful and committed to the cause of a canal at Panama. He promised to fund the conspirators with his own money and persuaded his US contacts to send the cruiser *U.S.S. Nashville* as a show of strength to Colón at a critical moment.

Trouble: Colombian troops at Colón, November 4, 1903. Only very quick thinking by the head of the Panama Railroad averted what could have been a very ugly confrontation.

NA 185-R-01-05

Fast Thinking in Colón

As soon as the chief conspirator, Dr. Manuel Amador, arrived back in Panama, things started happening very fast. Herbert Prescott, who worked for the Panama Railroad and was a US canal booster, wisely ordered all extra trains and cars to be shifted from Colón on the Atlantic to Panama City on the Pacific. Prescott knew that if any Colombian troops arrived, they would do so at Colón, but, that without the railroad which he controlled, they couldn't move across the isthmus to Panama City.

Around 5:30 on the afternoon of November 3, the *Nashville* anchored off Panama and the coup plotters breathed a huge sigh of relief, taking it as a sign that the ship was there to stop any Colombian interference in their plans.

But then around midnight, the Colombian warship *Cartagena* arrived with 500 troops, ready for any contingency. Imagine the shock of Amador and his co-conspirators when the troops landed the next morning without any resistance from the *Nashville*.

Enter one very cool character, Colonel James Shaler, head of the Panama Railroad. He was very aware of the plans for a coup, but also that the *Nashville* probably wouldn't actively intervene until the plotters had proclaimed the new republic, so he had to play his cards very carefully.

Shaler arranged for a special short train to take the Colombian generals to Colón, but there was no room for the troops. Shaler explained that another train would shortly arrive for the troops.

The second train never came. It was a stroke of genius. The move gave the plotters in Panama City a few hours' notice to plan and cut off communication between the Colombian generals and their troops.

The plotters quickly arranged to buy off the small Colombian garrison in Panama City. When the train arrived with the generals, they were warmly welcomed, only to be quickly surrounded and disarmed. Amador and his co-conspirators quickly proclaimed a new Panamanian Republic, and immediately sent word to Washington, D.C.

Less than 72 hours after the coup, a telegram was received back from Washington, recognizing the Republic of Panama. There had been but a single fatality: a Chinese store owner was killed by a shell from the Colombian gunboat *Bogotá,* which had disappeared as soon as its fire was returned.

It was a brilliantly executed coup, aided liberally by good luck. If the *Nashville* had arrived 24 hours later, or Shaler not managed to separate the generals from their troops, the outcome might have been very different.

Also, the US had been able to facilitate the coup without any direct involvement, other than the appearance of the *Nashville*. The denial of rail transport to the Colombian troops was legally questionable, but once the coup took place the point was moot.

However, "Gunboat Diplomacy" took on a new meaning. Within hours of the coup, more US Navy ships began arriving to station themselves off both the Atlantic and Pacific coasts of Panama, to prevent, by force if necessary, the landing of new troops from Colombia. The reality of the situation was that the new Republic of Panama had almost no armed forces, and had it not been for what was essentially a blockade of the Panamanian coast by the US Navy, the Colombians could have retaken the isthmus relatively easily.

In a larger sense, the Panamanian Revolution of 1904 was simply a manifestation of Roosevelt's and America's new sense of power. This new foreign policy was guided by a sense of national destiny and willingness to exercise this power to further what it perceived as national interest, without being overly concerned with the sovereign rights of other nations.

While giving many Americans great satisfaction in their newly used powers, this action was seen by most Latin American countries as a blatant power grab. This created difficult relations in this region for decades to come. If Roosevelt had waited a bit, it is likely that the Colombians might have come around and an arrangement could have been concluded that would have been equitable to both sides without the bitterness caused by the Panama Revolution.

What did the Americans get for their 40 million dollars in Panama? While some of the equipment like this submerged bucket excavator wasn't much use, a surprising amount of the French equipment was in good shape, well maintained and eventually used as part of the US effort.

NA 185-G-1359

The New Treaty: Where Were the Panamanians?

If the 1903 treaty negotiations with the Colombians and the subsequent intrigue and plotting by Bunau-Varilla and others had been like a spy novel, what happened next was positively Machiavellian.

In exchange for the $100,000 he had promised to pay the coup conspirators, Bunau-Varilla got himself appointed Minister Plenipotentiary. Presenting his credentials at the White House on November 13, Bunau-Varilla was formally introduced to President Roosevelt in the official ceremony that marked the recognition of Panama by the US.

As David McCullough so wryly noted in his excellent book, *The Path Between The Seas*, there were neither any Panamanians present, nor a word of Spanish spoken.

The real Panamanian delegation was then aboard a steamer from Panama to the US. Their mission was to sign a new treaty between Panama and the United States spelling out the arrangements for the Canal Zone and the relationship between the two countries. Before they arrived, Bunau-Varilla got a copy of the treaty from Secretary of State John Hay.

Instantly realizing that the treaty as written would face stiff opposition in the US Senate, Bunau-Varilla took it upon himself to rewrite those sections that had to do with the proposed Canal Zone, as well as the definitions of US power in the Zone and length of the concessions to be granted by Panama. Within 36 hours, he had rewritten the treaty, making it extremely advantageous to the US, in particular widening the Zone from 6 to 10 miles, and granting the US complete sovereignty within it. Furthermore the grant would be forever.

The steamer carrying the Panamanian delegation arrived at New York on November 17th just as the last draft of the treaty was being finalized between Hay and Bunau-Varilla. The latter had convinced the Secretary of State that he was empowered to act on behalf of the Panamanians. Bunau-Varilla sent word to the Panamanians to wait in New York while he frantically tried to wrap up all the loose ends of the treaty.

No fools, the Panamanians headed straight for Washington and were actually on the train while Bunau-Varilla was at the residence of the Secretary of State, signing the treaty on behalf of the Panamanians.The ink was hardly dry when Bunau-Varilla met the Panama delegation at Union Station to give them the good news.

The Panamanians were understandably furious and insisted to Hay that Bunau-Varilla had no authority to negotiate on their behalf. Hay, of course, knew an advantageous treaty when he saw one, and insisted the delegation take the treaty, unchanged, back to Panama for ratification.

Bunau-Varilla sent a cable to the Panamanian Secretary of State declaring that if the Panamanians didn't ratify the treaty without change, the US would pull their Navy back from the Panamanian coast and negotiate a new treaty with the Colombians. Without any army, this would essentially mean the end of the Republic of Panama, as well as a hangman's noose for the short-lived Republic's leaders.

Would this ever have happened?

No. Bunau-Varilla was delusional if he believed that the US would undo the coup in Panama. He was just continuing to play that game of high stakes poker he had been playing ever since the French effort had collapsed. In reality this last card was a joker, but to the Panamanians it was an ace because of what Bunau-Varilla had already accomplished for them.

The Panamanians capitulated; the treaty was ratified; the pro-US changes that Bunau-Varilla had inserted at the last moment were permanent.

The US Senate ratified the treaty with little serious debate. How could they not? It was slanted in favor of US interests.

The vote on February 23, 1904, also ended Philippe Bunau-

Varilla's quest. Against all odds, a foreigner with nothing on his side but dogged persistence had changed the opinion of a Congress, a President, and a country.

His last gesture was wonderfully fitting. He resigned his post with the Panamanians just a few days after the treaty was signed.

Philippe Bunau-Varilla, who had essentially created modern Panama, asked that his salary be used for a monument in Panama for the man whose vision had made his own quest possible: Ferdinand de Lesseps.

Ditch by ditch, pond by pond, mosquito eradication was carried out along the route of the Panama Canal. The Americans came to Panama with the newly discovered knowledge of the link between mosquitoes, yellow fever and malaria. If only the French had known!
NA

"Oh, Death, Where is Thy Sting?" Mosquito Control: The Key to Success

Between the failure of the French in 1888 and the ratification of the Treaty between the US and Panama in 1904, a new fact had emerged in the battle against yellow fever and malaria–the diseases were transmitted by mosquitoes. And not just mosquitoes in general, but two species of mosquitoes, each with very particular characteristics.

The malaria-mosquito connection had been made around 1899 by a Dr. Ronald Ross, an English doctor working in India, where malaria routinely killed perhaps a million souls a year. He found that when a particular species, the *Anopheles* mosquito, bites a human infected with malaria, the disease grows within the mosquito's body and eventually spreads to the salivary gland. Once there, the mosquito could spread the disease to the next person that it bit.

His book, *Mosquito Brigades*, was a revelation to the medical establishment and to public health authorities all around the world. The way to defeat malaria was to break the connection between mosquitoes and people who were sick with malaria.

That yellow fever also was carried by mosquitoes had been ferreted out around 1885 by a Cuban doctor, Carlos Finlay. The culprit was a different mosquito, the *Stegomyia*; but, with yellow fever, the disease path was harder to determine. It was only when Dr. Walter Reed came to Cuba in 1900 with the Army Yellow Fever Commission that the curious path was discovered. It went like this: if a mosquito manages to bite a yellow fever patient who has contacted the disease within the previous 72 hours, the insect gets infected. But then there must be an additional incubation period of up to three weeks before the mosquito can then pass the disease on by biting another person.

No one, especially Teddy Roosevelt, wanted to see the American experience at Cuba repeated. For every man killed by a Spanish bullet, a dozen had been felled by disease, primarily yellow fever and malaria.

After Dr. Reed arrived in Havana and determined that mosquitoes were a disease path for yellow fever, he and his staff approached the problem with typical American efficiency. Standing water was the key. Mosquito larvae needed to hatch in water. Accordingly, health workers fanned out around Havana beginning early in 1901 to empty or spray with oil all bodies of standing water. The mosquito larvae cannot grow in water that has a film of oil on the surface.

The result was stunning. Yellow fever dropped from around 1500 cases to 37 in a single year; malaria incidence was halved.

So in the same period that the US was gearing up to build a canal, the key to solving one of the biggest problems that France had faced in Panama was found.

1904: Teddy says "We'll Make the Dirt Fly."

Now that the Americans were in charge, Teddy Roosevelt asserted, "We'll make the dirt fly." The underlying message was something like this, "We'll show the world what Americans can do." The thought was that American horsepower and ingenuity were enough to overcome whatever had defeated the French at Panama.

One of the first groups to arrive in Panama was the medical team charged with ridding the isthmus of mosquitoes.

As soon as the team got their bearings, they were humbled by the immensity of the task ahead of them. Panama seemed to be one vast perfect breeding area for mosquitoes. The rain was incessant. Standing water was everywhere and the whole canal route was surrounded by swampy jungle. Havana had been a

Fumigation brigade, Panama, circa 1905. Incoming US Chief Engineer John Stevens gave Dr. Gorgas a big budget and a green light to do whatever he needed to rid the Canal Zone of mosquitoes. These workers broke up into teams and went street by street, house by house, searching for open water containers, putting up screening, and spraying insecticide.

NA 185-G-1429

small discrete area: teams were dispatched, lists were created and standing water oiled, covered, or eliminated. By contrast, eliminating mosquitoes at Panama was a daunting task.

Fortunately, the man chosen to head the yellow fever/malaria eradication team was Dr. William Gorgas, who had worked alongside Dr. Walter Reed in Cuba. Unfortunately, the lesson of Havana–that mosquitoes, malaria and yellow fever were intimately linked–was not shared by Gorgas' superiors in the new canal effort's managing body, the new Isthmian Canal Commission.

Imagine Gorgas' frustration. While he himself was immune to yellow fever as a result of having it as a child, he was intimately familiar with the stunning success of the mosquito eradication program in Havana. Furthermore, while there was little yellow fever in Panama in the summer of 1904, he knew that the arrival of thousands of new workers in Panama could trigger a devastating epidemic.

Meanwhile, as Gorgas and his team struggled with few resources against a huge task, the workers began arriving.

The first American in charge of the effort on the ground at Panama was John Wallace, a railroad man, who was quickly overwhelmed with the challenges of picking up where the French had left off. Who could blame him? The jungle had taken over much of the many work camps, dredges were half-sunk around the shores of Colón, equipment was rusting in the jungle, and food, housing and working conditions were all terrible.

Furthermore, the canal plan, which was based on building

Hundreds of laborers from Barbados arrive aboard the *Ancon*, Colón, 1904.
NA 185-G-1128

a huge dam to hold back the Chagres River at Bohio, was undermined by doubts about the site.

Panic of '05: Yellow Fever Appears; 75 Percent of Americans Flee

As Gorgas had foreseen, bringing new workers to Panama without an effective mosquito control program was like throwing dry kindling on a smoldering fire. It didn't help that the Panamanian undertakers, used to the devastation that the fever had wracked in the French era, had stacked up piles of coffins outside their businesses in anticipation.

By November of 1904 the first worker of the American era had died of yellow fever, and by the spring of 1905 the regular funeral trains were running once again to Monkey Hill. It was beginning to seem like the French era all over again and the panic was on. In reality only a mild epidemic was occurring, but it was enough to send most of the newly arrived Americans in Panama headed back home on the first available ship.

Shortly thereafter, Chief Engineer John Wallace, reportedly terrified by disease, left Panama with his wife to take up a more lucrative and safer position back in the States.

It had been a disastrous beginning. Wallace's departure, after less than a year on the job, along with the appearance of yellow fever, threw the entire US effort into disarray little more than a year after the first workers had arrived with such high hopes of showing the world what the US could do.

However, a new player that was little noticed in the beginning, but which would contribute greatly to the eventual success at Panama, had arrived. This was the Bucyrus 95-ton steam shovel, a monster excavator that rode on railroad tracks, took a huge bite out of earth or rock, then lifted and swiveled to dump its load onto a nearby railroad car. It had a daily capacity of at least three times the biggest similar machine operated by the French.

Just in time, John Stevens, a railroad man to his very core, and a legend in the construction community, came to Panama at a time when work was almost stopped. Americans were fleeing, and there was a very real chance that the American Panama Canal era would be over before it started. Critical to the success of the American effort was that Stevens immediately grasped that one of the key problems in Panama was setting up an efficient rail system to move the dirt from the cuts to the spoil areas.
NA 185-G-2108

The Right Man Arrives: John Stevens

When John Wallace left Panama, the entire project was in jeopardy. Yellow fever had come back, workers were fleeing as fast as they could book passage, little work was getting accomplished, and employee morale had collapsed. There was a very real possibility that the US effort might end in failure.

Into this immensely challenging situation came John Stevens. At that time he was probably the most experienced railroad builder in the world and a legend in the construction community. Son of a Maine farmer, Stevens had worked his way up from laborer to junior engineer to railroad magnate James Hill's right-hand man. A big-framed, hardy and plainspoken man, he'd surveyed the route for the Great Northern first over the Rockies under Hill and then had discovered the important pass over the Cascades in Washington State that still bears his name.

Stevens didn't waste any time getting to the crux of the problem–that efficient work could only come when the workers were well fed, housed, and healthy.

The fear of yellow fever was especially debilitating. While Stevens didn't totally believe in the mosquito connection, he quickly established a good rapport with Gorgas and realized that his only chance at attacking the dreaded disease was by supporting Gorgas' plan.

So if the dirt didn't fly in those initial months, the insecticide, the kerosene (to spray on exposed standing water), and screening did. After a deeply discouraging year of trying to attack the most pressing life and death problem in Panama with a tiny budget and no support from Washington, Gorgas was thrilled when Stevens essentially gave him a blank check.

Yellow Fever: Conquered at Last

The task ahead was huge, but Gorgas was the man for it and he knew the drill. As in Cuba, he hired fumigation brigades to go house by house through Colón and Panama City neighborhoods. The tight-fisted Isthmian Canal Commission had limited his purchases of critical pyrethrum insecticide to eight tons. Stevens quickly signed off on his request for 120 tons without hesitation. But it was the attack upon standing water that was the biggest factor in eliminating yellow fever and reducing malaria at Panama.

What Doctors Reed and Gorgas discovered at Havana would have shocked the French: the very jars and buckets of water that surrounded and filled the French hospitals turned out to be the perfect environment for breeding the *Stegomyia* mosquito. Additionally in 1905, there was no running water in Colón or Panama City. In place of running water in their homes, residents usually kept one or more open containers of water for daily use. These could also be excellent mosquito breeding spots.

Armed with this information, Gorgas' teams set out with a vengeance. Backpack sprayers were devised to take kerosene to the most remote pool of standing water. Swamps were drained, and if that wasn't feasible, regularly visited by kerosene spraying boats. Running water was brought to the cities and screening was installed by the acre.

It was astonishingly successful: Less than 18 months after Stevens had given Gorgas his full support, yellow fever had disappeared from Panama. For Gorgas and his team, it was nothing less than a stunning victory.

A Railroad Man's Solution

On his first visit to the great cut at Culebra, Stevens understood what the French never fully had. A railroad man to his very core, Stevens could see the immense amount of dirt that had to be moved and the Panama Railroad's very limited capacity to do so. He instinctively grasped that the biggest problem at Panama was moving the dirt efficiently, and for that railroads were the solution.

And everything had to be bigger: heavier rails, stronger bridges, bigger freight cars, more powerful locomotives. The 95-ton Bucyrus shovels couldn't work at capacity if they had to wait for empty train cars.

Dirt trains became the dominant feature of the Panama

Panama breeds innovation. One of the problems in getting rid of all the dirt that was being excavated from Culebra was spreading it after it was dumped from the trains. This double plow device saved a lot of backbreaking manual labor with shovels.
NA

Railroad. Special equipment was devised like the Lidgerwood plow, pulled by cable from a locomotive, emptying a dozen cars in a few minutes.

One of the key features of the Canal Zone was the well constructed open and airy housing. Married workers were encouraged to bring their families. With the dreaded yellow fever eliminated, it was critical to provide an environment that would encourage workers to stay.

Before Stevens, food purchased through Panamanian merchants had been both expensive and bad. Stevens quickly instituted a system of ordering everything possible from the States, and even built a large cold storage facility on the Colón waterfront. He also had the trains take out fresh food each morning to the new settlements being constructed all along the canal route.

In 1904 and 1905 getting good quality workers from the US was a challenge. Many had heard about the disease and the poor working and living conditions at Panama. By late 1906, a different word was spreading in the US–yellow fever had been almost eliminated, the food and the housing were good. Panama could be an exciting place to work.

While thousands of whites came down to fill the administrative, supervisory, and many of the craft or trade jobs, the majority of the work at Panama under the Americans, as with the French, was hard manual labor–shoveling dirt, building railroad, moving tracks, etc. This work fell mainly to natives from island nations in the Caribbean, particularly Barbados, Martinique and Guadeloupe, where many natives survived on a few months of work in the cane fields each year at 20 cents a day. At Panama the going rate was 10 cents an hour.

The good housing and the imported food were primarily for the white workers. Although a number of barracks were built for the black laborers, most preferred to both cook their own food and find their own housing, either in the slums of Colón or Panama City, or in little shanty villages all along the line of the canal.

The first workers that arrived under Stevens concentrated on the infrastructure. They rebuilt the Panama Railroad, and laid a parallel track (the original railroad had been a single track, with occasional sidings for trains to pass), as well as built hundreds of new structures and rebuilt some French buildings.

Finally, early in 1905 Stevens felt comfortable that the immediate problems of housing, food, and dirt transportation had been solved, and excavation could commence. By then, almost 20,000 laborers and supervisory personnel were at work.

But the effort was still handicapped by the absence of a clear plan of attack. Was the canal to be at sea level, or was it to have locks?

A Sea Level Canal: The Idea That Never Dies

To the uneducated, a canal meant sea level without locks despite the fact that there were many canals with locks already in the US. The Soo Locks in the Great Lakes, for example, carried almost three times the tonnage of Suez each year without a problem.

The decision was to be in the hands of yet another board, who after a quick visit to Panama, voted for a sea level canal.

By then Stevens, who had come to Panama assuming that he would be building a sea level canal, had seen the light. He had witnessed the sobering power of the Chagres River after the rains

The Zone Transformed

As the yellow fever program was moving ahead, Stevens attacked the two other major sources of worker discontentment, food and housing. Instead of buying at high prices from local merchants, Stevens instituted a program of shipping food from the States and selling it through Canal Zone stores at cost. Mechanical refrigeration, a relatively new invention, was installed at a large cold storage facility at Colón. A bakery was built, and fresh food and bread went up and down the construction line on the Panama Railroad.

Not popular with the locals. A typical ICC commissary store, offered hardware, food, meats, etc. to Panama Canal workers. Panamanian shopkeepers bitterly resented the loss of business, and Panamanian locals were angry that the shops weren't open to them as well. However, it was an important ingredient in keeping good workers, especially Americans.
NA 185-G-1256

had swept in from the Atlantic and filled its watershed.

The experience had transformed his views. Before, he viewed a sea level canal as just a lot more excavation than a locks canal. After seeing the power of the Chagres he was convinced that a sea level canal was impossible.

His conversion came at a very opportune time. In testimony before the Senate and in private conversations with Teddy Roosevelt, he managed to persuade policy-makers to avoid what would have been a very costly mistake.

Finally, on June 19, 1906, in the last of a series of deliberations that essentially began in Paris in 1879, the choice of a canal design was finally and truly made. The US Senate voted for locks, 36 - 31.

The die was cast and when the news arrived at Panama, the engineers breathed a sigh of relief: finally they knew exactly what they had to do.

Teddy Roosevelt Visits: First Foreign Trip by a Sitting US President

By the summer of 1906, the dirt was finally flying. The cumbersome organization of the ICC had been streamlined to concentrate authority in Stevens' hands, the shape of the job ahead was finally defined, yellow fever had been defeated, and the infrastructure was rapidly being constructed for the task ahead. Most importantly, excavation, the single largest task at Panama, was accelerating.

It was a good time, the President decided, to see the Canal.

Traveling aboard the new battleship *Louisiana*, his short trip was a major media event that electrified the country and indelibly identified his administration with the Panama Canal.

He had purposely chosen to visit in November at the height of the rainy season and the weather obliged. He was able to see the Chagres in all its fury; even the railroad was underwater in places.

He was also delighted to get out of Washington. In *The Path Between The Seas*, David McCullough relates a wonderful anecdote of when Stevens and the official welcoming party arrived at the dock at 7:30 a.m. to greet the President as he arrived from the ship. There was no sign of anyone until suddenly Teddy hailed them grandly; he had come ashore at the crack of dawn and had been exploring Colón on his own.

His vitality and interest in the project surprised and was remembered by everyone who encountered him. The famous photo of the President sitting in the operator's seat of a Bucyrus steam shovel was actually an impromptu event. When Roosevelt saw the huge shovels working, he halted the train to rush down and clamber aboard, peppering the engineer with questions.

He was a man totally enthralled with the excitement and drama of the project, and naturally, that he himself had been such an important part in its creation. Upon his return he made an enthusiastic report to Congress.

Stevens Leaves; Why?

Inexplicably, at the peak of his career and success at Panama, John Stevens resigned in February 1907, just two months after Roosevelt's trip and glowing praise for Stevens afterwards. Everything seemed to have been going very well.

What happened?

Most probably, he was simply exhausted. In an amazing year and a half he had been the guiding spirit that had transformed the canal project from dispirited workers in a disease infested jungle to a throbbing hive of activity.

It was not only his skill, knowledge, and vision that had reinvigorated Panama, but his personality as well. Walking the line daily, talking to the men, taking a personal interest in all that transpired, he had been a remarkable leader at a critical crossroads.

Stevens' legacy was a railroad system that was state of the art for the task at hand. The huge steam shovels could only work as fast as the dirt trains that they had to fill. Stevens had made sure that everything was in place for the most efficient excavating.

Tamping dynamite. Huge amounts of dynamite were used during construction. At least one specially adapted ship was occupied full time bringing explosives from New York down to Panama. In the background is the Panama RR bridge over the Chagres at Gamboa.

NA 185-G-783

George Goethals and the Army Corps of Engineers

Needing someone who wouldn't be able to resign, Roosevelt turned to George Washington Goethals, a dour career officer in the US Army Corps of Engineers and experienced in the construction of locks and canals.

Stevens' easy manner was a hard act to follow and the American workers, as well as the residents of Panama, didn't hide the fact that they adored Stevens and resented the US Army "taking over" the work of creating the canal.

A tall, aloof, athletic man, and a constant smoker, Goethals wasn't interested in winning a popularity contest. He had been transferred to Panama to finish the canal and he wasn't going to let anything stand in the way of getting it done.

There was plenty to do and for much of the next eight years, a lot of it would be in the place named for a snake, Culebra.

The War at Culebra

Details in the old photographs are often obscured, murky from the steam, the smoke, the dust. The workers are all long dead. All that remains is the great cut itself, and a few aging, brittle movies in the National Archives where some hint of the dimension of the great feat that was accomplished there may be glimpsed.

As ships now move smoothly through the canyon where the thousands struggled and died, travelers marvel at the neat-

The machine that won the war at Culebra, the 95-ton Bucyrus steam shovel. The triumph of the Americans was due to conquering disease, but also to building this remarkably durable piece of equipment that was able to handle the hard digging in Culebra and the other big cuts, day after day, year after year.
With a dirt train supplying a constant supply of empty cars, it was scoop, lift, swing, and dump, five tons at a bite, repeated all along the canal route, day after day and year after year.
NA 185-G-0022

ly terraced cuts, stair-stepping back from the water.

But make no mistake–what happened at Culebra beginning with the French in 1881 and continuing to the present day was nothing less than a war. No bombs were dropped, no shots fired. Yet armies toiled, strategies were developed and changed, the tide of battle shifted from one side to the other.

From an engineering standpoint, the problem could be boiled down to a simple goal–the sides of the canyon that had to be cut through the mountain range that was the spine of Panama had to be excavated back to the angle of repose. This was the angle at which gravity would simply keep the earth in place, and slides would be impossible.

That simple strategy assumes that for any cut, for any geological formation, there is actually an angle of repose that may be achieved.

The reality is that after almost 120 years of more or less continuous work, slides are still a problem in the great cut at Culebra (now called Gaillard Cut).

The problem lay with three elements: the geology of Panama, the inexorable geometry of slicing through a mountain range, and the legendary rains of Panama.

The wet earth constantly sloughed off, taking whatever was below it into the bottom of the cut. That meant trains, tracks, steam shovels, sometimes workers, would be buried in a great morass of earth and mud.

The great cut at Culebra in a rare quiet moment. This photo was probably taken on Sunday morning before the maintenance crews arrived to service equipment like the steam powered drills in the foreground. In the distance is the foot bridge at Empire.

NA 185-G-0666

When John Stevens was ready to call the steam shovel operators back from the States and resume work after he and Gorgas had exterminated yellow fever, he moved his office to Culebra, where he could look out and see the great work underway.

Historians developed all sorts of examples to show how much earth had to be moved–dirt trains that would reach around the Earth, etc.

But the best description is simply that for seven years under the Americans, the largest excavation effort the world has ever seen, before or after, tried to cut a trench through a low pass in the Panamanian mountains. It was, in a nutshell, hell in a very small place. Every day five or six thousand workers

Those Changing Estimates

The French had discovered early in their work a crucial truth about Panama: the more you dug, the more you had to dig.

US estimates of the total to be excavated grew steadily:
1906 estimate – 54 million cubic yards
1908 estimate – 78 million cubic yards
1911 estimate – 89 million cubic yards
1913 estimate – 100 million cubic yards

Source: David McCullough, *The Path Between The Seas*

would descend by train into the great trench. Temperatures regularly reached 100 to 130 degrees; the humidity was always very high. The noise level was deafening. Three hundred crews with their clattering air drills were almost always at work; 50 or 60 of the largest steam shovels ever built, served by hundreds of trains, worked to load rock and earth loosened by dynamite into the long trains to carry away the dirt. On an average day during the high production years of 1909 - 1915, over 450 long trains of spoil would rumble out of the great cuts to be disposed of.

Dynamite ships with special wood-lined holds would deliver up to a million pounds at a time to be unloaded and taken to special magazines near the great cuts. There, workers would carefully load the explosives into the drill holes for maximum effect.

By the time the cut at Culebra was filled with water, more explosives than in all the previous wars in the history of the world had been used at Panama.

When the US took over the project, it determined that at the bottom of Culebra the channel had to be widened to 300 feet wide, vastly increasing the amount of material that had to be excavated.

At Culebra and in the other cuts, steam shovels and trains worked on terraces. Where the rock face was exposed, drilling crews would blast and the big Bucyrus shovels would dig into the shattered rock, taking 5-ton bites and typically filling a single train car in 8 or 10 minutes. Each big shovel was attended by a crew of ten including an operator, an engineer who tended the steam engine, making sure there was enough water in the boiler, two men shoveling coal into the fire, plus at least six others who cleared debris from the tracks on which the shovel traveled, and also laid new track ahead as it dug. These terraces were typically 50-feet wide, with similar terraces 12 feet above and below it. In some places steam shovels were working on six or seven terraces simultaneously.

Keeping the trains moving was a sophisticated balancing act. Making empty cars available meant that emptying the full ones had to be done quickly and efficiently. When digging was in full swing, from 1908 - 1914, this meant that the crews working the spoils or dumping areas had to unload up to 500 long trains of full dirt cars each day!

American ingenuity in every aspect of transportation was needed and the engineers were up to the challenge. First the Lidgerwood plow was developed to empty dirt cars quickly. Hundreds of workers would then spread the dumped dirt with shovels, a brutally hard job that quickly became a bottleneck as production rapidly increased. Quick thinking railroad men next devised a dirt spreader that was just a rail car with a plow sticking out on either side to spread and flatten the piles of dirt after

dumping. Even so, the volume of dirt mounted so quickly that tracks had to be moved repeatedly, sometimes daily to keep up with the flow. Again, a job that required a crew of hundreds of laborers was streamlined with a clunky invented-in-Panama contraption called a track shifter, essentially a big crane that could lift and move long rail sections at a time.

There is nothing like competition among crews to get production up, and the daily Canal Zone newspaper instituted a section with weekly production numbers, steam shovel by steam shovel. With personal reputations on the line, the steam shovel and railroad crews essentially became individual units, each racing the other to be the highest producer for the week.

The cumulative effect of bigger and better equipment and a more sophisticated rail system allowed the Americans to achieve excavation figures that would have astounded the French. Just three years after John Stevens restarted excavation, the big Bucyrus shovels and long dirt trains moved an incredible two million cubic yards of dirt and rock from the cuts at Culebra to the dumping areas in July of 1909. This was ten times what the French had managed to move in their best month.

High production depended on keeping a steady supply of empty cars next to the big shovels. John Stevens and his staff put together a very sophisticated system to simply keep the shovels digging and the dirt moving. Notice the train moving high up on a terrace above and to the right of the shovel.

NA 185-G-0004

And the Walls Came Tumbling Down

Slides had plagued the French. Their ambitious goal of a 45-degree angle (or one-to-one) for the walls of the cuts at Panama was wishful thinking. The only way to reduce slides was to cut back the slopes at a flatter angle, gaining stability at

Slide at Culebra, circa 1913. There have been landslides in this area almost since the first steam shovels started biting into the unstable clay. Often the slides occurred at night and daylight would reveal months of work wiped out. To say that the slides were disheartening would be a considerable understatement.

NA 185-G-0644

the cost of increasing the amount of dirt that had to be removed.

The Americans had the same problems, particularly at Culebra. The deeper they dug, the more the walls had a tendency to slide. At first the slides were relatively small. For a time, Wallace and Stevens, the first two American project managers, had felt as if the slide problem may have been finally reduced to manageable proportions.

Then came the night of October 4, 1907. The area called Cucaracha, east of Culebra proper, had always been a source of problems for the French, sliding several times and forcing them to angle the cut back considerably from the 45-degree angle they had hoped would be sufficient. It was the height of the rainy season and the layers of heavy clay that overhung the deepening cut had become saturated. When they finally ripped loose, they issued in an era of slides that were an order of magnitude beyond what the French had ever experienced. The first slide buried steam shovels and hundreds of yards of track. But then it kept just sliding slowly, until after 10 days, almost a half million yards of mud, rock, and muck had slid into the cut.

There were no easy solutions, no magic way to stabilize the slopes above the cuts in the face of the rains of Panama. The only answer was to dig the slopes back at a flatter and flatter angle, dig the dirt that had slid into the cut, dig and then dig some more. Plastering the walls was tried, digging diversion channels above

Steam shovel damaged by landslide, Culebra, 1910. "Dig it out, again, boys!" Weeks and sometimes months of work would be wiped out in a few moments by the big slides in the cut through the mountains of Panama. Even today, after almost 120 years of more or less constant work, slides are a problem along the canal.

NA 185-G-0131

the cuts, but nothing seemed to work. The smaller cuts could be cleaned up in a few days, but the larger ones took months.

The engineers had anticipated that the clay that overlaid the rock at Culebra would have a tendency to slide, but had assumed that once they began digging into the rock itself, conditions would begin to stabilize. It was not to be. The heavily fractured nature of the rock in that part of Panama, combined with the shattering effects of almost daily blasting, had destroyed its integrity. What followed, particularly at the site of the town of Culebra, would occur even in dry weather. It was simply a function of the exposed sides of terraces not being able to support the tremendous weight of the hillside above them.

These slides were of a dimension greater than the slide of '07 –3 million yards of rock slid into the cut in 1912. Had it not been for cracks appearing in the earth among the buildings of the town of Culebra and thereby alerting the residents to move their homes, much of the town would have disappeared into the cut.

And a new phenomenon–never seen before–began occurring at Culebra. The bottom of the canal cut actually rose up in places due to the pressure being exerted by the sides. In a few well-recorded instances, it happened while workers stood amazed as the earth rose five or ten feet in as many minutes.

When Stevens went home and Goethals took over, the

Dredge pipe sections moored alongside the canal, Culebra, 2001. During the construction of the Gatún Dam, material from the bottom of the Atlantic in the approach channels was pumped almost a mile into what was to be dam's core.

work at Panama had evolved into three distinct tasks: constructing the locks and associated structures, building the huge Gatún dam, and the nine-mile-long cut through the mountain heart of Panama at Culebra.

The lock gates were to be of monumental size. Special locomotives had to be designed running on tracks with cogs or gears to ascend and descend the inclines between lock chambers. Huge valves and immense tunnels had to be designed to move the water in and out.

At Gatún, a giant earthen fill dam had to be constructed. Naturally it would be the largest yet built anywhere.

Yet the challenges of each of these separate and immense projects were still small compared to Culebra.

The Chagres: Dammed at Last

If the most exciting place in the Canal Zone to see was the struggle against the clay and the rock at Culebra, the second key piece in the Panama Canal puzzle was beginning to take place at Gatún with the damming of the Chagres River.

As in many of the elements that comprised the Panama Canal project, the Gatún Dam was to be the largest of its sort in the world. As designed, it would be 90 feet high, 1,700 feet wide and 1.5 miles long. It was to be an earthen fill dam, relying on the weight of the dam itself to resist the force of the water.

The dam was to be a lightning rod during the sea level vs. locks debate in Congress. The reason was because in 1889, some 3,000 Pennsylvanians died when an earthen dam failed, causing the infamous Johnstown Flood. That dam, a 90-foot-high struc-

ture, failed after several days of heavy rains.

Soaked by water, and undermined by multiple streams coursing through its interior, the center of the dam failed suddenly and completely and the water from the 700-acre lake thundered through the valley at approximately 50 mph. The wall of water destroyed everything in its path and was the biggest disaster of its kind in US history.

Only the patient testimony of John Stevens and the fact that the gates of the locks would be constructed by a Pittsburgh contractor–Senator Philander Knox, a key Canal proponent, was from Pennsylvania–swayed the Congress to overcome their doubts of earthen dams and vote for a dam and lock canal.

What was unique about the Gatún Dam was that much of the great mass of earth that was to hold back huge Gatún Lake–163 square miles–was to be pumped in, in the form of a slurry. This "hydraulic fill" was to be created by several large

Business end of a suction dredge. Very large engines were required to pump the sediment-filled water over a mile to the Gatún Dam. The business end, or cutter head, is suspended from the crane arrangement at right, and is slowly swung back and forth as the pump sucks up the muddy slurry picked up by the rotating blades. NA 185-G-0170

THE JOHNSTOWN FLOOD: COULD IT HAVE BEEN AVERTED?

Another tragedy of Johnstown was that it possibly could have been prevented with some routine maintenance. Basically what makes earthen dams fail are leaks that create channels through the interior which undermines its integrity. The dam that failed above Johnstown had been weakened by leaks caused by high lake levels in the spring of 1888, a year before it failed. Herbert Webber, who watched awestruck on the shore when the dam failed, said later that had repairs been undertaken to stop the leaks, the disaster could have been avoided.

Webber also estimated that the entire 700-acre, 50-foot-deep lake had emptied through the crack in the dam in less than 10 minutes.

In addition to creating Gatún Lake, Gatún Dam had to generate electricity for operation of the locks and be able to handle the impressive flow of the Chagres River after powerful rainstorms.
NA

suction dredges that were working to dredge a channel between the exit of the Gatún Locks and the Atlantic Ocean.

These huge suction dredges moved the spoil, or the mud and dirt excavated from the channel, substantial distances. The idea was simple: a pipe, approximately two feet in diameter with a rotating cutter head, would be maneuvered along the bottom of a channel to be dredged and a very large pump would suck up the dirt, silt, smaller rocks, etc. This material would exit the pump located on a large barge in the form of a slurry, pumped through floating pipes to the final disposal site.

At Gatún, the dredges were working up to a mile away from the Gatún Dam, requiring huge pumps. At the dam site, the soupy slurry would empty from the pipe into what was essentially a little artificial lake contained by the two walls and the two ends of the dam. The solids would quickly settle to the bottom, and eventually even the finest silts would settle out of the water, which would eventually find its way back to the Atlantic, minus its load of suspended dirt.

Once the dam's design was finalized, the "toes" had to be constructed–rock breakwaters which formed the upstream and downstream sides of the dam. They contained the slurry that would be pumped in by the big hydraulic dredges and protected the core of the dam from wave erosion.

To partially hold back the Chagres River while the dam was being constructed, a dike was built at Gamboa near the

Looking toward the three-step Gatún Locks from the Atlantic Ocean entrance. The locks and entrance walls comprise one of the largest man-made structures on earth, and took almost four years to complete.

western end of the great cut at Culebra. As the Culebra cut grew deeper, the dike at Gamboa would also serve to keep the waters of the Chagres River from flooding into the cut itself. Once construction started on the toes, the process of pumping fill into the dam's center could begin, a process that was to continue for more than two years.

Building a dam this large using so-called "hydraulic fill" was an act of faith. Nothing of its size and style had been attempted before. But as the toe walls slowly rose, along with the huge pond between them, fed by the two immense dredges, the silt and sediment settled out of the murky salt water to form a core that was as hard as cement. Like many of the other engineering firsts at Panama, the dam at Gatún was a resounding success.

Lost in the Fall of the Roman Empire: The Formula for Cement

The reason some of the buildings built by the Romans are still around is that the builders had discovered the unusual properties of cement. Unfortunately that knowledge disappeared with the collapse of their civilization. About 1,300 years later an English engineer rediscovered that a combination of limestone and silica, baked in an oven, made a remarkable cement. Mixed roughly 1:5 with sand and gravel, with water added, it makes a durable and cheap construction material.

The most notable feature of modern cement plants is the very long rotating kilns, where the mixture of limestone, silica and alumina is heated up to about 2,600 degrees in a four-hour journey from one end to the other.

Flooding was always a problem. View of Pedro Miguel locks looking South from the Gatún Lake side. Note the style of cranes. Rail cars brought cement from a mixing plant and cranes allowed the buckets to be delivered as needed.
NA

A Monument Rises in the Jungle: Building the Locks

By the spring of 1909, the work at Culebra was well underway, though it was to be constantly plagued by slides. Gatún Dam was getting higher and higher, and the design work had finally been finished for the last of the three major parts of the project, the locks.

Since the French had abandoned the project, technology had been rapidly moving forward in two areas that were critical to building the locks, concrete and electricity.

Concrete technology was advancing rapidly at the turn of the century, led by the development of steel reinforcing rods that added much strength to concrete designs. However, the small silos, bridge abutments, and the very rare concrete building in the US gave only the slightest hint of what the engineers were about to attempt at Panama.

At Gatún, for example, the complete structure of three step locks (actually three pairs of huge chambers) complete with the approach walls on either end was almost a mile long. Not only was it 10 times the size of the closest competitor, but when complete it would be the largest single structure of man-made materials on the entire planet.

Today's visitors see only a fraction of what was built. When in operation, much of it is covered by water and earth. But when it was being constructed, rising cathedral-like from an area of flat ground between the Atlantic Ocean and the rising dam at Gatún, it often stunned visitors into awed silence.

To create these remarkable structures, an impressive infra-

structure had to be assembled from scratch. At each coast, sources of sand and gravel had to be found and a fleet of tugs and barges assembled to bring the raw materials to the mixing plants. At each plant a separate automatic electric railway was built to move the sand and gravel to the big rotating cement mixers and to move the filled six-ton buckets to where they could be lifted by crane or cable tramway to wherever around the construction site they were needed.

Look at the size of those blocks, or pulleys! Concrete is being dumped from a rail car to a dumping bucket, just under the big blocks that connect to a tramway or crane overhead. The man with the telephone headset is in contact with the crane operator.

NA

At Gatún several parallel sets of railroad tracks on each side of the site were constructed to serve the unique traveling tramway towers. Two of these 85-foot towers moved on tracks set about 50 feet apart, and each tower was connected by cables to its counterpart approximately 800 feet away on the other side of the construction site. Heavy counterweights tensioned the tramway wires, allowing them to pick up and move the buckets of concrete.

The topography at the Pacific lock sites, Miraflores and Pedro Miguel, about a mile and a half apart, wasn't suitable for the rolling tower tramway arrangement used at Gatún, so a different approach was used. Large T-shaped cranes were built, also moving on tracks. One style of these cranes even had the cement mixing plant built into its base.

Concrete engineers were working on the leading edge of their profession at Panama. They created the world's largest concrete structure (before it was eclipsed by Boulder Dam in 1930) at a time when concrete technology–the science of what

A number of safety features, including a double set of lock gates and this safety chain, were designed to reduce the chances of a ship damaging the locks. This chain might work on a small freighter as in the above picture, but would be hard pressed to stop an 85,000-ton cruise ship in some kind of maneuvering mishap.
NA 185-G-1911

was the right mixture–was imperfectly known. Almost 100 years after the first bucket of concrete was poured at Gatún, the concrete still supports the immense strains put on it every day. Work crews patch as needed here and there, but for the most part their work is cosmetic. That such a huge structure–built when so little was known about concrete construction, in such a challenging climate–has survived so well, is an engineering triumph.

Electricity: Pushing the Envelope

Had the French wanted to build a canal controlled by electric motors in the 1880's they would have been very challenged to do so. Electric lighting was just spreading across US cities. The alternating current (AC) motor wasn't invented until 1888 and the infant technology hadn't yet advanced enough to support such an ambitious project.

But when the first bucket of concrete was poured at Gatún in 1909, it was mixed in a drum turned by an electric motor, transported by an electric-powered tramway and guided by electrically telephoned instructions. In many areas the electrical technology that allowed the creation of a US Canal at Panama was being used by the builders as quickly as it was invented.

General Electric, which made most of the motors and switches, created a showpiece for electricity that both served to push the growing company into the very forefront of technology and also showed the world the wonders that electricity could do.

Control was the key word. Electrical controls allowed the complicated series of operations involved in moving vessels up and down to be managed both from a central point, and also in a

Big enough for a subway train. One of the 18-foot diameter tunnels that carries water from Lake Gatún into the various lock chambers. At intervals smaller tunnels branched off and into the floor of the 1,000-foot-long lock chambers. The trick was to have enough water flow for speedy operation, but not enough to create currents that could damage ships.
NA 185-G-1789

manner that reduced or eliminated the possibility of operator error damaging the locks. GE developed a mechanical interlock system that made it impossible to operate a valve or a lock gate out of the proper sequence of operations.

Furthermore, in each of the three control rooms that controlled the three separate sets of locks was a scale model of the locks that dominated the room and was itself the key control apparatus. It wasn't just a model. All the appropriate controls to control the lock gates or doors, as well as the multiplicity of valves that controlled the water flow, were located in the correct places on the models.

Moving the Water Around: Tunnels Big Enough for Subways

The men who designed the locks set the very ambitious goal of lowering or raising the water level to the new desired height in 15 minutes. This required moving large volumes of water by gravity through tunnels that could have served for the New York subway. In order to reduce turbulence within the immense lock chambers to a level that wouldn't cause ships to rip their mooring lines loose many smaller tunnels were required to distribute the water throughout the big chambers. Gate valves larger than any used anywhere before in the world had to be fabricated. Wooden forms to create the tunnels and smaller channels had to be built and installed.

As the walls rose higher and higher from the floor of the locks, their construction began to rival that of Culebra for the attention of visitors. Newspapers all over the US and the world sent correspondents. The word was getting out that something very special was happening at Panama.

Massive wouldn't be adequate to describe the great doors that closed off the Pacific end of the Canal. 82 feet high by 66 feet wide and 7 feet thick, they weighed 745 tons. And like most of the other engineering firsts in the Panama Canal, they functioned amazingly well. NA 185-G-0538

Big Iron: The Lock Gates

As soon as the walls of the locks were high enough, iron workers began assembling the great gates, or miter valves, as they are called. Wisely, the design of the canal was for parallel locks so that both Atlantic-bound and Pacific-bound ships could transit the locks at the same time. Although each lock chamber was 1,000 feet long, lock chambers were divided in half by an additional set of gates so that smaller ships could pass without the huge water use that the full lock would require. Additionally, each set of gates was actually two sets of gates, one behind the other, in case one failed to close, or God forbid, a set was rammed and broken by an out of control ship.

This made for a total of 92 separate doors or gates. Each was 66 feet wide and 7 feet thick, constructed somewhat like the hull of a ship–riveted steel plates over an inner framework. Even the smallest of these gates was five stories tall. The height of the gates varied from lock to lock; the tallest was at the Pacific side of the Miraflores Locks. In order to accommodate the occasionally very large tides on the Pacific Ocean, each of the gates was 82 feet high, and weighed 745 tons.

In order to reduce the strain on the operating mechanism, the engineers cleverly designed the gates to be watertight, so that the buoyancy of the water would carry a lot of their weight, also making for easier operation.

Imagine walking down one of the lock chambers after the concrete work was done, but before the doors had been started.

It would have been like a concrete canyon, five blocks long, with eight-story walls. But then when the framework of the great doors was in place and the riveters began putting on the great steel plates what would create a watertight structure, the effect was totally different. Tall as buildings, the immense riveted doors were an image that once seen could never be forgotten.

Of course there were a few minor problems once the Canal opened for business. This is one of the early style locomotives being hauled out of the water after it got dragged off its tracks by a ship. Even though the locomotive weighed only around 20 tons, the crane had to exert over a 100-ton pull to break the suction on the muddy bottom. Notice the turret-like structure between the cabs–this was the winch to keep the wires to the ship taut. Today's locomotives, or "mules" as they are called, have the winch arrangement at the bottom of the car. It makes the mules a lot more stable, handy for obvious reasons.

NA 185-G-0722

The Canal Zone: A Worker's Paradise (If You Were White)

For the French, living and working in Panama always had a large element of danger–death from disease always lurked nearby. But under the Americans, the Canal Zone became a unique place to live and work. First, by almost eliminating mosquitoes, yellow fever, and malaria from the Canal Zone, the fear of working in Panama that made it so hard to recruit in the early US years was gone.

Next, a wide array of housing was built that, in many cases, was better than what was available to the workers back in the US.

Eighteen excellent commissary stores, carrying a wide selection of goods at subsidized prices, were located throughout the Canal Zone. Recreation facilities were constructed, all paid for by the government.

For many workers and their families the experience of working and living in the Canal Zone during the construction of the canal was the most exciting period in their lives.

Good housing and stores were certainly a part of the reason, but probably the biggest was the genuine excitement of working on the canal. It was the largest construction project any nation had ever attempted. Many families took the train several times a month just to look at the awesome structures rising from the jungle. Though the construction of the locks was to take four

Is it some kind of weird submarine? Actually a place like the Panama Canal requires all sorts of odd specially constructed equipment. This is a floating caisson. It can be fitted into special slots in the walls of a lock and then flooded so it touches the bottom of the locks, and seals it off in case work needs to be done to the big lock gates.

years, each week a visitor would have been able to notice a little more progress, the walls a little higher. The only comparable experience any people might have had would have been the medieval French farm families, at seeing the great cathedrals at Chartres and other towns slowly rising from the wheat fields.

> "I had come rather with the hope of shouldering a shovel and descending into the canal with other workmen, that I might some day solemnly raise my right hand and boast, 'I helped dig IT.' But that was in the callow days before I had arrived and learned the awful gulf that separates the sacred white American from the rest of the Canal Zone world."
>
> – Harry Franck, *Zone Policeman 88*

If you were an American living in the States while the canal was being built, you could easily fall under the impression that all the work to build the canal was being done by whites. All the many articles showed whites at work–operating the biggest machinery, designing the great works, driving the many trains. The elegant houses with their wide-screened porches all showed happy white families.

The reality was very different; only about one in eight workers at Panama during most of the construction years was white. During the peak years, when about 50,000 workers toiled in the Canal Zone from the Atlantic to the Pacific, there were only about 6,000 whites, for the most part engineering, administrative, and support staff.

MEAN STREETS - COLÓN AND PANAMA CITY

Back streets of Panama City, circa 1910. If you were white, you wanted to be pretty careful about where you went if you left the secure, spic and span "Zone." There was a deep feeling of resentment among many Panamanians over the treatment they received from the Americans, and mugging, robbery, and murder were common.
NA 185-G-1398

If the Canal Zone was a great place for whites to work, you didn't have to go too far to get a sobering dose of reality. All you had to do was to step across the border into Panama proper to become a potential victim of hostility, mugging, robbery, or murder. A very unfortunate legacy of the American takeover of the Canal Zone was very bitter feelings among the Panamanians towards the Americans.

It wasn't unjustified. The Revolution and subsequent treaty was sold to the Panamanians as something that would bring a new level of prosperity to a very poor country. At the very least, Panamanian merchants were excited at the prospect of having so many new customers for their goods.

The establishment of the commissaries in the Canal Zone, essentially selling subsidized goods including fresh food to all canal employees and their families, was a bitter blow to Panamanian merchants. If the loss of business was crippling, an even greater cause for resentment was seeing that only the well-paid canal workers had access to such an abundance of low-priced goods.

It was clear to many Panamanians that they were essentially second class citizens in their own country. Many of the most senior American officials neither spoke Spanish nor showed any inclination to learn.

As the waters of Gatún Lake rose, it began to displace whole villages whose residents were often given little or no compensation and who were forced to relocate to sites much inferior to the homes they had left.

For the blacks, many of whom were from Barbados and other Caribbean islands, the experience at Panama was more mixed. Under the Americans it was a lot better than under the French, when many blacks couldn't wait to leave once they understood the working conditions and the chances of contracting a fatal disease.

The good housing was for whites, as were many of the recreational facilities. While the free housing provided to whites was excellent, the free housing for blacks was in many cases nothing more than a string of boxcars pushed from place to place around the Canal Zone as labor was needed. Black married workers received no special treatment at all. In consequence, many black workers chose to live in shacks in the jungle, as they had during the French Era, or in unsanitary tenements in Colón or Panama City.

In fairness, it should be said that for the most part the working and living conditions under the Americans were better than what they would have experienced in a sugar mill at home, and the pay was substantially better and included free medical care.

Many of the blacks that worked at Panama were from Barbados or other English-speaking Caribbean nations. Many came from communities where no medical care of any sort was available and a job that offered benefits of any kind beyond pay was a totally new experience.

There was a larger issue as well, which might be called the Good Old Protestant Work Ethic. The vast majority of the Americans who came to Panama came to do a job and viewed the canal as a genuinely exciting endeavor to be involved with. They came from a nation in the middle of probably the biggest transformation in modern times–from rural to urban, from agricultural to industrial–within their own lifetimes. And most of all, these Americans were doers, raised in a culture where work was both rewarded, and seen as an end in itself.

Panamanian culture and society were very different. First of all, life in the tropical heat created a culture that naturally moved at a much slower pace than Americans were accustomed to. When the Americans first arrived, the Panamanians that weren't living in the few towns and cities were subsistence farmers, on the very outskirts of the cash economy. They lived in simple huts, clustered in small villages. The concept of working five or six days a week, eight or ten hours a day, was as foreign to them as electric lights or telephones.

For the average Panamanian the prosperity that the canal was supposed to bring wasn't evident. In the American zone were neatly mowed lawns, roomy, newly built houses, baseball diamonds, excursion boats to Taboga Island on Sundays, and stores full of cheap goods unavailable to Panamanians.

This resentment was to continue until the Panama Canal Treaty of 1979, which ceded the operation and revenues of the canal over to Panama, and continues, to a lesser extent, today.

> "Greater perhaps than the building of the canal is the accomplishment of the United States in showing the natives how life can be lived safely and healthily in tropical jungles. Yet the lesson will not be learned, and on the heels of the last canal builder will return all the old slovenliness and disease, and the native will sink back into just what he would have been had we never come."
>
> —Harry Franck, *Zone Policeman 88*

For many of the Americans who came to Panama with the Canal effort, there was a palpable excitement at being present at the creation of such an immense work. Especially during the period starting in 1909 with the beginning of lock construction, progress was visible week by week all throughout the Canal Zone, and the weekend excursion trains were usually full of excited families visiting the site.

Sherman

The Glory Years: 1909 - 1914

When the first bucket of concrete was poured for the first lock, in August of 1909, it inaugurated easily the most exciting period in the 33-year-long construction of the Panama Canal. With work proceeding on breakwaters and harbor dredging at each end, three massive locks, and in the great cuts, the entire Canal Zone, from Atlantic to Pacific, was a construction frenzy.

A long supply chain extended from steel mills and fabrication plants in the US midwest, by train to the east coast, and by ship to Panama. Among the community of steel fabricators the buzz was Panama. Called upon to create immense castings and metal fabrications, workers on unrelated projects would wander over to where the crews were working on the huge pieces of the Panama Canal orders.

As the walls of the locks began to rise from the sea of muddy construction debris around them, pictures of the progress were a regular feature of newspapers and magazines all across the country. More than ever before, the whole country was aware of and proud of the progress at Panama.

There had been tumultuous years: revolution, the "Panic of '05," when yellow fever fear drove Americans from Panama, the full court press to conquer disease, the immense challenges of the work itself. But starting in 1909, progress was visible–the cuts were vast and deep, the forests between Culebra and the Gatún locks were beginning to disappear under the rising water of the lake. The cranes at Miraflores and

A huge day. Two big steam shovels finally meet at the bottom of Culebra Cut, May 13, 1913. There was still much digging to be done and another huge slide would thunder down a mile away, but the meeting of the two shovels marked the beginning of the end of 33 years of construction. See text on bottom of opposite page.

NA 185-G-0017

Pedro Miguel, and the tramway towers, could be seen from miles away as a beehive of workers toiled beneath them.

As the number of projects under construction at the same time grew, so did the labor force, rising to 40,000 and then at the peak to almost 50,000 workers of many races and skills. The pressure was on; many worked overtime week after week. Yet morale was amazingly high and there was a spring in people's steps; if they went home for a vacation (Panama Canal workers got an amazing 42 days of paid vacation a year, when the average worker back in the States was lucky to get two weeks) they were eager to get back.

Good pay, good benefits, free housing, cheap food and free medical care were all part of the reason. But there was something much bigger at Panama–just being there at the creation of such a monumental project of such immense benefit to the entire world.

> "It is as if each were individually proud of being one of the chosen people and builders of the greatest work of the modern age."
> – Harry Franck, *Zone Policeman 88*

Culebra's Last Gasp: The Cucaracha Slide of 1913

By the end of 1912, David Gaillard, in charge of the complex excavation in the Culebra section, thought he could see the light at the end of the tunnel. If he walked from his office on the hill above Culebra to the edge of the great man-made ravine, he could see the two teams of steam shovels, working toward each other. Already they had finished excavating the particularly difficult section at Cucaracha, site of so many previous slides, and removed the tracks. Now all that remained was to connect and widen the channel at the base of the cut before him–two or three months at the most would see it done –the greatest excavation in history.

Then on January 19, 1913, came the worst slide yet. It occurred at Cucaracha, about a half mile south of Culebra, which the engineers had thought they were done with. The whole side of the cut just collapsed and slid into the cut, completely obliterating the channel and even sliding up on the far side. According to David McCullough, Gaillard was almost in shock, but as in all the other slides, there was nothing for it but to dig it out again.

We're gonna move two million yards of dirt with shovels???? The huge slide in January of 1913, after engineers thought that section was finished, was particularly disheartening. Note another slide in the distance, a classic example of the Panama axiom: the more you dig, the more you have to dig...

NA 185-G-0549

And dig they did, though they had to start first with hundreds of men with shovels, because the tracks on which the steam shovels and dirt trains needed to run on already had been removed. It was a huge and discouraging task.

On the morning of May 13, 1913, two of the biggest steam shovels in the world were still working in the Culebra Cut only a hundred or so yards apart. All day long, shovel No. 230, operated by D.J. MacDonald, and shovel No. 222, operated by J.S. Kirk, got closer and closer to each other. Finally at the end of the day they stood nose to nose. The bottom of the vast cut at

Ladder dredges working on the Cucaracha slide, in the summer of 1913. The excavation of this part of the cut was finished and the railroad tracks had been removed when the slide occurred. Letting the water in–the Gatún Dam was complete–and letting the bucket dredges remove the dirt seemed the best option. The area that slid will be off the right-hand side of your ship, about two miles after leaving the Pedro Miguel Locks, headed from the Pacific to the Atlantic.

NA 185-G-0557

Culebra had finally been reached!

There was still much to do. The Cucaracha slide still blocked the canal to the south, but it was truly a moment that marked the beginning of the end of the years of struggle in the immense cut.

The bottom of the cut was 40 feet above sea level, but as soon as the lake filled, there would be enough water in the great trench to float ships through.

It was also a sobering revelation–the Americans with all the money and equipment at their disposal that they could possibly need had taken almost eight years to get to that level.

To have dug a sea level canal would have required going down at least another 80 feet. To stand on the bottom of the cut that the Americans had struggled for so long to achieve, and to look up at the great walls and imagine the effort it would require to go down still further, could have only reminded a person of what one observer had remarked early in the digging–that all the money in the world wouldn't have been enough to dig a sea level canal at Panama.

Now things were progressing very rapidly. Less than two weeks after the steam shovels met, the last bucket of concrete was poured at the Gatún Locks. Four weeks after that spillway work was completed on Gatún Dam the lake began rising to its final level.

There were still millions of yards of dirt to be removed from Cucaracha, a task that could take months and would have

The excavation of the cuts and the construction of the locks weren't the only huge projects at Panama. The building of the breakwaters that protected the ship anchorages at either end of the canal was also an immense job. These barges are loading rock for the construction of the Naos breakwater that extends from Panama City to some nearby islands.
NA

required that the low dam at Gamboa be raised to keep the rising lake waters out of the cut.

Instead, Goethals decided not to delay the flooding of the cut, but rather to allow the rising lake to float big dredges to where they could do the excavating at Cucaracha.

Would the great locks, larger by many times than any others ever built, open and close smoothly? Would the complex system of valves and tunnels move the water fast enough, but without damaging ships in the locks?

Such questions were answered with positive results when the flag draped tug *Gatún* made the first passage of the locks it had been named for on September 26, 1913. Though this wasn't to be an official opening, the word was out and some 10,000 spectators crowded the area around the lock chambers for the historic moment.

The complex control system wasn't fully installed, so instead all the valves and lock controls had to be carefully operated so that nothing was done out of sequence.

The mechanisms all worked as smoothly as expected, and in just the thinnest remaining twilight the gates to the lake opened. The *Gatún* entered, tooting her steam whistle wildly to an enthusiastic crowd.

Four weeks later, a mixed fleet of American and left-over French dredges made their way through the Pedro Miguel and Miraflores locks from the Pacific to attack the slide. They

The steamer Ancon makes the first "official" transit of the canal on August 15, 1914. Where are the flag draped warships, the cheering crowds? Such a huge project – so many lives lost, so much money spent. But when it opened, war had broken out on the other side of the world and the long awaited "Grand Opening" passed with little notice.
NA

loaded barges which were then towed to dump the dirt in part of Gatún Lake away from the ship channel.

Then in December of 1913 came another historic moment. The French ladder dredge *Marmot*, in a scene Ferdinand de Lesseps would have been truly proud of, carved her way through a thin spot in the still huge dirt pile to the water on the other side, and the end to a gargantuan task was truly in sight.

A Not-So-Grand Opening: Eclipsed by the Guns of August

The completion of the Panama Canal was nothing less than one of the greatest human accomplishments in history. Almost 90 years has passed, yet the achievement hasn't been diminished. The completion of this project deserved a grand opening with hundreds of boats and dignitaries from all over the world.

Plans were made for a great fleet of US Navy ships to gather off Virginia and travel to San Francisco via the Canal. Their transit would be the official opening. The old battleship *Oregon*, whose frenzied transit around Cape Horn had stimulated Teddy Roosevelt's canal interest, would lead the parade through the canal. President Wilson would be aboard for the transit; the festivities would be huge, as fitted the occasion.

It was not to be.

In Europe, August of 1914 heralded a world-shaking event of a very different sort. A regional struggle began that was to quickly become World War I. The assassination of archduke Franz Ferdinand, heir to the Austrian throne, served as the

And the digging goes on: *Sun Princess*, looking back at the great cut through the continental divide at Culebra. Working alongside, keeping the channel clear, is a dredge and a barge. Digging, digging, digging continues at the Canal, even today.

match that lit the fuse to long smoldering regional feuds. Austria declared war on nearby Serbia on July 28, and in a world-stunning rapid sequence of events, Germany declared war on Russia and France and invaded Belgium on its way to Paris. In a few short weeks, Europe was in flames.

> "The lights are going out all over Europe; we shall not see them lit again in our lifetime."
>
> - Sir Edward Grey, British Secretary of State, 1914

The war news quickly eclipsed news from Panama and filled the front pages of papers all over the US. Two weeks after the opening guns, the French lost tens of thousands of soldiers in a two-week battle with the Germans; and a few days later, the first German aircraft begin to bomb Paris.

In the midst of these world-shattering events, the passage of the first real oceangoing ship through the Panama Canal created little fanfare. She was the humble cement ship *Cristobal*, which for the last four years had been round tripping between New York and Panama City with part of the 5 million sacks of cement that went into lock and breakwater construction.

But on board and looking thoughtfully over the side as she transited that great work that had cost so many lives was Philippe Bunau-Varilla. He had much to think about. Without his efforts, the French canal at Panama would have remained just a wide ditch in the jungle, filled with rainwater and surrounded by rusting equipment covered by vegetation.

PANAMA CANAL SCRAPBOOK

The End of an Era

Full rigged ship *John Ena* at Culebra, passing the Gold Hill Slide in January of 1915. In the background three ladder dredges work to clear the slide. A few months earlier, the canal had been closed for two weeks when two slides blocked the

canal. About nine months later, an immense slide–some 20 million cubic yards of material–thundered into the cut at Cucaracha, closing off the canal for seven long months, to date the longest closure in the history of the canal.

Standing on the right-hand side of the bridge deck on the stern of the square rigger is a lady in a white dress and large hat. Most likely the skipper's wife, she probably would not have been on board if the itinerary of the ship had included a rounding of "Cape Stiff," as sailors called Cape Horn.

The ship is most likely loaded with wheat from Australia, bound for England. In the second decade of the 20th century, wheat from Australia and nitrates from Chile were about the only bulk cargos a sailing vessel could make money on. If the *John Ena* had been loaded with nitrates, which are much denser, she would have been noticeably deeper in the water with her load, especially in the fresh waters of Culabra Cut and Gatún Lake.

In Better Days – HMS Hood

HMS Hood, the pride of the British Navy, seen at Culebra, circa 1932. Built for speed, her designers made her deck armor thinner than usual to conserve weight. But by doing so, they knew that in certain situations her ammunition storage areas or magazines would be vulnerable.

Then in the early days of World War II, the Germans finished the mighty *Bismark*. Also very fast and equipped with long ranging 15 inch cannons, she slipped through the British naval blockade and into the North Atlantic in May of 1941.

Anxious that the *Bismark* would attack vital food and supply convoys coming from Canada and the United States, the British send every available ship to find and try to sink the powerful German battlecruiser.

Just at dawn on May 24, 1941, the British ships *HMS Hood* and *HMS Prince of Wales* found the *Bismark* and smaller *Prince Eugen* in Denmark Strait, between Iceland and Greenland. The *Bismark* started firing from 14 miles away. With stunning accuracy, shortly after opening fire, a German shell penetrated the *Hood's* deck, and in an immense exposion, the *Hood* blew up. Of her crew of 1,419 officers and sailors, only three survived.

Ingenuity Gets It Through

When it was built, the 110-foot width of the locks seemed plenty big. But by World War II, the largest battleships, like the US Navy New Jersey Class, at 106 feet wide, were pushing the envelope. Ushering such very large ships carefully through the locks took much longer, and their transits had to be scheduled in advance.

As part of the Pacific war effort, this floating drydock had to transit the canal, from the Atlantic to the Pacific, but at 130 feet wide, there was no way that it would fit. Ingenious Navy engineers arranged for one of the huge floating cranes, built to lift the 750-ton lock gates, to exit the canal and meet the drydock. Workers installed braces so that the drydock wouldn't collapse like a house of cards when it was tipped on its side. Next, the crane very carefully lifted the drydock so that it could float on its side and make the transit. Were the canal to be built again today, designers might have built it wider yet, as there is a whole class of very large tankers, cruise ships, and special purpose ships like floating oil rigs whose owners would be pleased to pay a stiff toll in exchange for weeks of steaming around Cape Horn.

THE TWO-HEMISPHERE NAVY

If only Teddy Roosevelt could have seen it in its glory. One of the key reasons for the US involvement was for the US Navy to have access to it during wartime. With naval actions simultaneously in the Atlantic, Pacific, Mediterranean, and other oceans, the Panama Canal was a critical link, protected by naval cannon, patrol craft and aircraft.

Most of the participants of those naval battles have passed away, and today only a few survivors, historians and keen readers have an appreciation of the number of ships and sailors that participated.

But while I was in the National Archives researching the Panama Canal, I came across a remarkable series of photographs. Taken during the Pacific naval campaign against the Japanese, it was an aerial photograph of a great fleet at anchor in the vast lagoon of an unnamed coral atoll:

Hundreds of ships, either resting after a major battle or resting up for one. Then I took a magnifying glass and looking closer, grasped the size of the individual ships. In the foreground were aircraft carriers–I counted eight of them and past them were battleships and cruisers, landing ships, destroyers, support vessels. An immense fleet, ships almost beyond counting.

Note the electric locomotives or mules in the picture–these are the old style, with the tow wire winch assembly located on the top of the machine. The operators of the canal found out the hard way that for maximum stability, the best location for the winch/wire assembly was low, down by the loco's wheels.

SUN PRINCESS
A PANAMA CANAL PASSAGE

Don't miss any of it–some canal transits have to be scheduled early in the morning. So get up early on canal day if your ship is making an early entrance into the locks–there's a lot to see.

One of the particular challenges of the Panama Canal was developing a system to carefully control the movement of the ships in the locks. Designed to take ships larger than any canal to date, the worry was that if the ships transited the locks under their own power, a mechanical failure or operator error could send a ship smashing through the gates. So the concept of using electric locomotives, nicknamed "mules," to move ships through the locks was developed. Special winches had to be designed so that wire would pay out rather than break under extreme strain, and yet stop a heavy ship quickly. Even though the mules were very heavy, a heavy ship could easily just drag them along the steel tracks while their brakes were set and the wheels locked.

So a cog system was incorporated as well, consisting of a slotted center track, and a gear wheel on the locomotive. The gear wheel engaged the slots in the track, allowing both immense pulling and stopping power. The cog railway system also allowed the locomotives to climb and descend the steep incline between the lock chambers, as seen in the above photo.

And, just in case, a special emergency dam was built that could be lowered into slots in the lock chamber walls to stop Gatún Lake from emptying into the ocean if the worst did occur.

Would these ships even have been able to go around the horn? Much of today's international commerce travels in these ubiquitous containers, aboard immense ships that barely fit through the locks. Designed for the milder sea conditions of the mid-latitudes, a winter passage around Cape Horn would have presented a major challenge for these ships with their acres of exposed surfaces to catch the wind.

What is also apparent to any passenger that makes a transit of the canal is the immense volume of freight that passes daily. The installation of lights in the locks and along the ship route in Gatún Lake allows ships to transit the canal day or night.

Right: A Cuna native from the San Blas islands displays her needlework in the craft market in Colón, 2000, a cruise ship port facility near the Atlantic entrance to the canal.

Right: one of the biggest pieces of moving equipment ever built–the 745-ton lock gates at Miraflores, where the Pacific tides required especially tall gates. The key design factor that allows a 40-horsepower motor to move them easily is that they float–they are hollow and watertight, meaning that when immersed in water, their weight is much reduced.

Below: Passing the Culebra area, just north of the Pedro Miguel Locks. Since the digging started in the 1880's, there has seldom been a time when excavation was not being carried out along the canal. Here the canal channel crosses the Continental Divide in the Culebra area where the channel had to cut through hills that were almost 300 feet high. The *Sun Princess* passes close to the area where slides gave both American and French engineers so much trouble. As you can see, the digging still goes on.

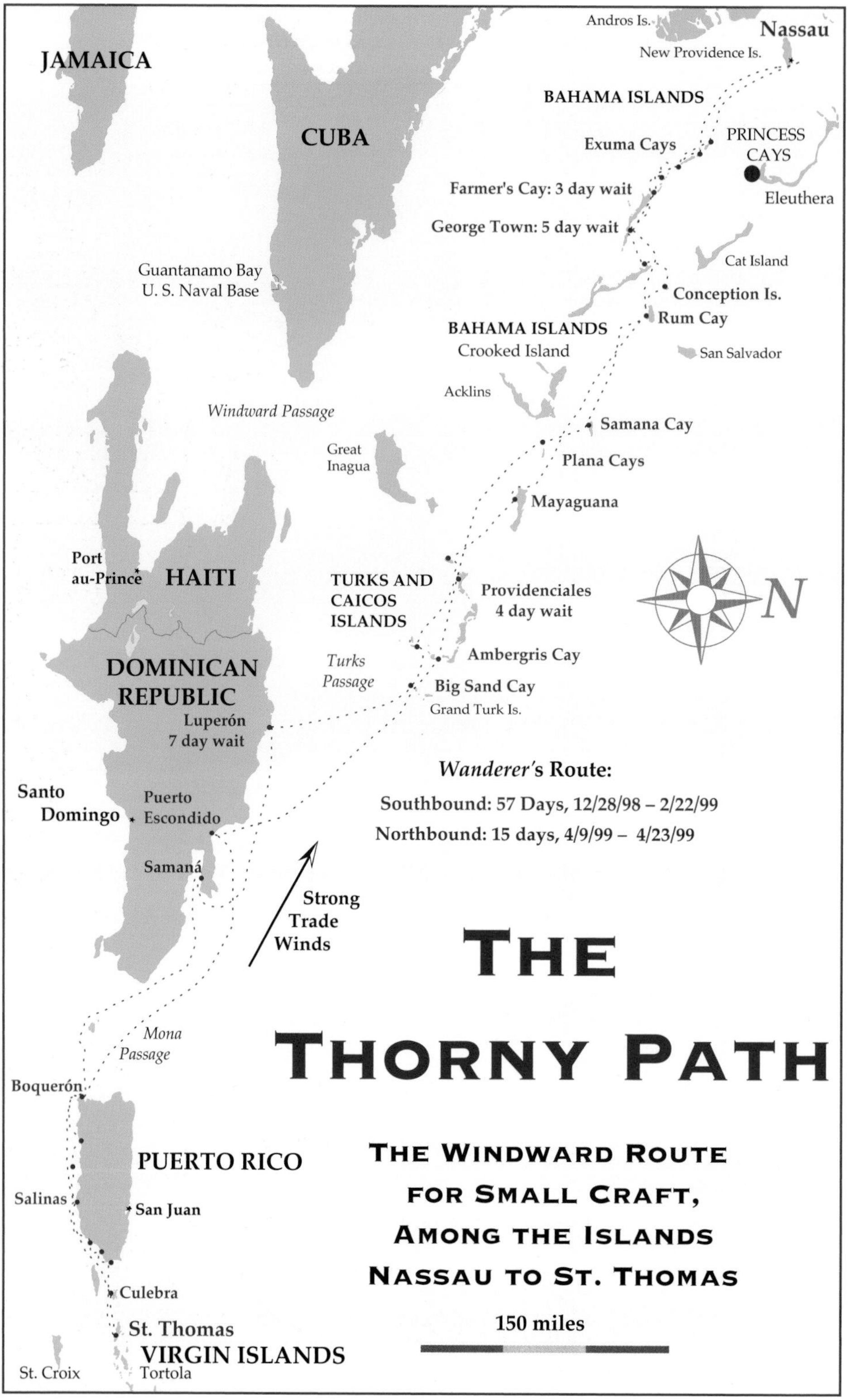

Andros Is.
Nassau
New Providence Is.
JAMAICA
BAHAMA ISLANDS
CUBA
Exuma Cays
PRINCESS CAYS
Farmer's Cay: 3 day wait
Eleuthera
George Town: 5 day wait
Cat Island
Guantanamo Bay
U. S. Naval Base
Conception Is.
Rum Cay
BAHAMA ISLANDS
Crooked Island
San Salvador
Acklins
Windward Passage
Samana Cay
Great Inagua
Plana Cays
Mayaguana
Port au-Prince
HAITI
TURKS AND CAICOS ISLANDS
Providenciales
4 day wait
N
Turks Passage
Ambergris Cay
DOMINICAN REPUBLIC
Big Sand Cay
Grand Turk Is.
Luperón
7 day wait
Wanderer's Route:
Southbound: 57 Days, 12/28/98 – 2/22/99
Northbound: 15 days, 4/9/99 – 4/23/99
Santo Domingo
Puerto Escondido
Samaná
Strong Trade Winds
THE
THORNY PATH
Mona Passage
Boquerón
PUERTO RICO
THE WINDWARD ROUTE
FOR SMALL CRAFT,
AMONG THE ISLANDS
NASSAU TO ST. THOMAS
Salinas
San Juan
Culebra
St. Thomas
150 miles
VIRGIN ISLANDS
St. Croix
Tortola

THE THORNY PATH

A FAMILY JOURNEY

Even from the beginning we sought out the remote and little visited islands. In the Gulf Islands of British Columbia, on our shakedown cruise, the kids scaled a steep bank on shore to tie *Wanderer's* stern to a tree.

Beginnings

It seemed like we barely saw the kids, hardly had a meal together. Between work and kids' sports, someone was always driving somewhere. It was the fall of 1997, I was a writer, my wife a second grade teacher. We lived on a rural island near Seattle.

But I could see the time looming ahead, when the kids would be off to college, into their own lives. What would they remember of their teenage years–this blur of rushing here and there?

We'd get a boat, I thought, take off for a year–sail around the Caribbean, have some real fun together as a family.

Of course, no one in the family took me seriously. For years I'd talked about it, but we didn't have a boat; we were barely sailors. And then some friends had bouts with cancer, my son entered high school, and I realized that it was now or never.

We borrowed, found a boat, a big, strong 1979 Kelly Peterson 44, and on a fine August morning set out on a shakedown cruise, along the British Columbia coast.

We sought the sleepy out of the way places. We anchored in coves so narrow the kids would row a line ashore and tie it to a tree. We played touch football on one deserted beach, softball on another. The cruise was everything that we had hoped for and our first sailboat was safe, fast, comfortable and strong.

The kids were adamant about not missing their fall water polo and soccer seasons, so we made a new plan: truck the boat to Florida, have friends take it to Puerto Rico, where we'd join it after Christmas.

Between publishing projects, kids' games, and packing, I went over our boat carefully, making sure everything was ready for a long trip far from good stores. Mary Lou and I loaded her with canned goods, spare lines, spare sails, spare parts, until every cupboard and locker was full.

Bad weather delayed the truck. When the boat arrived in Florida the window for the crew to take her to Puerto Rico had closed; we settled on Nassau instead.

Our family would have to do the difficult "Thorny

Path"–the windward route through the islands that I'd hoped to avoid. I was apprehensive, knew that many cruisers had set out with high hopes but had been defeated by contrary weather and had never gotten further than the Bahamas.

But the important thing was just to start. As in life, I knew that it was the journey that was important, not the destination.

On a snowy Christmas Eve we left our Puget Sound home with our 14 bags and boxes. We'd rented out our house, taken leave from our jobs, hoped that all the loose ends would come together.

Twenty-four hours later we were aboard *Wanderer* at a marina in Nassau. Clutter was a problem: clothes, school books, computer stuff, food, etc. all competed for limited space.

We needed a few days to sort things out, get used to that new life, before we set out for the Exumas–a thinly settled island chain that was the first stop on The Thorny Path.

Iguana on the beach at Allan Cay. They would rush down to greet any people that approached the shore in their dinghies. Note the color of the water in the anchorage. It was about nine feet deep around our boat, which needed seven to float! Navigation in the very shallow waters of the Bahama Island chain is often by "eyeball"–getting to know the subtle color changes between the channel and the shallows. The main danger in these waters is coral heads–refrigerator-sized outcroppings of concrete-hard coral that stick up from an otherwise smooth sand bottom. Fortunately, they are easily recognized by their darker color.

> "Having now secured your ship in one of the most interesting ports of call in the world, look around you and you will see everything to delight the soul of the sailor and artist. Watch the Out Island boats come in laden to the gunwales with handsome Out Islanders, youngsters singing calypso chanties, giggling girls, pigs, goats, sheep, chickens, sometimes a cow, all this on a small sloop only 25 or 30 feet long. Once we saw a Turks Island sloop come sail into Nassau Harbor with a deck load of sheep. Whenever the skipper yelled 'hard-a-lee' the sheep all ducked their heads.
>
> A lesson no doubt learned the hard way on their long ocean passage."
>
> –J. Linton Rigg, *Bahama Islands, A Boatman's Guide to the Land and the Water*. New York, 1949

NASSAU, BAHAMAS, DEC. 26, 1998

"C'mon, get up. Let's go." Mary Lou was shaking me. Groggily I looked at my watch: 4 a.m.

"Ah, that's west coast time," Mary Lou said. "It's seven o'clock, we got to hustle or we'll miss the parade. Sleep when you're dead."

I stumbled into the cluttered main cabin of our sailboat. Every flat surface was covered with half unpacked bags and boxes. I poked my head up into the forward cabin; the kids were still sleeping, surrounded by piles of clothes.

My wife thrust a paper cup of coffee into my hand.

"C'mon, let's go; I think it's over at eight."

I followed her up into the sunlight, blinking. The morning was delightfully warm and fair. Just 36 hours earlier we'd left our Puget Sound island home on a snowy Christmas Eve, where sunshine in winter was rare.

More unpacked bags and boxes filled the cockpit and overflowed onto the dock, but Mary Lou was already halfway to shore.

At first I doubted the taxi driver's "Don't be missing the parade, mon." We walked down empty and littered streets with nothing moving anywhere.

But we finally turned a corner to a surreal scene. Wildly dressed marchers wearing costumes that towered high over their shoulders were slumped against buildings, exhausted from marching and drinking all night. As we watched, more marchers and musicians, like wind-up dolls running down, came to the end of the parade route, and stood around exhausted, fumbling with costume straps and pads to finally sit and rest.

The Jukunu Parade, which starts at midnight on Christmas Day and goes until daylight the next morning, is a highlight of the holiday season. Different teams compete with their floats and bands for awards. The ornate floats often take months of work by a team of workers to complete.

Another block and we were in the thick of it–pressed back against the shuttered and gated shops by the crowds as the parade writhed and twitched along the narrow street, the color, the noise, the intensity of it all assaulting us.

Half a block away, the crowd's favorite, "Barrabas and the Tribe," approached with its own band: wildly blown trumpets, frantically beaten drums. The crowd picked up the urgency of the moment–began pounding on the corrugated steel shutters of the store windows around us with fists and pieces of wood.

We retreated tactfully back a block or two; we had noticed we were the only whites to be seen.

Then squads of police appeared, nightsticks at the ready; the pounding stopped and in a little cul-de-sac filled with parked floats we spoke with a lanky fellow, bleary eyed, gluing a bit of foam back to an ornate arm on a float representing the characters involved in Bahamian Independence.

"Ooooh, Prince Charles, he be *hard* to make mon, very hard. A mon like dat, he has to be just right, just *right!* And Prime Minister Pindling, you got to get him just right too! We be working for months to get them just right."

Clutter was a problem. Moving from a three-bedroom house to a boat with around a tenth of the floor space presented some challenges. We couldn't leave Nassau until we'd found a place to put everything.

From my son Matt's journal: Nice to finally be out of Nassau. Good crossing in fair weather. Only problem was on our way out of Nassau Harbor we ran aground! It was easy to get off but it will take a while getting used to water that's ten to fifteen feet deep even when you're out of sight of land.

Arrived and prepared to head ashore. Once we got within a few feet of the beach we spotted the iguanas. Mom was not impressed and opted to stay on board. The island was an iguana sanctuary and one of a few in the world where they can breed. There were fifteen of them on the beach ranging from small to the size of a small dog. Pretty crazy.

Went snorkeling with Mom and was amazed by all the fish that live here. They come in all kinds of shapes and colors. I hope we get an underwater camera because it's really quite a sight to see all the bright colors in a school of fish as they swirl around the brain coral.

Mom and I were swimming along not far from the inflatable where Dad and Katie were. Dad can't seem to nip the cough that he's caught in the bud and is a little under the weather. So it's just M.L. and I snorkeling. Mom grabbed me and pushed me in front of her. Not ten feet away from us was a barracuda! I struggled to free myself from her grip–it was as if she was using me as a shield! We both sprinted for the dinghy and practically fought each other as we tried to get in. Dad and Katie were laughing and I suspect that the barracuda, or the "cuda," was as well.

ATLANTIS

On Treasure Island, across a bridge from Nassau, is the Atlantis Resort, one of the more unique of the Caribbean. Built on an artificial lake on the spit between Nassau Harbor and the open Atlantic, the 14-story pink hotel has a deluxe suite that's a bridge between two buildings. More than just a beach resort, the basement of the complex includes an aquarium that is the equal of some of the best in the world, featuring plexiglass tunnels that pass through some of the specimen tanks, so that it's pretty easy to be eyeball to eyeball with some startling critters like a huge jewfish or a 3-foot big lipped Nassau grouper.

Of course, no Caribbean resort would be complete without the glitter of a casino, and the artwork here is spectacular. The highlights include a number of extremely large glass sculptures by Northwest glass artist Dale Chihuly.

Our daughter, Kate, exploring, Exumas. Nothing in our experience prepared us for the underwater world of the Caribbean. Our fins, masks and snorkels were the most used equipment of our entire trip. After each exploration, we would look in the field guides to mark down each new species that we had seen.

ALLEN CAY, EXUMAS, DEC. 29, 1998

We made it! Out of winter, away from the rain and the wind and the grey and the cold. All the struggles of getting the boat ready and shipped, all the difficulties of getting out of Dodge melt away with the turquoise waters and warm breezes.

This is my bell ringing–sliding out of bed early and quietly, making a coffee and sitting up in the cockpit, in just a t-shirt and shorts, feeling the cares of the last months fade away. After a while Mary Lou came up and we just sat together, looking out at it all–the scrub palms, the white sand beach, the other cruisers laying easily at anchor.

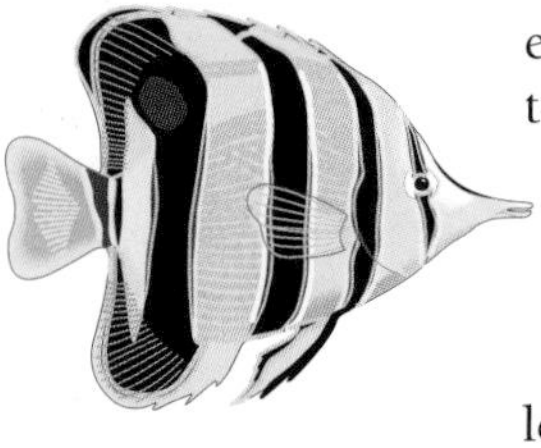

The ubiquitous **BANDED BUTTERFLYFISH** often travels in pairs and is seen in shallow water around coral reefs.

We launched the "new" secondhand inflatable dinghy, lowered the outboard motor down and hooked it up.

I had a cold, with aches in my lower back, a reminder of the north we'd left behind. So stayed aboard, reading in the cockpit, taking in the sun, while Mary Lou, Kate and Matt jumped in the skiff with the brand new snorkels, masks and fins.

I'd look out now and again, sometimes seeing just the three snorkels sticking out of the water near the anchored inflatable, sometimes hearing laughter from the water.

Just this is what we have come so far for.

THE EXUMAS

This chain of low-lying islands and shoals, running for about 150 miles southeast from Nassau, has been called by some cruising guides "The Pièce de Résistance of West Indies Cruising." Mostly empty, with but a few modest and hurricane battered settlements, the visiting yachtsman finds exquisite little harbors and remote anchorages; water clear as glass and beach after lonely beach. The trade winds blow strong and regular; the big resorts and casinos are away to the north. It is hard to believe that such an unspoiled archipelago exists so close (150 miles) to the boating hordes of South Florida. That it remains so is a tribute to the sobering power of the north flowing Gulf Stream, which runs like a river between Florida and the Bahamas, and when opposed by a northerly wind, creates a fearsome sea.

ALLAN CAY, DEC. 30

Comes at 2 a.m. with Mary Lou poking me awake. "Hey," said she in alarm, "we're hitting the bottom." I lifted myself up on one elbow, felt the faintest bump as our keel touched the sand beneath us.

"C'mon," she said, poking me a little harder, "get up, we got to move to deeper water." I looked at my watch: it was just half an hour until low tide.

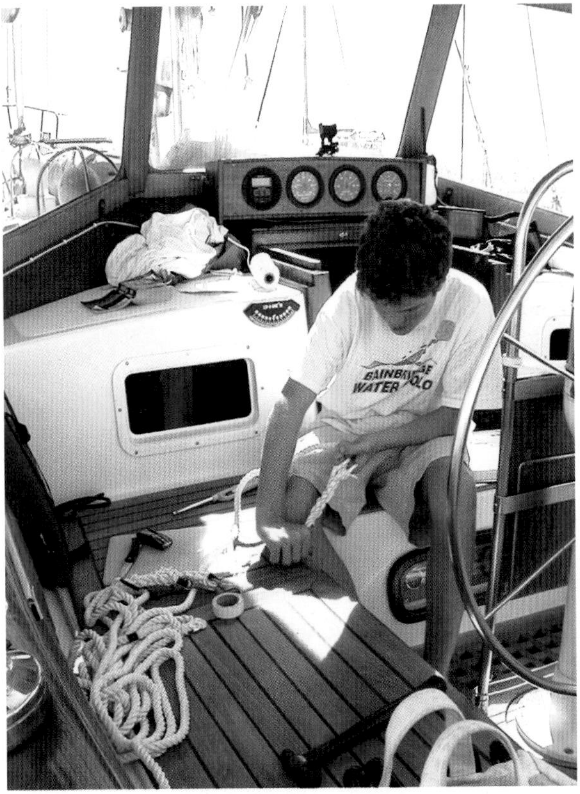

Matt splicing eyes into the lifting bridle for the dinghy. Cruising is sometimes called "working on your boat in exotic ports of call." Our kids shared in the boat and navigation work, learning a lot in the process.

"Where we gonna go? Pick up both anchors and try and find some place six inches deeper? This whole harbor's shallow." I'd spent most of the last 10 summers fishing commercially in the very shallow waters of the bays off the eastern Bering Sea, in Alaska. Bumping on the sand bottom for an hour or so at the bottom of the tide was something I was used to. The tides here were small; in a couple of hours we'd be floating again anyway. I went back to sleep.

"All the other boats are pointing the other way. And they're not leaning over either..." Mary Lou was poking me again.

When day came, it was fair, with a fresh breeze from the west: a traveling breeze. The five cruisers that came into the anchorage last night, Caribbean-bound by the look of the gear lashed to their decks, were off at first light, for they, like we, have many miles to travel. I suppose it would have been wise to have taken the dinghy over last night and visited, perhaps joined their little entourage, for the waters past the Exumas are lonely indeed, and we have no wish to travel alone. But I am still a bit stiff; we need just one more day to hang out, explore, snorkel and swim before moving on.

But also there is something I do not share with my family: I am anxious. One is on one's own here–the settlements are very far apart, and any kind of help or service difficult to obtain. Ahead lie many thousands of miles of challenging navigating and sailing. We have rented out our house; our budget is adequate but tight. A misstep here could change our plans dramatically for the worse. I'd rather have an extra day to shake this ache than to get out there, out of sight of land, and make a mistake.

Wanderer at Warderick Wells Cay. The line of darker blue water is the channel. When we entered, from the right of the picture, the tidal current was flowing very strongly with us. The challenge to pick up a mooring buoy was this–to turn around and head up into the current to pick up the mooring without hitting the sand bars at the edges of the very narrow channel! This is a typical Bahamas out-island scene–many low uninhabited islands surrounded by shallow water.

WARDERICK WELLS, EXUMAS, DEC. 31

Comes with strong southeast trade winds. Brought windsurfer aboard, tied dinghy close astern, secured all for sea and underway by 10:00. In an hour the low islands disappeared over the horizon and we were alone, heeled over, driving hard to windward. This is *Wanderer's* wind–18 to 20 knots, a good fresh breeze, and didn't we eat up the miles! But where are all the other boats? A bit disconcerting in a way, this pounding along in 8-10 feet of water, heeled over, throwing spray to leeward and never a bit of land or another boat in sight around the whole horizon.

Finally at 4:00, we picked our way every so cautiously into the narrow lane of deeper water to pick up a mooring buoy–all a marine reserve here; no anchoring allowed.

Then a nattily dressed older man with an Australian accent came by in a skiff and invited us for drinks at the park headquarters, a rambling frame structure on the bluff. So cleaned up, and we motored with the kids past the five other boats in the harbor to meet other sailors and park volunteers, coming each winter from distant homes to work on park improvements.

Wonderful spot with the deck overlooking the stunning blue waters of the harbor surrounded by low islands and the shallow waters of Exuma Bank filling in the distance to the horizon.

Motored back at dusk to a sad note. Matt was a bit blue, so quizzed him and it all came out in a rare teary rush: how the trip was ruining his chances for good grades this semester (he'd had to leave school before the end of the term and had brought the work with him); how he was missing his friends; how we hadn't met any kids his age, etc.

It brought back all those things one worries about at the beginning of any long trip. Would the family get along, would anyone get hurt or sick, would we break down, hit a rock, run out of money? Would the kids do OK with their home schooling? A lot of worries and no answers. So much for bringing in the last year of the century on a cheery note.

Matt's Journal: Jan. 1, 1999:

Snorkeled a nice reef with some big coral heads that you could swim through. Best part was seeing the spiny lobsters for the first time.They're huge! Spiny lobster are a lot bigger than their brother species in Maine. There were two of them hiding in a coral tunnel. We couldn't catch them for dinner because it's a park. Too bad.

Hiked up Boo Boo Hill where a huge pile of junk has accumulated over the years from the cruisers. The tradition is that you take a piece of junk from your boat–it may be anything from a toilet seat to part of an oar. You carve or write the name of the boat in it as well as the crew and throw it on top of the other memorabilia that has collected over the years.

"The supermarket was pretty sad though. It was in a dimly lit shack containing rows of old food. Most of the cans had rust on them and the 'fresh' food had bugs flying around it. Very different from Safeway." – from Matt's journal. Our children, like many Americans, were used to the well-lit and well-stocked aisles of our local grocery store. It was very good for them to see the much more modest lifestyles of other cultures.

STANIEL CAY, JAN. 2, 1999

Underway at 10 with reefed main in ESE 20 to 25 knots, the fresh breeze creating a very short and wet chop on the shallow Exuma Banks. Wet and hard going, but *Wanderer* did just fine. Pastel colored houses of Staniel Cay settlement visible from many miles at sea. Very glad to drop sail in late afternoon and motor the last few miles, creeping in over very shallow water, hitting all the high spots to anchor off village. All hands ashore for shopping. Tidy small town with modest bungalows.

One of the larger villages in the Exumas, Staniel Cay features two modest marinas, and a store. "Busy" would not be a word one used to describe the settlement: dogs sleeping in the streets didn't have to worry about traffic.

Thunderball Cave

One of the more spectacular sights of the Exuma Chain is Thunderball Cave, near Staniel Cay. It's named for a scene that was filmed here for the James Bond movie of the same name. The cave is inside a high, dome-shaped limestone island, and is entered through several passages that are covered by water at high tide.

When the sun is high, its rays shine directly down into the cave through a series of fissures in the top of the island, creating an underwater scene that is extremely dramatic, to say the least.

We anchored our dinghy 30 feet off the eastern side of the cay and swam into the cave through a narrow, winding passage. Once inside we surfaced and looked around in awe–the cavern was perhaps 80 feet in diameter, with a ceiling 40 feet over our heads.

But it was the schools of fish that were the most dramatic–totally unafraid and, indeed, used to visitors who had brought bits of bread or perhaps frozen peas to feed them; they literally surrounded us.

Keeping your children on board is critical. Kate is wearing a harness, which is clipped to a strong point with an 8–foot tether. We would all wear harnesses and clip in at night or in stormy weather. Additionally, at night we would wear life jackets equipped with whistles and strobe lights, whenever we were on deck or on watch in the cockpit. We also practiced how we would respond to a man overboard situation. Fortunately we never had to use any of the skills we practiced.

Of Kids and Boats

As we were to quickly discover, our two teen-aged kids were incredibly social and gregarious. Their prime consideration was finding other kids and keeping in touch with their old school friends or new cruising friends. As we approached any anchorage they would have the binoculars glued to their eyes, inspecting other boats for signs of other teens. Those peaceful secluded coves so attractive to their parents were rarely of interest to them for obvious reasons. And so, we learned to accommodate their wishes by occasionally modifying our cruising plans to travel or remain in port with boats that had newly made friends on board.

Quickly memorizing the names of the boats of their friends, they would regularly use our several radios to communicate with them.

We learned a lot about letting go, although somewhat uneasily at first. More than anything else, in the beginning, letting go meant letting them take off by themselves, or with friends, in the little outboard powered inflatable boat that was the equivalent of our family car. The rules were: tell us the plan, stick to it, and take a walkie-talkie so that we could be in touch.

We also learned quickly that the cruising community of 30- and 40-footers crewed by families that travel these waters, is a larger family in themselves, watchful for all its extended family.

One breezy evening, while we were anchored amongst a group of several dozen cruisers in the George Town area of the southern Bahamas, several teens from other boats were aboard playing board games with Matt and Kate.

Needing another game, one of the boys, a 14-year-old, headed off in his inflatable dinghy across the anchorage to his parents' boat. My wife, Mary Lou, looking out as he sped away, called out in alarm, "He's gonna flip it!"

The boy was sitting way back in the stern, and as Mary Lou watched, a gust of wind lifted the bow of the inflatable as he came over a wave and flipped it completely over backwards.

By the time I got up on deck, my daughter already had her life jacket on and I joined her, heading out across the choppy anchorage in our inflatable.

When we got to the overturned boat, another inflatable was already alongside, pulling the startled boy out of the water. Knowing it was a dark and breezy evening, and that there were kids about, most of the fleet had had their radios on and watched to make sure our guest made it home OK.

With no TV and VCR aboard, we were also viewed by our kids and their friends as the Grinches of the cruising community. Instead we had board games: Scrabble and Backgammon, as well as a great selection of books.

We encouraged writing, and over the course of our six-month cruise, Matt and Kate produced some wonderful journals and letters, some of which are reproduced here. Before our trip we purchased a digital camera. With a Macintosh laptop computer and a small color printer, the kids were able to illustrate their journals and letters to friends.

The indispensable laptop–where would we have been without it? Actually one of the biggest sources of conflict among the kids was whose turn it was on the laptop. Not only did they prepare and read e-mails (sent when we found a phone at a port), but each had a journal spiced up with photographs from our digital camera. More sophisticated cruisers would have had a navigation program on their laptops which would also display their vessel's position in real time on an electronic chart!

It was a perfect situation for e-mail, and we used it to the fullest. Cruisers with a bit more technical sophistication than I use a modem in conjunction with a so-called single sideband radio–essentially a ham radio–to connect to the internet while they are aboard.

By necessity we chose a lower tech approach. As we traveled away from towns, we would all write our e-mails, and just save them until we were in a port that might have a telephone. Then the kids or I would go ashore and see if there was a way to hook up. To our delight, we found that often even in remote settlements, if there was a phone, we could connect and get our mail.

The cost of overseas calls required us to be a bit creative–you connected, downloaded all the waiting incoming e-mails, but without reading them, then sent off the outgoing e-mails one after the other as fast as you could. Then, when we got back to the boat, we would all open our e-mails one by one and catch up with friends as well as my business.

Matt and Kate lived together for most of those six months in the fo'c'sle, or forward cabin area, of our Peterson 44. They had a space roughly 8 feet long by 10 wide, narrowing to 5 feet wide at one end. Each had a couple of drawers, a shelf for books and a long hammock, strung close to the overhead for all their clothes. Mary Lou had made a curtain that ran down the middle of the sleeping mattress, so that each child could have a modicum of privacy as well.

Aside from the inevitable, "Get your smelly feet on your side," and the like, the kids did remarkably well in that small space.

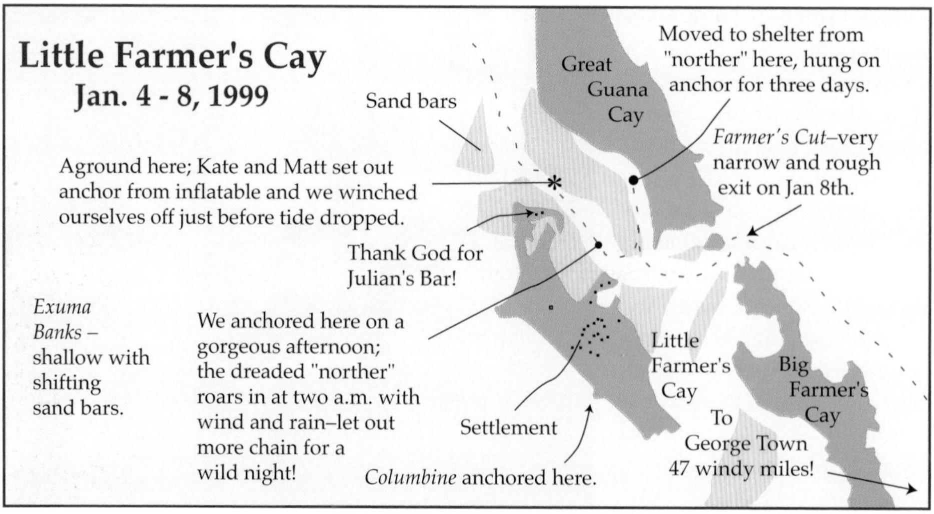
Little Farmer's Cay
Jan. 4 - 8, 1999
Sand bars
Great Guana Cay
Moved to shelter from "norther" here, hung on anchor for three days.
Farmer's Cut–very narrow and rough exit on Jan 8th.
Aground here; Kate and Matt set out anchor from inflatable and we winched ourselves off just before tide dropped.
Thank God for Julian's Bar!
Exuma Banks – shallow with shifting sand bars.
We anchored here on a gorgeous afternoon; the dreaded "norther" roars in at two a.m. with wind and rain–let out more chain for a wild night!
Little Farmer's Cay
Big Farmer's Cay
Settlement
Columbine anchored here.
To George Town 47 windy miles!

Typical of the smaller Bahama settlements, the people at Little Farmer's Cay make a modest living at fishing and a bit of subsistence agriculture. Farmer's Cut, like many of the narrow passages between Bahama Cays, has to be transited carefully, especially when the tidal current is running against a wind.

LITTLE FARMER'S CAY, JAN. 4

We slid onto the sand bar at the edge of the channel and lurched to a stop. "Oops," Mary Lou said. "So much for a day without hitting the bottom."

"Put the kids in the skiff, have them drop anchor in the channel. . . " A man in a red shirt was waving from the shore of a nearby island. The tide was dropping fast, so I hauled the dinghy alongside, waved Matt and Kate into it, and passed down the anchor and line we kept ready on the stern for such occasions. The kindly man directed the kids where to drop the anchor and I put the end of the anchor line around a bow roller and back to the winch to pull us back into the channel.

"Ohhh, the channel ain't like the chart now, mon," our benefactor, Julian, who ran the Farmer's Cay Marina and Yacht Club, told us that evening. A modest bar with a fancy name and a rickety dock, we were the only paying customers. Our children played pool with his at a toy pool table, and when we asked for rum and tonics, we learned the standard refrain of the islands:

"Oh, tonic be coming on the mailboat, any day now, mon."

As we dinghied out to our boat afterwards, we marveled at the transparency of the water in which we were anchored and the peacefulness of the scene around us.

The kids brought out a few small gifts and homemade cards, and I went to bed on my 53rd birthday feeling as if the strains and the worries that accompany the beginning of any long journey were at last starting to pass.

LITTLE FARMER'S CAY, JAN. 5

Comes at 3 a.m. with a great north wind ripping open the night. Stumbled up on deck and up to the bow with flashlight to let out 10 more fathoms of anchor chain. Just made it back to the cabin when the skies opened up with slashing rain as well. The wind stayed steady and strong at north even after the rain had stopped, and I realized it was the "norther" forecast for several days now. After several days of warnings that had yielded no change of weather, I had dismissed it. Foolish me.

So for uncomfortable night rolling and pitching in short steep seas. First light brought a mean looking scene with white capped seas and trees on shore bent low in the gusts. Picked up anchor at morning high water and motored cautiously over shallows to narrow gutter of deeper water along Great Guana Island. Here the tide ran very strong, and we laid out two anchors so as not to hit the shore or the sand bar when the tide turned.

Young pool sharks, Little Farmer's Cay. While we hung out in this sleepy bar, waiting for the wind to ease, the satellite TV showed a blizzard that covered much of the eastern US, and whose strong winds were to reach even into the Bahamas.

The weather was too inhospitable to go ashore but it provided a needed opportunity to organize below. Piles of stuff disappeared into cupboards and lockers, journals and colored pencils came out, Mary Lou and I caught up on our writing and the kids their schoolwork.

The night settled in, black, windy, and cold.

But there was a good, thick stew for dinner, and hot rolls, and afterwards, we took turns reading out loud. Now and again a particularly angry gust would roar down on us from out of the darkness and howl through the rigging. Twice I excused myself, took the big flashlight, went up on

THE DREADED "NORTHER"

"It came up so quick–we got our anchor up and were able to move around to the other side of Conception Island, but one couple was ashore, exploring when that wind just came out of nowhere. They couldn't launch their dinghy through the surf to get to their boat. Their anchor couldn't hold and the surf pounded their boat to bits in front of their eyes. We walked across the island when the wind let go, and helped them pick out valuables from what was left. One of the other cruisers gave them a ride back to George Town. They had everything they owned on that boat. They were devastated."

– a cruiser's tale

Regularly in the wintertime, cold fronts will sweep across the US and penetrate into the Bahamas and occasionally as far south as Puerto Rico. The air temperature may drop to as low as 50 degrees, and the wind will come violently out of the north. A "norther" may last several days. The prudent mariner will always monitor daily weather forecasts and when a "norther" approaches, seek protected harbors.

These weather fronts do have benefits, however: as the front passes, the change in wind direction allows southbound cruisers, who may have been waiting for days, and sometimes weeks, a period of perhaps a few days or more of favorable winds.

deck and forward into the wind to see that all was well.

Of course, it always was, but still, it was unsettling to feel the power of the wind and see the dark land so close. But then there was the treat of making my way carefully aft, looking down to the chatter of voices, the cozy glow of lamplight, such a contrast to the wild and unfriendly world around us.

WEATHERBOUND AT FARMER'S CAY, JAN. 6 - 7

Very cool and windy. Each afternoon we'd dinghy a half-mile through the wet chop to the settlement and walk around very clean and modest homes with conch shells everywhere in evidence as part of the local building materials–used with cement for walls, lining walkways, etc. But we met some other cruisers, Steve, Deb, and Kathy, Caribbean–bound like us. Their 38-footer, *Columbine*, was anchored on the other side of the island. We sat at Julian's bar, and they shared their many experiences and advised us as the big screen satellite TV showed scenes of ice and cold and snow from the big cold front sweeping across the States.

Ninety–nine percent of the time when we were sailing, one anchor was all we needed. But at Farmer's Cay, with a strong northerly blowing, and anchored in a narrow little gutter of deep water with the strong current switching directions every six hours, two anchors were required. An ideal cruising boat would have two separate anchor rollers in the bow. We just had one, which meant that the second anchor had to be unlashed from the life lines back in the stern and carried forward.

Just before dark, we'd say our goodbyes, put on our rain gear, and get into the dinghy for the wet ride across the choppy sound to *Wanderer.* We'd climb aboard, tie off the dinghy and clamber below to the coziness of our cabin with the wind moaning through the rigging outside.

Matt was all for heading for George Town, some 40 miles south, weather be damned. He had been told it was where there were lots of cruising families with kids. I tried to explain to him the "prudent mariner" theory of cruising–of traveling when the weather was cooperative but he wasn't listening.

This month's book was *Grain Race* by Alan Villiers, a true tale of bringing a big four-masted square rigged ship loaded deep with grain around Cape Horn to England in 1932, the last such race before this trade was taken over by steam-powered craft. Their trials in surviving a storm in the vicinity of the much feared southern tip of South America put any difficulties we might think we were having in these warm waters in sobering perspective:

> "The seas mount in height terrifically; the ship is small now, for all her three thousand tons and her mighty spars. There is no moon. The great seas rise black hills beside her, behind her, all around her, towering above her, foam streaked and angry. They froth and roar as they go, while the ship, lurching wildly and rolling as if she would roll right over, staggers on. Blindly she runs now, staunchly she conquers, barely she survives. Green seas pour over the length of her as she rolls; no longer is it possible to venture on the main deck for all its life-lines and its nets spread from rigging to rigging. Her side goes right under, nets and all."
>
> –Alan Villiers, *Grain Race,* Charles Scribners, New York, 1933

"You must also be aware that rough seas can build up within hours on the barrier reefs fringing the Atlantic Ocean, and normally navigable passages through the reefs become impassable. This is the deadly sea state the Bahamians call a "Rage." . . . You will not survive to relate the experience if you attempt to force your way through a reef passage during a Rage".

– Mathew Wilson, *The Bahamas Cruising Guide,* International Marine, Camden, Maine, 1998

PASSAGE TO GEORGE TOWN, JAN. 8

For genuine excitement, give me today again.

This morning, with just inches under our keel, we motored cautiously out into the tide and wind ripped waters of Farmer's Cut. Outside in the Atlantic, we found a truly ugly sea running–6 and 8–footers with the wind blowing their tops downwind at us.

Matt and I put on our safety harnesses, got up a double-reefed main, rolled out a bit of jib and off we went. For the first hour hardly anyone spoke. Not only was it our first time out in the big ocean, but we had to make it through a narrow and reef strewn passage before dark, or go offshore for a long ugly night before daylight allowed us to try the shallow entrance again.

But the weather gods smiled on us, and with the very last of the light, we ever so cautiously entered the harbor where the anchor lights of many other yachts shone out cheerily.

Finally we picked a spot, the anchor chain sang its little song, and the first leg of our journey was done. It was two mightily relieved adults that poured out the rum and toasted a difficult passage made at last.

Matt's Journal:

"After five dreary days of waiting for a mythical 'weather window' we are free from Farmer's Cay and headed for the cut. YES! Going through the cut is going to be pretty crazy. It's a really narrow opening in between two huge boulders and the seas are really running hard."

And later:

"Very rough crossing from Farmer's Cay. Had to wear life lines and everything. 7- to 9- foot seas and 25-35 knots of wind. Mom and Katie were not feeling very well so Dad and I ended up doing most of the sailing."

Not for the faint of heart–the Family Islands Regatta, held in George Town each spring, features boats from many of the smaller or "family" islands of the Bahamas. The races start with the boats anchored so each crew must hustle to get the anchor and sails up to get onto the course. When the boats tack or change the side of the sail that the wind is on, all the crew and long boards must be shifted to the other side at just the right moment.

George Town, Bahamas: Summer Camp for Adults

"Mom, Dad, there's kids here!"

I stumbled groggily up into the sunlight to see what all the excitement was about. Matthew and Kate were already dressed in bathing suits, looking at the beach, where half a dozen teens were throwing a frisbee back and forth.

Our kids grabbed their life jackets, jumped in the dinghy and headed eagerly for the beach, to quickly melt into the group, as if they had all been friends since kindergarten.

A little later, as Mary Lou and I were sitting in the cockpit, drinking coffee and savoring the hot sunny morning, the kids motored breathlessly out to the boat.

"We got invited for lunch aboard a boat, and they want us to come over to play cards tonight and watch a movie. Can we? Can we?"

Both of us nodded, immensely relieved that the kids had at last found some friends.

So began a remarkable interlude while we waited for the right weather window to continue our trip to the Caribbean.

George Town had the flavor of an adult summer camp. Each winter almost 400 yachts, mostly from the US and Canada, would work their way down the coast to these miles of protected anchorages and wonderful white sand beaches.

About half the fleet were retiree couples, opting for the cruising lifestyle while they still were limber and active. But many were couples like ourselves, who had put careers on hold to step back from the rat race and just sail for a while, with children if they had them. We became acquainted with many, and everyone had a tale of the path that led them to their boat and to George Town.

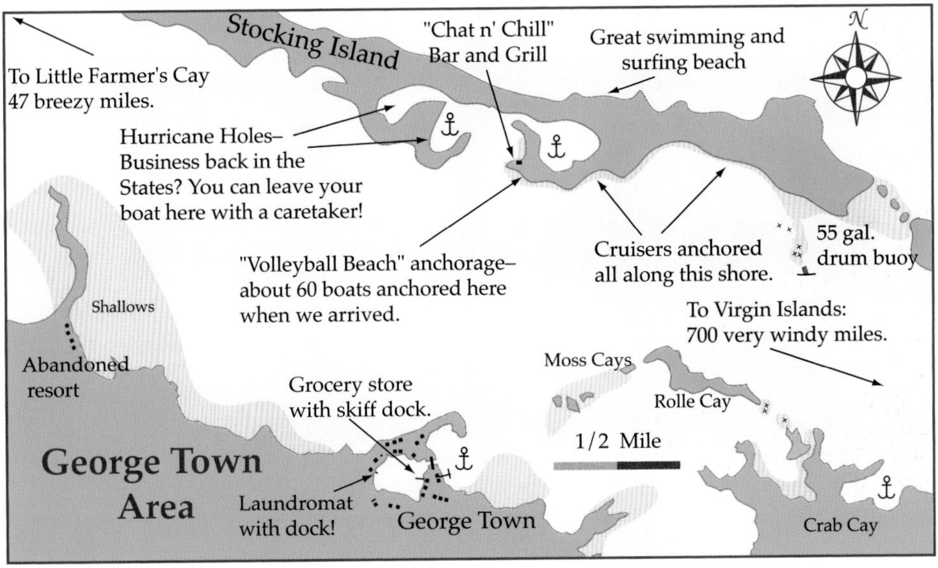

Most of the kids were involved, like ours, in some sort of correspondence schooling. Usually, they would work on their schoolwork for two or three hours in the morning, and then make plans to meet their friends on the beach. Sometimes they'd hike over to the back side of Stocking Island to body surf in the cuts between the reefs. Usually someone in the group would have a handheld radio, so they could all keep in touch with their parents.

A few miles across the bay was the village of George Town. Once every few days, most boats would motor across the bay to anchor for an afternoon to shop, or do laundry, and always, except for those few boats with water makers, to fill up the plastic jugs with fresh water and shuttle them out by dinghy to fill their boats' water tanks.

Cruiser's Crossroads

George Town was also a popular stop for circumnavigators, cruisers who are working their way slowly around the world, usually with the prevailing winds, east to west.

Often with wind generators, solar panels, and decks cluttered with cruising gear, the circumnavigators were easy to distinguish from the more common coastal cruising yachts.

Robin Stanley and Sophia Dracos, from England, were taking a break in George Town in January, 1999, after a transatlantic passage in their Kelly Peterson 44, *Zinfandel.* Their plans included a trip to the USA east coast before they headed west for Panama.

While Matt and Kate would have been content to winter in George Town, we needed to be ready to move on down the Thorny Path when an easing of the trade winds, or a "weather window," allowed.

Between George Town and the next provisioning stop were almost 300 lonely miles, broken only by a few uninhabited or sparsely inhabited islands. What we needed most was another boat to travel with.

With a regular schedule of school work every morning and playing with their new found friends each afternoon and evening, our children would have been happy to have spent the entire winter at George Town.

> "This is Kevin O'Sullivan on the *Shannachie II*. We're headed down to St. Thomas and the Virgin Islands down through The Thorny Path and hoping for a little company for the trip. So if anyone is headed that way and wants company we'll be on channel 69. Thank you."
>
> – *heard on the morning "cruiser's net," an informal daily call-in hour, when vessels may listen on their radios for items for sale, sailing parents needing babysitters, sailors needing crew, etc.*

From Matt's Journal: "We got back from town just in time for 'fun volleyball at volleyball beach.' Every day at two o'clock everybody gathers to play volleyball. There are different games for all of the different skill levels. I was playing with the experts or snob ball. Most of the guys who were playing were middle aged and were really serious about it–almost too serious if you ask me. They have a system where the first hit goes to the guy in the middle and he is the only one who gets to hit. One time when there was a ball coming right at me I hit out of turn. The guy in the middle was an old fogey all decked out in sweatbands and a white t-shirt. He said ' Son, that second hit always goes to me unless I tell you otherwise.' Yikes."

"Chicken Harbor"

"George Town earns the moniker of 'Chicken Harbor' every season. Cruisers gab about stopping off at Conception Cay on the way to Puerto Rico, or sailing to Rum Cay in one shot, as though they were just stopping by the convenience market before ramping up onto the interstate. Their biological clocks are still set on high from the hassle of getting the boat ready, from the bustle of provisioning, even from the social whirl among the yachts at George Town. One after another finds an excuse to return to Florida and "go south next year": a water maker filter goes bad, an autopilot is on the fritz. The road south looms long and treacherous.

"Unprepared cruisers that take the plunge and head out have their clocks cleaned by the Equatorial Current and the incessant trade wind. They slow down to island time. They begin to see the wisdom of this guide's constantly drummed advice: *wait for weather*, leave early, get in early, and *never pass a safe anchorage*."

– Bruce Van Sant. *The Gentleman's Guide to Passages South*, Cruising Guide Publications, Dunedin, Fl., 1998

GEORGE TOWN, EXUMAS, JAN. 13

This afternoon motored to a lonely anchorage at the eastern end of Elizabeth Island, to get boat and gear all squared away for sea. After being anchored for a week, our little cabin becomes cluttered with books, computer stuff, games, etc. and we need to set aside some time to get all ready for sea, lay out the courses, bring the dinghy and outboard motor aboard and generally get ready for whatever the weather may throw at us.

Anchored near by were *Columbine* and *Shannachie II*, our new traveling partners We had been encouraged by the morning's weather report of moderating winds, but occasionally a strong wind gust heeled us over and howled through the rigging. This was not what we expected.

This was the allure of George Town – so many secluded anchorages, white sand beaches, even a great little beach bar with fried conch and cold beer.

The night came early and black with lots of wind. Before I turned in, I stepped outside to check our position, to make sure we weren't dragging in the strong squalls. I stopped, just before heading down into the cozy warmth of the cabin: something wasn't right. *Shannachie II*'s anchor light was moving rapidly through the darkness–their anchor must have broken loose in a squall.

I tried the radio: "Kevin, Kevin, KEVIN! Your anchor's dragging, better start up quick... can you hear me?"

By very good fortune, Kevin and his wife, Ann, still had their radio on and pretty soon the deck lights went on, a splash of light with Kevin on the bow working the anchor winch.

And I was thankful for *Wanderer*'s all chain anchor tackle. *Shannachie II*, like many yachts, had a short piece of chain–perhaps 30 feet-long attached to the anchor, and a long nylon line connected the chain to the boat. Nine times out of ten it was fine –but in strong gusty winds, the boat would surge back, lifting the short piece of chain and giving the anchor an opportunity to break free. *Wanderer*'s all chain arrangement was more tedious to set and took longer to retrieve, but when the wind blew and the night was wild and black, one rested a bit more securely with the weight of the chain holding the anchor securely to the bottom.

But still, sleep came hard. The wind moaned through the rigging, and I knew that what lay ahead was very different from that which was behind us. We'd heard a few tales of cruisers who had headed south as we were, only to return a few weeks later, defeated by contrary winds or mechanical failures.

Whatever The Thorny Path held for us, we were about to find out.

Heeled over, pounding hard and throwing spray wide, so our journey along The Thorny Path began.

The Thorny Path

CALABASH BAY, LONG ISLAND, BAHAMAS, JAN. 14

Whoaaaa... another white knuckle departure–we had our life jackets and safety harnesses on when a big roller drove green water over us in the cut between the reefs! It only lasted a moment and then we were out in the deeper water.

When we were clear of the land, Matt and I clipped our tethers into the wire jack stay that runs along the deck and got up a reefed main, rolled out a bit of jib, and off we went.

We were still getting the hang of this big boat sailing, but each day we gained a little more confidence. The wind was southeast 22 to 25 knots, with higher gusts. A sailor with real gusto and a newer mainsail might have gone without a reef at all, but if we "blew out" our mainsail, we'd have to limp back to George Town and wait weeks to get a new one shipped out from the States.

That morning, we could see each squall or strong wind shift as a darker area of water approached us, and we would "feather" the boat slightly up into the wind, easing the strain on the mainsail until the wind eased.

After a long day, we approached the break in the long reef that led to the anchorage at Calabash Bay in the late afternoon.

Like most anchorages in the Bahamas, this was only to be approached in daylight, with someone (me) up on the bow, pointing the way through. The little slot of deeper water was perhaps 20 yards wide, a single break in the wall of coral that lurked just below the surface along the whole west side of Long Island.

Next was our perpetual challenge in these waters–trying to get far enough in to the shelter of the land to be out of the persistent swell, but without hitting bottom. Finally we settled on a place where there was perhaps just a foot of water between us and the sandy bottom.

On the way in we passed a sobering sight: the wrecked hull of a big schooner–someone's dream, high and dry on the coral reef that lay just a foot or two underwater, a warning of the risks to all who passed.

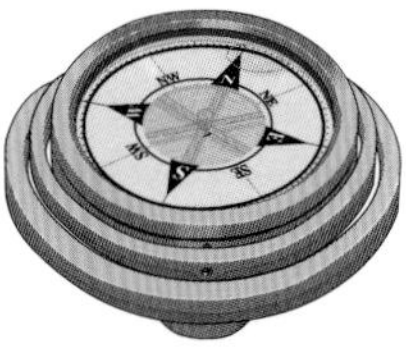

Unfortunately for a deep draft boat like ours, many of the anchorages in the Bahamas were marginal–either we couldn't get in at all or we had to anchor so far from shore we were exposed to the rolling effect of ocean swells. Just being a foot shallower meant that our friends were able to anchor a lot closer to shore.

January 15th came cloudless with a perfect breeze, and we had a truly exhilarating sail over to uninhabited Conception Island, where we found some of the best snorkeling of our entire trip. As we approached the anchorage, Steve, on the *Columbine*, climbed his mast with a camera to get this photo. Look at the shadow our boat makes on the bottom.

Conception Island, Jan. 15, Matt's Journal: "God, what a beautiful spot. There are five other boats in here moored inside of the reef and off the sandy beach. The entire place is a natural preserve, meaning I can't do any spear fishing.

The reef is absolutely amazing. The coral formations are huge and riddled with tunnels that you can duck through. It's exactly as Bruce Van Sant describes: 'With heads towering over 20 feet over white sand bottom, you'll feel like Superman flying between the towers of Metropolis. The bad guys on the streets below are 10-20 pound groupers, snapper and 5-10 pound lobsters.' It was amazing. We snorkeled, then broke out the windsurfers. Kevin had a fancy short board and really fast! So we rigged the sail on our board and everybody was flying around the harbor on it. Dad even got up. Everybody's coming over to our boat tonight for drinks and appetizers. It's also Kevin's birthday.

The party was great; everybody gets along so well. The Aussies and New Zealanders were making jokes about each other and Steve broke out his guitar and was playing all kinds of songs including 'The Wanderer.'"

Tilefish friends–just the smallest part of the richly varied sea life to be found on the reefs on the north side of Conception Island.

Kate paints a scene in the Bahamas. An avid snorkeler, she was always the one in the water first, and the one to search through the field guides to identify what she had seen. She also quickly discovered a disconcerting habit of barracudas–they like shade, and usually one is hanging out just under any anchored boat. So when you are ready to jump in to explore in the morning, there is this sinister looking 4-foot fish with a mouthful of ugly teeth, just waiting . . .

Kate's Letter To Friends: "Caribbean Cruise. That's what I call what we are doing. My week consists of days such as this: I wake up around 8:30 if it's a school day, have breakfast, do 2-3 hours of schoolwork, go swimming or snorkeling, read, play cards or Scrabble, check out the new town or country we have just arrived at, go for another swim or snorkel, shower, eat, read, and sleep. Usually there's a barracuda waiting just underneath the boat! Sometimes we go ashore and walk on really white sandy beaches.

That's mostly what my daily journal says. I might go more into details, but you get the point. If I were to say what I missed the most it, would be: hot showers (not freezing cold ones at a local marina or the sun shower), my bed (the hard pad that I sleep on doesn't cut it), my friends (Matt and the tropical fish don't cut it), and my bathroom or head, as they call it, stinks and is way too small for 2 people to have to share. That's about it. There are numerous more little things but they don't totally affect us much.

Oh I forgot one: the food! I miss Dove Bars, coffee ice cream, and Safeway Chinese food! In the Bahamas you always end up eating conch, which is an elasticky food that the Bahamians here eat with just about anything. To sum things up, I miss all the people that I'm sending this letter to. I feel real bad that you have to deal with rain, but I'll drink a strawberry daiquiri or piña colada for ya!

Luv, Katie"

RUM CAY, JAN. 16

Comes perfect and still–up with Mary Lou for beach walk, swept clean by the night's tide, ours the only tracks. Motored over to Rum Cay in very light airs. The landfall is a wrecked freighter, which, bound for Haiti with a load of Salvation Army clothes, ended up on the reef. Until the sea breached the hull, many a passing cruiser stopped here to freshen up their wardrobe.

Picked our way through the coral heads to anchor just ahead of Kevin. One guidebook put it this way: "As with the pudding in the school cafeteria, it's best to avoid the dark spots." Kate and I wasted no time getting into the water with our fins and masks, and almost immediately saw our first sea turtle, moving incredibly gracefully.

Life ashore, with a weekly mailboat and just a hundred or so residents, was on island time. The small marina/restaurant seemed deserted; when Matthew asked a groundskeeper where

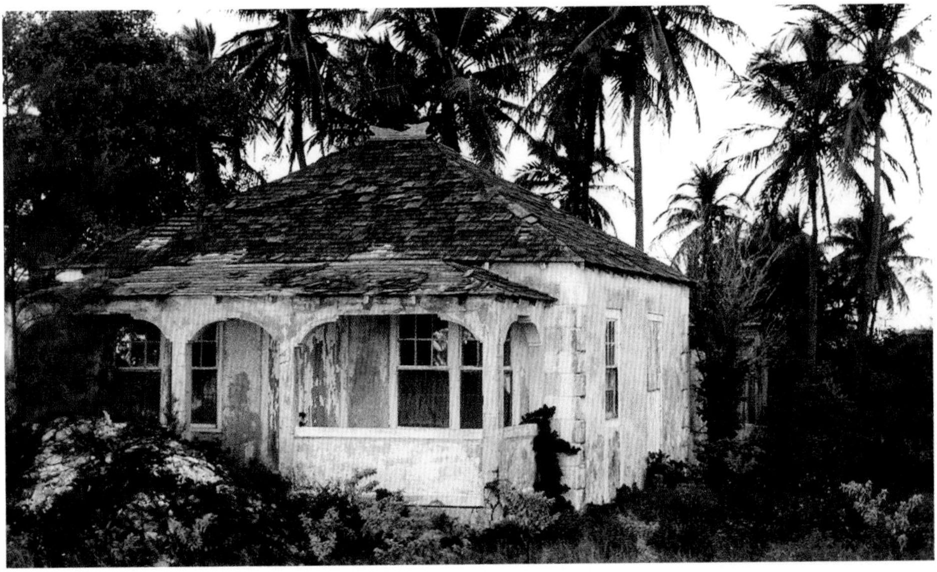

Abandoned home, Rum Cay. Broken houses and the skeletons of ruined resorts and developments are common features of the Bahamian landscape. Were it not for the unpredictable ravages of hurricanes, many of this region's islands would be more developed.

the staff were, he got this answer: "Oh, they be surfin', mon..."

Hurricanes, the bane of the Caribbean, had taken their obvious toll. The dive club, a very modest resort–whose operator knew where a friendly 500-pound jewfish would allow his photo to be taken with guests–was only ruins, as were some homes, overgrown, and empty. At Ted Bains' Oceanview Bar, Ted's wife took our orders, said it'd be an hour or so, and we wandered the beach to Kay's Bar, where sand had drifted in deep around the tables and chairs.

We savored our room temperature Kaliks, the local beer, and Steve told us of their two attempts to get over to the Bahamas from the US, crossing the Gulf Stream in poor conditions:

"Twice we got beat up in the 'Stream.' Twice we limped back into Charleston. We were going to go offshore–straight from the Bahamas to Tortola (in the British Virgin Islands), but after that we decided to take it a bit easier–take the intracoastal waterway to Lauderdale, cross from there, go down The Thorny Path."

When the dinner was over, we stepped out into the darkness. There were no house lights anywhere, only the wide sweep of the Milky Way arching above the palm trees over our heads. We found our beached dinghies by flashlight and motored out carefully into the still and black anchorage. There were no lights to be seen anywhere on shore; and only the motion of our masthead anchor lights, as our boats moved gently in the swell against the panoply of stars, showed us where they were.

Just that little thing–walking down to the silent and dark shore and setting out into the night with only the twinkle of anchor lights against the stars to guide us– filled me up. Do the kids feel this? Will they remember it?

A thrash to windward –*Columbine*, a 38 footer, on The Thorny Path near Rum Cay. There's a good breeze and Steve has rolled in a bit of jib to reduce sail area and have a better ride.

ON PASSAGE TO MAYAGUANA: OUR FIRST OVERNIGHT!
JAN. 17

Just at 2 p.m. after a morning of snorkeling and a few small boat jobs, we followed *Columbine* through a narrow crack in the reef, made the deep water, and hoisted full main and jib in SE 20.

This was our first real one to one sail against Steve and the gals, and didn't we pour it to 'em. With a deeper keel, taller rig, and slightly longer waterline, we quickly drove to windward past them with Matt doing a great job at the helm. Meanwhile Kevin was lagging behind badly, and we finally rolled in a bit of jib to slow down and stay with them.

As the forecast was for more wind after dark, we put a reef in the main, also called "shortening sail." To accomplish this requires the boat to be steered up slightly into the wind to reduce the pressure on the sail, while Matt and I lower the mainsail about four feet and tighten up on a winch that tensions the bottom of the sail. This reduced our sail area, slowing us down a bit, but giving us a better ride. In any case, I'd rather put in a reef in daylight than in the middle of the night.

We are "hard on the wind", sailing as close to the direction that the wind is coming from as we are able to. For most boats, that is about 45 degrees away from the wind direction, and means sailing with the boat well heeled over, making many

In Harm's Way – Sailing at Night

When a tanker sailed into San Francisco a few years ago, the pilot boat told the horrified skipper that there was the mast, sail, and rigging of a sailboat hanging from its huge anchor. The crew of the tanker had never seen the boat they'd hit. Was the sailboat showing proper lights, did it have a radar reflector, was the tanker's bridge crew standing a proper watch? These questions were never fully resolved.

The hard truth is that sailboats out on a big ocean are hard to see, even in daylight, if there is a sea of any size running. At night, it can be a bit easier, if the yacht's masthead light is working. (If a masthead light burns out at sea, it is probably impossible to replace it until the yacht is in a harbor again.)

Big ships frequently travel at 20 knots or more (a knot is 1.1 mph), which means that in just 20 minutes a ship can travel from over the horizon to a few hundred yards away or worse.

Fortunately we carried radar, which alerted us to the presence of ships. Whenever we encountered a "target", we would track it carefully, and if it appeared as if it would come within a mile of us, we would endeavor to contact it by radio.

onboard tasks like cooking, eating, or moving around, difficult. There is a well-known expression in the cruising community: "Gentlemen don't sail to windward."

The opposite to sailing to windward is running with the wind behind you. It is an immensely more comfortable way to sail–your boat travels upright, there is much less apparent wind and flying spray is reduced as well. On much of the open oceans of the world, the trade winds blow from east to west, so the preferred way to travel across oceans is from east to west.

Our route was called The Thorny Path for specifically that reason: we had to sail to windward. When the trade winds were blowing strongly, progress was almost impossible and you had to anchor up and wait for a weather window when the trades eased, or shifted to the north or west as they often did after a "norther" had passed.

Like most cruisers, we use an autopilot, which makes being "on watch" immeasurably easier. When the rest of the family went to bed, I made myself comfortable in the cockpit, and just stared up at a sky totally full of stars. Now and again a shooting star would streak silently overhead, and it was immensely peaceful.

MAYAGUANA ISLAND, MON, JAN. 18

At 3 a.m. spoke on the radio with tugboat skipper with heavy Alabama accent, who passing astern of our little group, wished us a safe passage. First light found us just north of the Plana Cays, with Mayaguana just on the horizon. After some 18 hours of port tack, we all had to tack again and again to clear the reefs, with the wind getting gustier and stronger as we approached Mayaguana.

Lowered sails and finally picked our way tediously between the coral reefs to anchor off the ruins of an old US Air Force fuel dump on a bleak looking bit of low shore. This island was once part of the Atlantic missile range.

Steve on *Columbine* was just swimming around the anchored fleet, checking to make sure our anchors were well dug in, when a very high tech US helicopter appeared out of nowhere, in a beeline for us, and hovered, probably for a minute, off each of our sterns. It was really strange and sort of Star Wars. The pilots didn't respond to our waves or radio calls and we supposed they were on routine drug patrol on this lonely highway. So ended our first overnight, with everyone really tired–the anchorage a bit choppy–but did we sleep–yes, deep and long–lights-out in the fleet by 8:00!

Our tax dollars at work –from a leased airport in the central Bahamas, US Drug Enforcement Agency helicopters track vessel traffic entering Bahamian waters.

Matt rinses off in a sudden downpour south of Mayaguana. Water is scarce all throughout the islands, so we soaped up on deck and rinsed off whenever a squall brought rain.

WEST CAICOS ISLAND, JAN. 19

"Yo, *Wanderer*, you see those waterspouts?" A waterspout is a tornado on the ocean) "There's one between you and us...!"

We'd been sailing along in a full sail breeze, out of sight of land, when *Columbine* disappeared into the rain haze, maybe a mile ahead. When he called about the waterspout, a squall had just hit us and I called down for Mary Lou to hand up the rain gear.

"You haven't got time for that...you've got to get those sails down if there's a waterspout out there..." She pushed Matthew, who was studying at the table, out the companionway. We both stripped to our underwear and dropped the main and rolled the jib in record time, all the time looking around to see if the waterspout was approaching. Mary Lou turned on the radar, and I attached the thick copper grounding cables to the heavy wire stays that supported the mast, and dropped the other ends into the water. The theory was that if lightning hit the mast, it would be able to find an easy path to water without damaging the boat. (See below.)

When the radar picture came on, it showed the rain squalls clearly, but something else as well–two very well defined small dark circles to the north of us. We swung south to avoid them.

"The waterspout we saw was nasty," Steve told us later. "Once the bottom lifted off the water, and swung back and forth slowly, and when it hit the water again, we could see the water flying, like an explosion, and we were almost two miles away."

As we approached the land, we wished very much that

Lightning at Sea

While the steel ketch *Windseeker* was anchored peacefully, a sudden thunderstorm approached and a lightning bolt hit her mast. The wooden mast exploded as the intense heat boiled the moisture in the wood, and her anchor chain disintegrated, but none of the electrical equipment was damaged. On another occasion, a different boat was tied to a dock and connected to a generator operating on shore when lightning apparently hit the generator. Though there was no obvious external damage to the boat, every single piece of electrical and electronic equipment aboard (and like most world cruisers, there was a lot) was destroyed.

On *Wanderer*, when a thunderstorm approached, we attached heavy copper cables to the stays that held up the mast, and draped the other ends of the cables into the water in the hope that if lightning hit the mast, it would travel safely down the stays, into the cables and into the sea.

we'd started just an hour earlier. The night, when it came, was very black and instead of the shallow anchorages we'd become used to, here the water was deep right up to the shore, with only a very narrow and steep shelf. On our first attempt to anchor, I dropped it in 40 feet of water, but "missed" the bottom–in the minute or so while I lowered the anchor, we had drifted off the edge, and anchor and chain were hanging straight down 150 feet. On the second try, the anchor got a good bite, but I slept uneasily, with the wash of the sea on the bold shore loud and close.

JANUARY 20 - PROVIDENCIALES ISLAND

"Anchoring, grounding or wrecking that causes damage to live coral within the National Park will usually result in a fine."

– Gascoine and Minty, *Turks and Caicos Islands, 1998*

The government of the Turks and Caicos Islands had realized that their greatest resource was the abundance of marine life that flourished on the hundreds of square miles of shallow and reef strewn waters that surrounded them. Setting aside large areas as marine sanctuaries, a modest local dive industry developed. Several large dive boats take passengers for a week at a time around the islands, stopping to dive several times a day.

Seeking fuel, we cautiously entered a shallow channel carved out of the limestone shore that led to a South Florida-like maze of canals and channels dug to create waterfront lots. The big cranes, dredges and excavators had done the hard work, but then the investors had bailed, or the money had run out, without a single structure built. A rundown boatyard offered modest services: a dock, fuel, cold showers and 20 cents a gallon water.

When customs showed up with a drug sniffing dog, I had a sudden sharp pang of fear. I'd hired a crew to take our boat from Fort Lauderdale to Nassau; what if they'd been pot users, left an old roach end on the boat? The uniformed dog handler pulled a plastic bag containing an obvious joint out of his pocket, and quickly put it up behind the bookcase on the port side.

"Hey, whadd'ya doing?" I asked, afraid of what was going to happen next.

The drug sniffing dog immediately went in to a point at the bookshelf, whining frantically.

The official triumphantly pulled the marijuana cigarette from behind the bookcase.

"Just testing," he said with a smile.

Our neighbors here were a Montana couple with a craft business, but they flew south each year to get away from winter and cruise the islands. The gentleman was also a chemistry Ph.D. and was able to help Matt with some homework! In the background cranes wait to restart on a resort project that ran out of money, not uncommon in such places.

In the glass clear waters of Caicos Sound, the water and the sky seemed to join, seamlessly, without a horizon.

Later we set out walking to a nearby beach. We came over a little rise and I stopped, confused, for ahead the land fell away to what appeared to be a vast expanse of sky, as if seen from a very high vantage point, though we were but a few feet above sea level. Then I understood–it was the water–the vast, shallow Caicos Bank–stretching away to the horizon, but the water was so totally still and clear that there was no horizon: the reflection perfect, water and sky joined.

In the evening we set out cheese, crackers and beer on an old table. The yard work at the boat shop was over and the workers came over.

"Oh, the drug business is serious, mon....you cannot be fooling with them fellows," said a big well-spoken black. And at the side of the shipyard was a sobering reminder of what a careless mistake on the banks could bring–a wrecked 40-foot sailboat, her bottom torn out by an encounter with a coral head.

The *Strider*, tied astern of us, had a different problem–they'd been planning on heading to the Virgin Islands. Two hours east of town their engine had thrown a connecting rod, destroying it.

"It'd cost nine grand to get a new one delivered here," her skipper said. "We're thinking of just slapping a used outboard on the stern and heading for Florida–we can get a used diesel there and put it in ourselves."

Steve had caught a big dorado on the way over from Mayaguana, and grilled it on the cruiser's standby: a stainless barbeque mounted on his stern railing.

The fresh-caught fish, the still evening with the sun dying in the west, the shipyard workers stopping by for a beer and a talk –it was a true treat and we all savored it.

Laundromat Tales

Only the largest and most well-equipped cruising sailboats have a washing machine, let alone a dryer, so at each stop the ritual is finding a laundromat. In George Town, there was a great facility–with its own dinghy dock even–but only about a third of the machines worked, and water pressure was just a trickle.

But the set-up at The Caicos Shipyard did them one better–no water! The two machines were located in a battered old shipping container facing the docks, but the tank that supplied them was empty and the water truck wouldn't arrive for a day or two. However, we discovered that the showers, around the corner (cold only and be careful what you step on) were fed from a different tank and they still worked. What to do? Wash out the trash can and bucket the water from the slow flowing shower nozzle to fill up the washing machine . . .

SAPODILLA BAY, TURKS & CAICOS ISLANDS, JAN. 20 - 24

Matt's Journal: Dad set up a cell phone account where the charges were only on outgoing calls. I called Anne and gave her the number. The phone was ringing until eleven o'clock at night! It was great; I talked to almost everybody I knew back in the rainy NW.

Naturally this was one of the most exciting moments of the whole trip for our kids: being able to talk to their friends! Here was the scene aboard *Wanderer:* black windy night and the cell phone rings (the first time since we'd left the States)!! Only weeks later did those parents get their phone bills, and wondered who'd called the Turks and Caicos for a $40 call . . .

This is when you miss the family car and the convenience of the local supermarket. Here, once we got the groceries to the beach, we had to lug them over the shallows to the skiff and then up to the boat, where they had to be lifted up to the deck. The canvas bags that Mary Lou and Matt are carrying are called "boat bags" for a reason!

Groceries: It's Not Like Running To The Store

Of course for yachtsmen, just transportation from remote anchorages to shops can be a challenge in itself. At Providenciales Island, in the Turks and Caicos Group, a Mr. Morris, the only taxi operator in town, posted a note on a tree at the beach where cruising sailors beached their dinghies that he could be contacted through VHF radio. So with lists in hand, we called on our radio and Morris picked us up in his van. By the time we finally completed our other errands and finished up at the grocery store, several hours had passed, and as we were at the checkout counter, I tried to call Morris with our small handheld radio, to come and pick us up.

After several unanswered calls, our groceries were piling up and there was no Morris, and no Plan B.

"You be looking for Morris de taxi driver now?" the gal who was bagging our groceries inquired.

We said we were.

"Well, he's fixing the bathtub in my house, mon..."

A quick phone call to her house and Morris was on his way.

Waiting for the Elusive "Weather Window"

"Leave Sapodilla Bay on a day when the wind is north of east or under 15 knots for certain. Go at daybreak. Don't delay departure. You don't want to be caught out on the banks. Go at daybreak.

...If you have to anchor on the banks, do so at the risk of bending your anchor shanks, as I have done, while getting them up in a stiff chop the next morning, or chopping your foot off with the chain wildly snatching at the bow."

– Bruce Van Sant, *The Gentleman's Guide to Passages South,* Cruising Guide Publications, Dunedin, FL., 1998

One of the best things about cruising, whether it be on the luxurious *Grand Princess* or the little *Wanderer*, was this: the true magic of entering a new harbor or port for the first time. Just standing up there and drinking it all in.

Back in the USA, no big cold fronts were slamming Florida and Georgia so here the trade winds were honking. Sometimes at night a particularly strong gust would hit us and the rigging would hum, resonating with the force of it. And I'd get up with the flashlight, go up on deck, make sure the anchor hadn't dragged and look at the wind speed indicator: 25, 30, then a gust to almost 40.

When an especially strong gust rushed across the bay, I could see flashlights on around the decks of other boats as other sleepless souls did their checks too.

One evening as we were all cozy in the cabin playing Scrabble after supper, there was a knock on our hull and we quickly clambered up on deck.

"So sorry to bother you," an Englishman was alongside in his inflatable, "but I just happened to notice your dinghy drifting by, and thought you might want it back..."

We thanked him profusely, and retied the dinghy's bowline to our stern.

"It was Katie who used it last," said Matt, quick to accuse.

"Dad, I tied it up with a bowline, I was positive."

I got out a short piece of line and we all practiced tying bowlines until we could do it with our eyes closed.

We'd dodged a real bullet–the next land behind the sharp-eyed Englishman was Florida. If he hadn't seen it, our inflatable, basically our family car, would have been lost along with its outboard motor.

Matt's Journal: Bummer! Finally finished my chemistry and math and packed them all up feeling way relieved. But at the post office, the guy said, "There be no stamps, mon."

"Whadd'ya mean? This is the main post office in the whole country, whadd'ya mean 'no stamps'?"

"They be comin' on the mail boat, mon . . . maybe tomorrow, maybe next week. . . "

So I had to call all the way back to Bainbridge High School and explain that there were no stamps in the whole country and I didn't know when I'd be sending the stuff in.

Kate's Journal: Yuk, Kevin threw his eye at me last night! I couldn't believe it. We were over in their boat visiting with them and the guys from *Columbine* and he was telling some story about how hard it was to make a good landing at a dock with just one eye, and then I asked him what it was like just having one eye, and he took out his glass eye and threw it and it landed on my shirt. It was soooo gross! I couldn't believe he did that!

In strong trade winds, a short steep chop develops on the shallow Caicos Bank which can be very challenging for small craft. Deeper draft vessels (like ours) would run the risk of hitting the sea floor at the bottom of the seas in such conditions. The experienced owners of another deep draft yacht in the anchorage, a Tartan 40, elected to make the long outside route to avoid the shallow banks and stay in the deeper water. Smart.

"Cruiser's Potluck on the beach tonight." A Frenchman stopped by the boat the next day with the invitation. And while our kids joined some others scooting back and forth across the anchorage in our windsurfer, the topic with the adults was the weather:

"Herb doesn't make it sound like we're going anywhere for four or five days," said another sailor. He and his wife on their big CT 49 ketch were bound "down island" like us. They decided to leave their careers, sell their home and sail

The "Herb Show"

Every afternoon at 4:30 hundreds of sailors all across the Atlantic and Caribbean get comfortable in front of their single sideband radios (a type of long range marine band radio) and listen for the reassuring voice of Herb Hilgenberg, a retired cruiser turned weather forecaster, broadcasting from his home in Toronto, Canada. In a unique call-in show, Herb fields calls from sailors, asking their local conditions and telling them what to expect. One hears from huge tugs far from land, singlehanded sailors in frail sloops and worried families cruising for the first time. When the weather is good, Herb might be on for just an hour. But when the weather's "making up"–when a big mean low is on the move–Herb might be on for two or even three hours.

"Well, should I go?" an anxious sailor might ask. "Oh," comes Herb's reassuring return, "I can't make that decision for you, but if that low tracks like it seems it wants to, you'd probably be happier anchored up until it goes by."

and travel while they still were able and healthy.

"If we waited until we retired," he had told us earlier, "we might have gotten sick, or wouldn't have the strength to travel like this."

"Five *days?*" Mary Lou looked at me. We'd made the novice cruiser's mistake–arranging to meet someone on a certain date–the Virgin Islands, in five weeks. As we'd planned our trip on the map, it looked like just a pleasant trip down through the islands to St. Thomas. Now, we realized we'd be lucky to make it on time. There were so many unknowns–if the weather cooperated, we could make it in three weeks. But we'd heard of cruisers who had been stuck in Sapodilla Bay for five weeks and never gotten "down island" at all.

"*Wanderer, Wanderer, Columbine*. Ya there?"

I rolled over and looked at my watch: 5:30 a.m. But already I knew what Steve would be calling about–the trade winds had eased in the night, the morning was still.

"Yeah, Joe, Steve here. We think it might be a chance, so we're getting ready to go. I already talked to Kevin, they're going. What are you guys going to do?"

I clambered up into the cockpit and had a quick look around. It was a perfect still morning, with a cloudless yellow pre-dawn sky and only the lightest breeze rippling the water; we'd gone to bed with the trade winds howling.

"Hey, looks good. But by the time I get the dinghy and wind surfer and other anchor aboard, I might as well wait for the 7 a.m. forecast from BASRA." (Bahamas Air Sea Rescue Association gave the only early morning forecast for these waters.)

"OK, we'll be in radio range all day. Good luck!"

"*Columbine*'s leaving? Boo Hoo."

Mary Lou was already up, putting the coffee water on and starting to get things squared away in the main cabin

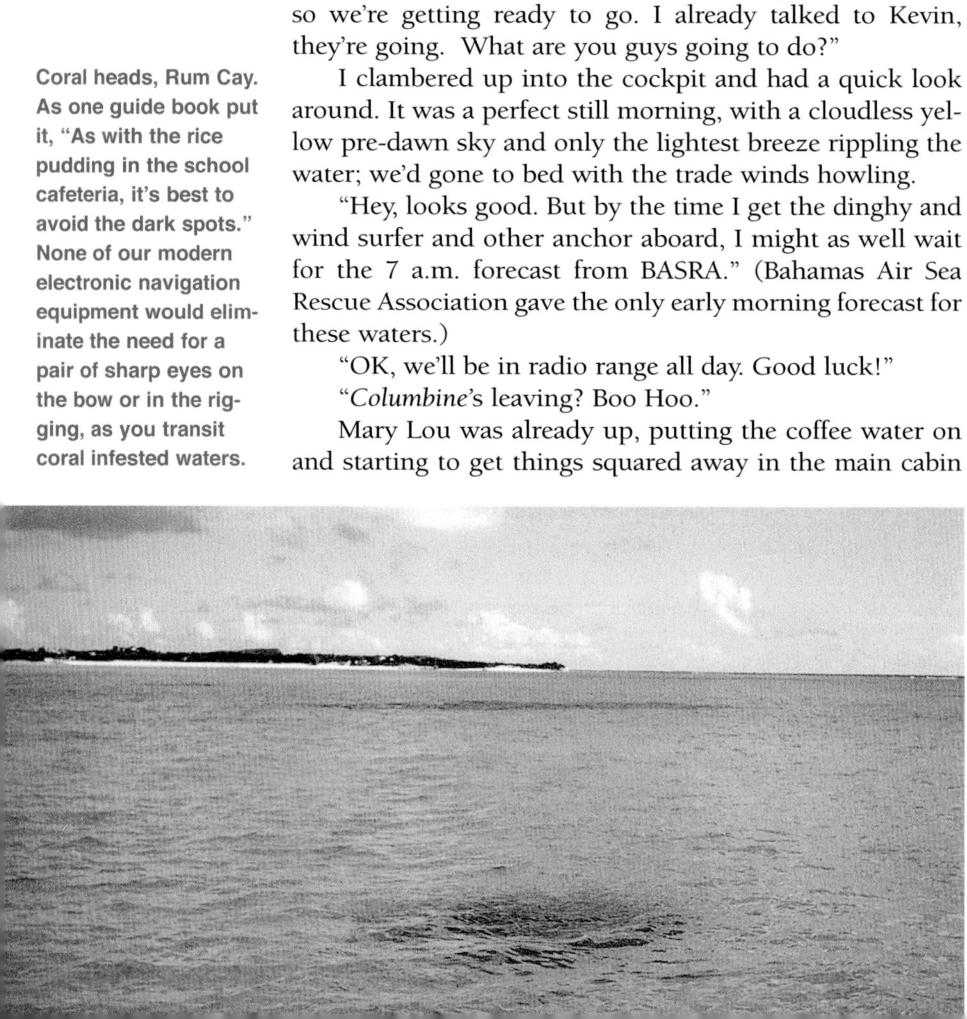

Coral heads, Rum Cay. As one guide book put it, "As with the rice pudding in the school cafeteria, it's best to avoid the dark spots." None of our modern electronic navigation equipment would eliminate the need for a pair of sharp eyes on the bow or in the rigging, as you transit coral infested waters.

to be ready for a sea passage. At six, I rolled a grumpy son out. We hoisted the outboard motor off the inflatable, took out the anchor, oars and gas tank, and then hoisted the inflatable itself and lowered it upside down over the forward part of the cabin, ahead of the mast. While Matt derigged the windsurfer, I took off and stowed the sail cover.

Just then *Columbine* swung by close aboard for a goodbye. They too had friends to meet in the Virgin Islands, but theirs were coming in just two weeks, so they were crossing the banks on a different course, and would head "offshore"– sailing day and night for 400 miles. They were experienced blue-water sailors; it was not a route we would feel comfortable tackling with our level of experience.

"Goodbye, goodbye, good luck!" They swung by once and were gone.

We'd miss them, had some truly wonderful times with them, and they had shared their extensive sailing knowledge with us, giving us a lot more confidence.

This was one of the hardest parts of cruising–meeting wonderful people and then separating, not knowing if our paths would cross again.

At 7:00 the radio reported no gales; it was a go. I immediately started up our diesel engine–time was of the essence if we were to get safely across Caicos Banks before dark.

On the way out I swung past another southbound yacht, the *Cherokee*. Nobody was up, but we passed close and I yelled over, "Hey guys, it's *Wanderer*. We're headed across to Ambergris Cay. It looks like a chance . . . "

The wind came up two hours after leaving Sapodilla

Heeled over, flying with a strong fair breeze–notice the reefed or 'shortened' sail–we raced across Caicos Bank with just inches beneath our keel. Avoiding the dark shapes that marked dangerous coral heads kept us on our toes all the way across. Did the rum bottle come out that night, once we were safely anchored? You bet.

So beautiful and so dangerous–the top of a coral head, extending from 15 feet of water to within 4 feet of the surface. Elkhorn coral consists of coral formations looking a bit like deer or elk antlers. But there is nothing delicate about its concrete hard consistency, which could easily rip the hull of a careless boat.

Bay, but it was a fair strong wind, and didn't we fly!

"Eight...eight...eight.....seven (in a louder voice) ...seven...eight." Mary Lou read the depth finder.

This was not comfortable–heeled over and flying along at 9 knots, there was less than two feet of water between us and the bottom.

"Coral ahead!" Kate called back from the bow.

I looked up–we were approaching two very dark patches, each perhaps 30 feet in diameter.

"I see 'em. Thanks!" I called back up to Kate and turned. As we passed, I could see a delicate-looking prong of elkhorn coral break the surface briefly between seas. Hard as cement, we would suffer the fate of the broken boat we'd seen in the shipyard should we hit one.

"Seven, seven, SIX!" Mary Lou's voice was anxious.

"SIX... SIX... seven... SIX... what are you going to do?"

Yaaaa! If I blew the sheets (released the sails), we'd slow down but heel less, and our keel would swing down, lower into the already too shallow water.

"Seven, seven, eight, nine, wow, ten... deep hole!"

We'd passed the hump.

Safe Cruising Tips

Never cruise these waters after dark unless off soundings. Never cruise the banks after 4 p.m., or with poor or dazzling light or murky water. Use caution when following the shallow water routes–post a bow or spreader lookout as there may be uncharted coral heads. Never attempt the north shore cuts when there is a large swell running.

– Gascoine and Minty, *Turks and Caicos Islands,* Wavy Line Publishing, Grand Turk, 1998

Beachcomber's delight–ghost crab and shells at Big Sand Cay. No evening was complete without us or the kids taking the inflatable ashore to explore and bring back treasures.

At 3:30, just as we finally got into the shelter of the land, the radio spoke; it was *Red Bear,* another cruiser who'd left Sapodilla Bay a little bit before we did.

"Hello, Kevin ... enough coral out there for you?"

"Oh well," came Kevin's distinctive New Zealand twang, "to tell you the truth, Dennis, I think this coral business is a bit over dramatized. On *Shannachie* we don't worry about it too much."

They were about a quarter mile away, near what looked like a dark patch of coral heads.

We came to where I wanted to anchor, and I did a slow circle. I wanted to make sure it was deep enough where we might swing to if the wind shifted in the night. Just then the radio spoke.

"Help. *Shannachie*'s aground!" Ann's voice was anxious.

I looked up quickly to see them jerking suddenly.

I called back, "Ann, I'm just anchoring; as soon as I can get the skiff in the water, I'll come over ..." There was only a low swell in the anchorage; whatever was happening over there wasn't life-threatening, and I didn't want to put my boat at risk by getting too close.

But by the time we'd dropped and set the anchor, I could see that they'd moved away from the coral and had anchored.

"Ahh, we're OK now, Joe," the radio spoke. "We had to back off. I just dove on it. There's just a little scrape in the gel coat. We're not leaking any ... no worries ..."

But there was worry in his voice; they'd dodged a huge bullet. If they'd punctured their hull, they could have easily sunk on

A lonely stop on The Thorny Path, Big Sand Cay offers cruising sailboats a place to anchor and wait for good traveling weather before crossing Turks Passage.

the reef where the swell and the sharp coral would have made short work of their boat.

This traveling in lonely, shallow, and coral infested waters was dicey stuff. Our whole family watched the drama unfold, realizing that the burden of the person up on the bow, looking for coral, was a heavy one.

After supper, I did one last patrol around deck in the rapidly falling dusk. Making sure the dinghy was securely lashed, the rigging all tight, the anchor snubber tied off properly; I checked the abandon-ship bag, made sure it had the flares, radio, food and water. Though we were sheltered from any rough seas, the cays were so low that they offered little protection from the wind, which seemed to be increasing, and the gusts would darken the water as they rushed across the anchorage.

The night was squally with some particularly strong gusts after midnight. Twice I got up to sit in the shelter of the dodger for a bit and look around. Clouds had covered the stars and all was black except for the anchor lights of our little band of travelers.

In the morning we picked our way tediously through a maze of coral heads in heavy rain squalls. More than once my heart was in my throat as visibility lowered to almost zero and seas broke on coral reefs close to port and starboard. The wind was directly against us and, having to continually zig and zag, we motored. If our little Perkins diesel had faltered even briefly, we would have been on the reefs before we could run out the jib and control her.

> Jan. 26, 1999, 10:45 a.m.: Deep water at last, steering 137 degrees for Big Sand Cay. Wind ENE 20-25 with 12 foot rollers. Pretty ugly at first, but sheeted main to leeward, and reduced jib, and boat making seven knots in heavy, wet going.
>
> – *Wanderer* log

On newer boats, the main halyard–the line that raises the mainsail–is controlled by a winch in the cockpit. The reason is safety. Unfortunately ours was located on our mast so Matt and I, in life jackets and with our safety tethers attached to the jack stay, waited for a chance between waves and went forward to raise and reef the big sail while Mary Lou steered.

Once it was up, we rolled out a bit of jib and what a ride we had! The coffee thermos broke free of its bungee cord lashings and flew to leeward in our first big roll, but we had a couple of spares so let 'er rip! The seas eased up a bit once we got a few miles out, and didn't *Wanderer* fly, putting her shoulder to the seas, and surging ahead like a racehorse leaving the gate!

But best was this–having the water turn from dark blue to emerald green as we came "on soundings" (in the deep ocean, most depth finders cannot "sound" or reach the bottom) in mid-afternoon and snuggling in as close to shore as we dared at Big Sand Cay.

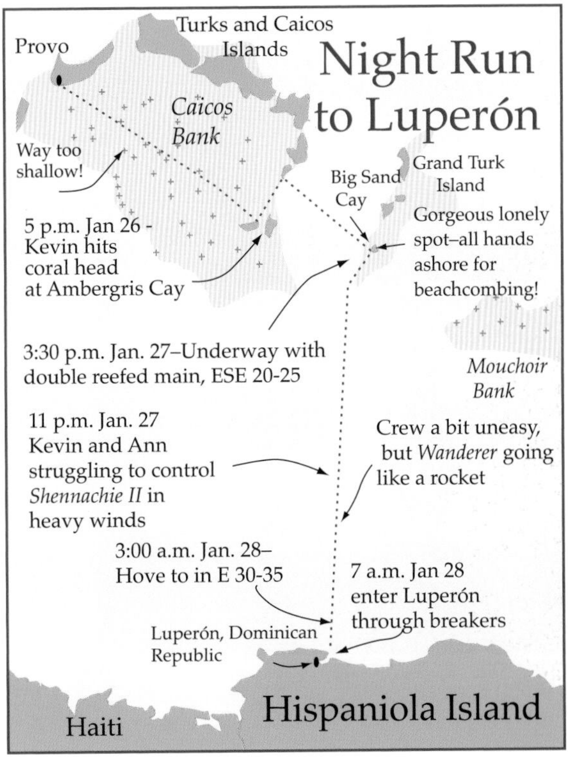
Night Run to Luperón
Turks and Caicos Islands
Provo
Caicos Bank
Way too shallow!
5 p.m. Jan 26 - Kevin hits coral head at Ambergris Cay
Big Sand Cay
Grand Turk Island
Gorgeous lonely spot–all hands ashore for beachcombing!
3:30 p.m. Jan. 27–Underway with double reefed main, ESE 20-25
Mouchoir Bank
11 p.m. Jan. 27 Kevin and Ann struggling to control *Shennachie II* in heavy winds
Crew a bit uneasy, but *Wanderer* going like a rocket
3:00 a.m. Jan. 28– Hove to in E 30-35
7 a.m. Jan 28 enter Luperón through breakers
Luperón, Dominican Republic
Haiti
Hispaniola Island

Matt's Journal: "Big Sand Cay is really a desolate spot in the middle of nowhere. All it really is is a big strip of sand on either side of an old rusted light tower on the hill.

The snorkeling isn't that much, but the beach facing the anchorage is very nice. It's great sand and the waves are breaking almost large enough to body surf on. The other side of the island facing the Atlantic Ocean is completely different. The entire beach is strewn with junk. There were bottles, light bulbs, plastic, the rear part of a car, and part of a refrigerator. I couldn't believe it; the place looked worse than a dump and there was stuff all over the place. Earlier visitors had made a shrine to the junk–piling hundred of bottles and light bulbs together and making murals out of them. It really wrecked my day, seeing it all.

Dad's been listening to the weather man and it looks like there's a massive cold front coming in which could leave us all trapped in Sand Cay for two weeks. That's not very appealing, so it looks like it's now or never for Luperón. Plus I have to get my school work in soon and those two weeks would mean I'd get incompletes in my classes."

There's a reason it's called The Thorny Path – yachts island hopping from the southern Bahamas to the Virgin Islands must face the shallow and coral reef studded Caicos Bank, followed by the notoriously windy Turks Passage.

"... and for those of you on The Thorny Path, in the area between Turks and Luperón, it looks like there might just be a very small window today and extending perhaps into tomorrow, until strong easterly winds return ..."

– heard on *The Herb Show*

"Depart only when favorable conditions prevail and shall be sustained for a day longer than you need to make safe harbor ...This will be when the winds back or veer to permit reaching or running, or if you must beat, when the easterly trades have moderated to less than 15 knots, with seas 3-5 feet."

– Bruce Van Sant, *The Gentleman's Guide to Passages South.*

Was it a window? That was the question on everyone's mind on the morning of the 27th. The wind was strong, but slightly north of east. If it held in that direction we could leave in mid-afternoon to arrive at Luperón at daylight. If it shifted to south of east, the normal direction of the trade winds, we would be forced to divert our course 40 miles further west to a port in Haiti, and add maybe as much as a week to our trip.

At first it was just the swells that were bad-we were traveling broadside to them and a couple rolled us over far enough that drawers flew out of their stops and across the cabin. Then after dark came the real wind....

I was the youngest and least experienced cruiser in our group. But I felt the pressure of getting my son's school work to a post office and off to the States. "How bad could it be?" thought I.

What did I know?

Wanderer, like many offshore cruising boats, was rigged with three sets of reefing points, to allow you to reduce sail area in stages, but the reefing lines are only rigged to the first two–the thought being that for 95 percent of situations, the third reef is not needed. If I had known what awaited us out there in the black, I would have taken the time to rig the third reefing line before leaving shelter.

The Abandon-Ship Bag

To prepare for our trip, I had read extensively of the experiences of other cruising families. I learned that the vast majority of yachts that travel the world's oceans do so without life-threatening events. However, if there was a single theme about emergencies at sea, it was that they can happen with little warning.

An on-board emergency is a highly stressful time–and not the right moment to be wondering where the flares or waterproof radio were.

So, like many offshore cruisers, we had a waterproof "abandon-ship" bag already packed. It contained flares, water, granola bars, fishing gear, flashlight, as well as a portable GPS or satellite navigation receiver. While traveling alongshore, within sight of land, the bag was often stowed away. But before any offshore passage such as this one, we brought it out, refilled the water jugs with fresh water, and put the bag in a place where it was readily accessible.

THE RUN TO LUPERÓN

The entrance to Luperón Harbor at 6 a.m. on Jan. 27, 1999. Would you want to enter here without a chart? As we approached it looked as if the breakers were sweeping all the way across the harbor entrance, but it was the only shelter for miles and the wind was coming on stronger.

At first, as if the weather gods were luring us out to where it would be too late to turn around, it was OK. NE 15 to 20 knots: rough but manageable.

It was the swells! Far out in the Atlantic a big gale had driven swells into Turks Passage–12 to 15 footers, on the beam, with the tops not really breaking. But every now and then one would give us a really good smack and we'd take an extreme roll to starboard, once enough to throw the drawers out of their stops and across the floor of our stateroom.

Then, after dark, the wind came on even harder, 25 knots steady, with gusts to over 30 knots, and I wished I'd put in the third reef.

At ten p.m. the VHF crackled with Kevin's twang,

"Say, Joe, we've a bit of a problem steering in these conditions and might have to heave-to."

Kevin's boat was really designed as a coastal cruiser, with lighter gear and rig than the stout *Wanderer*. Her rudder was too small for Kevin to easily control her in such conditions.

"Kevin, maybe you're carrying too much main," I suggested. "Let it out to the shrouds and roll out some more jib..." Such a move should make steering easier.

It worked, or enough anyway, and on we stormed through the night. I was immensely relieved. If they'd had to heave-to, a maneuver that allows a sailing vessel to jog slowly, into the seas, we'd have been faced with a difficult choice–leave our friends there at night, in deteriorating conditions, or put my family at risk by staying with them.

While we jogged off the breakers, debating a strategy, a good samaritan called on the radio and offered to guide us in. The transition from rough to calm, from the moan of the wind in the rigging and the slam of the seas to the twittering of songbirds and the stillness of a mangrove river, was one of the most moving experiences of our cruise. Our son is still wearing his harness, which tethers him to the boat in rough conditions.

If there is a single word to describe the Peterson 44, it is powerful. It was a mean night with a lot of wind and a big sea on. With double-reefed main and a handkerchief jib we were still a bit overcanvassed. But with vang, preventer, and running backstays all bar tight, the rig was strong and we were going like a freight train so it was hang on and let 'er run! We were dry and secure, life jackets and harnesses on behind our windshield-like hard dodger, but it was wild out there.

A big moon came up around 10. In its light the seas seemed truly huge, silvery, threatening us, lifting us, then dropping us once again as each one raced away into the darkness. Our first time sailing in such conditions, I had already worked out a long "what to do if" list, but hoped what other cruisers had said about sailing in bad weather was true: "Your boat can always take more than you can."

A couple of times when a sustained gust pushed the anemometer to almost 35, and a big swell lifted us just right, and gravity accelerated *Wanderer* briefly toward the trough, the knotmeter would push past 9, and edge up toward almost 10 knots–truly flying for a boat our size!

Once a big one swept us aft in a thunder of white water, and now and again we'd dip our bow, and solid water would run back and smack into the tempered glass of the hard dodger like a sea against a rock. My son, a great dinghy sailor, took it in stride, but Mary Lou and Kate were sick, finally huddling together in the leeward sea berth in the main cabin.

At 3 a.m., with the land looming high and dark ahead, we hove to. Luperón harbor was uncharted, and lacked navigational lights or buoys. Such a place can only be

attempted in daylight, in favorable weather.

Dawn came ugly with east winds at 35 knots and higher gusts. We approached the harbor but found only the smoking backs of big rollers.

Our only chart was a rough sketch, not enough to rely on. So we motored slowly, just off the line of breakers, talking on the radio with Kevin. The land was forested with high rolling hills that exuded a warm, moist, earthy smell totally different from the low dry islands of the Bahamas and Turks. So near, and yet so far.

Just then the VHF radio crackled with an unfamiliar voice. "Hello the boats off Luperón entrance. We're some American cruisers inside the harbor. Don't leave–we can come out in our inflatables and show you the way in! I'll be waving my life jacket. Head straight for that."

FIshermen, Luperón. For the first time in our trip we were anchored in a real active harbor, with fishermen leaving early each day to tend their fish traps set in the harbor mouth.

After a bit, we could just make out with our binoculars a person in a bobbing inflatable waving a red life jacket in a place where the waves seemed to be smaller, a path between the seas. As we approached, we could see that there were three inflatables waiting for us. As each yacht made it into the tricky entrance, an inflatable came alongside, hailed us with a "Welcome to Luperón" and led us up through the mangroves. The sudden transition from rough to calm, from danger to safety, the warm land smells, the birds singing, truly overwhelmed us, and when I looked around, there were tears in Mary Lou's eyes.

Matt's Journal: When we sighted the Dominican Republic I was overwhelmed by the huge mountains and cliffs that came right up to the water and were covered in trees and plants. It was a magnificent sight to see all of the greenery and mountains after such a grueling passage. What was most amazing to me was when we were still 3 miles out in the ocean, bucking the waves. You could smell the land which had sort of a cinnamon aroma to it and was amazing and unlike anything I've ever smelled before. I loved it.

High enough to catch rain clouds and thus able to grow crops, Hispaniola Island was a total contrast to the Bahamas and Turks and Caicos.

Luperón, Dominican Republic

Jan. 28 - Feb. 5

If the Bahamas and Turks were a verse in a Jimmy Buffet song, then Luperón was a chapter from a Joseph Conrad novel set in some Central American republic almost a century before.

Egrets by the hundreds sat in the trees that came to the water's edge. Sleepy guards watched over a concrete wharf. Fishermen rowed out to their nets at the harbor mouth. Boatworkers hammered away on a rusty fishing trawler nosed into the mangrove swamp.

And this was a place where you could set your clock by the trade winds. The evenings were still, and one could clearly hear the offshore report, the boom of the surf at the harbor mouth.

Then about 10:15 each morning, a few ripples would stir in the stillness, and within 15 minutes the strong and steady trades –15 to 20 knots–were creating white caps in the harbor.

We anchored close off the end of the dock, so that the kids, if ashore without us, could call out to the boat when they were at the dock and needed a ride

Perhaps two dozen other cruisers, mostly American, were laying in Luperón. About half were waiting for weather, headed "down island"–to the Virgin Islands and beyond. But for the others, Luperón was an end in itself, a low key respite, a very wel-

come change from the busy lives they'd left behind in the States.

For ourselves, we were hoping for five or six days before the next weather window. Time to get a few boat chores done, and to explore the town and surrounding country.

In the mornings Mary Lou and I would dinghy over to the shore for a long walk, along a path that led to a high point of land overlooking the entrance to the harbor, to get our weather report.

By then the trades would be booming and the surf rolling across the reefs; and the road east would be all feather white and we knew that it wasn't a "chance." So back we'd go, past sad, partially finished and then abandoned apartment buildings overlooking the ocean–financing seemed to be a constant problem in towns along our route.

The kids explored and once Mary Lou spent a day helping in the third-grade classroom of a young teacher she had met.

"There were no books," she told me that evening. Mary Lou taught second grade in our hometown. "The kids were all neat and very polite, but there were no books in the classroom, nothing to read, nothing to take home. The teacher would write the lesson on the blackboard, and the kids would copy the words down on their tablets. But no books. It was so sad. I just wanted to go out and buy some for them."

The trade winds would die in the late afternoon and the lightest zephyr of a land breeze filled in from the southwest, and our nights were truly delightful–not a swell to move the boat, almost without a ripple, and no wind to rattle halyards annoyingly against masts. It all made for wonderful sleeps and the moon was almost full. It was a treat to get up in the middle of the night and see the fleet laying so peacefully and the moon and the stars all around, plus the dimmest glow of town through the trees.

At the market, Luperón. There were no prepared foods here or freezer case. In a country where many had their own gardens, the food in the shops was incredibly fresh. "Chicken Day" was every Wednesday, when in addition to their other offerings, grocers would have live chickens and one would often see shoppers heading home with live chickens squawking noisily, strapped to the luggage racks of their bikes or motor scooters.

Luperón was a sleepy, family-oriented town, and we felt comfortable just letting Kate and Matt go ashore, wander around and practice their Spanish. Here two or three generations would often be living in one modest house, often just sitting out in the street in front of their houses on hot evenings.

Matt's Journal: My dad had been on my case lately about taking pictures with the digital camera because I wasn't really taking any. I imagined that the people wouldn't want their picture taken or it would make me seem like more of a gringo tourist. Like I wasn't one already walking around in board shorts and sandals.

I finally said the hell with it and went out into the poorer parts of town to take some pictures. I was away from the more touristy and yachtie areas and was probably the only white face within miles. My Spanish was a little rusty but I swallowed my pride and

doubts and proudly walked up to a bunch of kids and said, "Me pemieto sacar tu fóto."They surprised me with "si, si, si" and they posed in front of their house. I took the photo and showed it to them on the LCD screen. They screamed and I was mobbed with people all trying to get a glimpse. I was stalked by about ten kids all trying to get me to take their photo. The moms would drag me to their houses for a picture. It was really amazing.

Two worlds existed here side by side. The village of Luperón was a sleepy third world settlement. But just a mile away two fenced and guarded resort hotel complexes catered to tourists from Europe seeking cheap rum and sunny beaches.

Kate slides down one of the waterfalls near Luperón. After climbing each fall, we would swim through the clear water of a canyon little wider than our bodies.

Just a block from the head of the dock was a sort of general store fitted with six phone cubicles. Few of the villagers had telephones in their homes, so this facility was popular.

For Matt and Kate it was an opportunity to catch up with their friends via e-mail. The trick, as they quickly learned, was to write aboard the boat, put the laptop in the backpack, take the dinghy ashore, sign in at the desk, make the connection, quickly send their messages, save all the incoming messages, and then sign off. Unless there was a lot of incoming, they could usually get in and out for less than $1.50! Then came the fun part–gathering back around the laptop at the galley table to savor the news from home.

The Seven Waterfalls

An hour's drive and another hour's hike through sugar cane fields and up a narrowing creek bed with a local guide brought us to a deep pool at the base of a narrow waterfall. This was the beginning of the Seven Waterfalls, a popular local attraction. Our husky guide showed us the foot and handholds, or, in places, a rope that led up through the torrent. After climbing each fall, typically around 12 feet high, we'd swim a little ways up a canyon barely 6 feet wide whose walls disappeared into the forest above us. It was truly a magical place–in each fall, the stream had carved a corkscrewing path through the soft rock, each one a little different.

At the top came the really fun part–sliding down each waterfall in turn into the pool below. The best was the last, where the fall was the highest and a bump in the middle threw you out and into the deep pool where we had started.

The calm before the trade winds start, overlooking the entrance to Luperón. The boats are fishermen checking their fish pots. Here the trade winds started up around 10:00, just like clockwork, and made a passage to the east along this coast very challenging. The prudent sailor, we had learned the hard way, waited for a good "weather window."

"Sailing or motoring to windward on this coast during full trades is flat out suicidal."
– Bruce Van Sant, *A Gentleman's Guide to Passages South*

The boat jobs were accomplished in the first few days and we began to listen more carefully to the long weather discussions on the short wave radio and with other cruisers.

Ahead lay the most challenging part of The Thorny Path, along the exposed windward coast of the Dominican Republic and across the Mona Passage to Puerto Rico, some 230 miles.

The same trade winds that made motoring back to your boat from town a wet trip rushed around the great capes on the north coast of Hispaniola, creating rough and difficult conditions. Suicidal? Probably not, but uncomfortable and dangerous, yes.

Bruce Van Sant, the guru of these waters, whose book was our guide, also lived aboard his boat in Luperón, where his wife worked in a craft and jewelry shop. For 20 years he'd taken small and large craft on annual pilgrimages along this route.

"Well," he told us one evening at the little bar under the palm trees that called itself a yacht club, "everyone's boat is a bit bigger now, but when I started, what you'd see out here would be mom and pop from Ohio with this dream of getting to the Caribbean, but with just maybe a 34 footer and a 20 hp. engine. With boats like those you have to really have a different strategy for traveling against the trades."

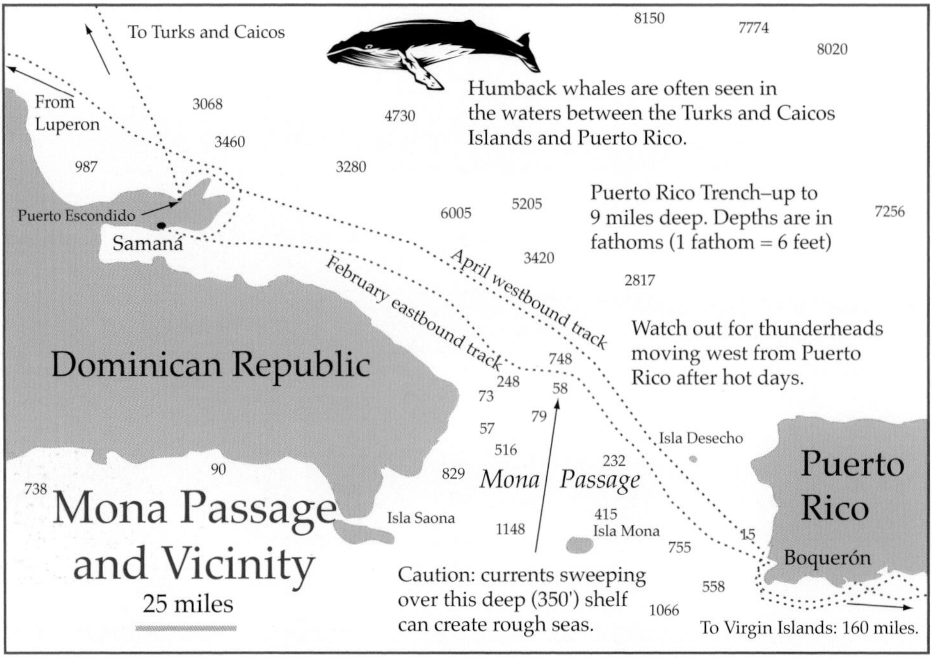

"Crossing the Mona with fingers crossed." Because of the danger from violent thunderstorms that often move westward from Puerto Rico in the late afternoon, this 150-mile passage must be planned carefully.

So Bruce had developed a carefully thought out guidebook on what he nicknamed "The Thornless Passage." The key to his strategy was to take advantage of the naturally occurring shifts in the trade winds and geographic features of each coast. It was also a book full of delightful anecdotes:

> "...It is smartest to sail into Samaná harbor shortly after daybreak in order to anchor unplagued by wind and before the dock has a pestilence of teeming idlers. Have an early G&T in the middle of the day and toast all the slicker clad yachties huffing and puffing into the anchorage from their offshore trials. Sit in Samaná Sams and listen to their tale of the ultimate wave."
>
> - Bruce Van Sant, *The Gentleman's Guide to Passages South*

El Despacho – "And for you folks on The Thorny Path between Luperón and Samaná, it looks like there might be a short window of very light trades starting on Friday." This short sentence on *The Herb Show*, on the afternoon of February 5th, was what we had been waiting for. Mary Lou and the kids immediately turned to getting the windsurfer aboard and otherwise squaring away the deck and cabin for an ocean passage. Meanwhile I motored to the town dock and walked across a rickety suspension footbridge to a low, dilapidated blue cement building–the local naval headquarters–to get our clearance papers or "despacho."

One of the most tedious parts of cruising in these waters is the need to obtain the necessary paperwork to

Third world contrasts. Local fishermen rowing a small seiner in front of a luxury hotel east of Samaná.

travel from port to port, even within the same country at times.

By then it was almost dark, and I had to knock several times on the door before a sleepy official came to the door. When I explained what I wanted, he said I would have to return in the morning. Only by pleading our case and finally making a contribution to cover the cost of such after hours work was the necessary document supplied.

Now I knew that some cruisers, a notoriously frugal group to start with, were adamant against paying the little bribes that sometimes were needed to ease over rough places with local officials. I felt it was just a way of tipping people who went out of their way to help us at a time when they really didn't have to.

By then it was dark, and as I walked carefully down the path, I could see the kerosene lamps in the houses on the outskirts of the village, and the lights on the mastheads and in the cabins of the anchored cruising fleet.

The next morning we got our weather report better than any fax–11:00 came and went without the regular trade winds sweeping through the anchorage. So it was away away!

But, oh, the tales we had heard of this coast! Creeping 20 or 30 miles each night, then laying over during the day when the trades blew–nasty seas, difficult anchorages and unfriendly natives.

So very wild and rugged, only here and there a town, and the rest only smoke in the hills to show that man existed. Then the dark came and it was really dramatic to see so much black and empty land, except for the little dots of light that were the cook fires back in the hills.

Unlike the sand bottoms of most Caribbean anchorages, Luperón's was soft, sticky, smelly mud. So getting the anchor and chain clean as it came aboard was critical–fortunately we had a saltwater washdown hose connection up on the bow.

Dangerous thunderheads over the Mona Passage. The challenge here is to pick a "weather window" ideally a dying cold front, which also reduces the chances of getting smacked by Puerto Rico's infamous thunderstorms.

But the weather gods smiled–the seas stayed small and at dark the wind came on a little stronger. After motor-sailing most of the afternoon, we stopped the engine, savoring the silence as we sailed along the dark and mysterious coast, a good safe three miles offshore.

"C'mon up, there's whales," I called down to Mary Lou; the pale light of dawn found us off Cabo Samaná–a particularly bold and unfriendly looking headland. But inshore were the unmistakable splashes and lifted tails of humpback whales.

For an hour we chased them. Then when I went below to check the chart, Mary Lou was rewarded by the best treat of all as a humpback breached less than 50 yards away, coming clear of the water, the rarest of sights for a whale watcher!

Just at 11 o'clock on February 6th we dropped anchor beneath the hills of Samaná to fuel up and plan our strategy for the last challenging leg of The Thorny Path: The Mona Passage.

Matt's Journal: Samaná is completely different than Luperón. When we got there a man had us pay him to act as a translator for the customs officials who he brought to our boat. Then when we went ashore to get gas a guy says "Here capitán, here capitán," so Dad and I drove the dinghy over there. He grabbed the gas tanks before we could say anything. My Dad says don't fill it up all the way 'cause we need to put in oil. He of course says "okay capitán no

Storm Cells on The Mona

During hot weather, thunder squalls develop from the heat rising off Puerto Rico. Sometimes these just dissipate in the late afternoon after dropping a bit of scattered rain here and there. But at least half of the time they develop into something larger and stronger–storm cells. With heads rising to 40 and 50 thousand feet, full of lightning, thunder, and hail, these can create surface winds, which though perhaps short lived, may reach hurricane strength. Planes with weather radar can often find alleys through these weather fronts, but slow traveling sailboats must plan their route to stay north of the storm track until late at night, when the storms have often moved far enough west to not be a hazard.

When the trade winds are blowing, the prudent yachtsman waits in Samaná for a forecast of light winds. The ideal situation is when a dying cold front creates favorable winds, and by lowering the temperature in Puerto Rico, reduces the chances of dangerous storm cells tracking across The Mona.

full, no full." Then the guy who helped us with the customs starts yelling at him to stop because we're *his* customers. The other guy with our gas tanks jumps on a moped and cruises off. That was pretty crazy but at least we got our gas tanks back overflowing with gas to the point where we had to pour some out just to put in the oil.

When we tied up our dinghy and locked it at the dock we were overrun with little kids fighting over who could "watch" our already tied up and locked dinghy. They would say "don't let the little kids watch the boat . . . I'm the biggest here . . . I'll take good care of her," yadda, yaddaa. When we got back and Dad handed pesos to the kids, they mobbed him and kept on reaching for his money. Yikes! I'll be glad when we're gone from here.

Dolphins meet us off the coast of Puerto Rico. Sometimes they would roll as they swam and look directly up at us.

Right now we're traveling with the *Mary Lou*. The capitán on it, Jay, is really cool. He says "gotcha" whenever you're trying to talk to him on the radio. We're going to do the Mona Passage which has the potential to be a hard crossing but Dad and Jay have been listening to the weather and think we have a dying cold front to cross the Mona. Mom's cooking up some Hungarian goulash so at least the grub will be plentiful and decent.

Good conditions for a crossing and the goulash sure warms you up. Katie and I have first watch which has gone well except for one freighter that was invisible on the horizon but a target on the radar. All of a sudden a voice out of the darkness says, "I'm on a collision course with the three sailboats on the Mona Passage!" Yikes! I got him on the radar and plotted his course and location and altered our course so we wouldn't get in an accident. This sure is more interesting than sitting in English class counting flies on the wall and watching the second hand slowly move: tick, tick, tick.

After we crossed the Mona Passage from the Dominican Republic to Puerto Rico and were entering the harbor of Boquerón we met up with three dolphins. I was up on the bowsprit looking for sand bars when all of a sudden three dark spots materialized out of nowhere. The dolphins rode our bow wave and were so close to the boat that they would bump up against it every few minutes or so. I was so excited that I was laughing and screaming at the same time! I could almost touch them with my feet. They were making that clicking noise which I guess is how they communicate. Every once in a while they would switch places and one would jump out of the water. It was great!"

Dinghy dock, and cruisers' anchorage at Boquerón, with locals passing the time of day. With good stores close at hand and easy living, Boquerón was the center for a small community of cruisers.

BOQUERÓN, PUERTO RICO, FEB. 9

Real milk, cash machines, a laundromat, ice cream, $2 piña coladas at the little beach bar–welcome to Puerto Rico –and didn't we savor it! Boquerón, at the very southwest corner of Puerto Rico, was a sleepy little beach town, "a Latin version of Myrtle Beach", as our cruising guide had it. With hundreds of tiny rental bungalows along the beach and every other storefront a bar, it seemed to be waiting for the weekend and the revelers.

With a good harbor and a bilingual population, it was also a haven for a small group of American expatriates, living aboard their boats, working a bit here and there, and finding life a lot slower than where they had come from.

We also breathed a huge sigh of relief–we had made it

Kate's Journal: This page is the start of my picture journal, which I will try to write in almost every day. This beach was about 6 miles from Boquerón, and it was a great beach full of these little horn-like shells called augers that I love and hope to make into a frame, if we ever get to a big enough city to go to a craft store. Here the water is about 75 degrees, but I liked this area because they had a buoyed-in swimming area! We swam in it like little fishes in the great turquoise sea of the Atlantic Ocean.

across The Mona in perfect conditions and the worst of The Thorny Path was behind us. But, even as we entered the shelter of the land at Boquerón, the window that had allowed us to cross slammed quickly shut. The cold front died, the strong trade winds kicked in, large swells arrived from a storm far out in the Atlantic, and it would be almost a week before yachts could cross again.

Matt's Journal: Boquerón was awesome.They had a nice little grocery store–probably the best we've been to since Turks and Caicos. They had everything including Ben and Jerry's ice cream bars. I had Phish Stick. It was heaven on earth. Chocolate covered chocolate ice cream with gooey bits of chocolate covered caramel. YYEESS–all from Vermont!

PUNTA AGUILA, PUERTO RICO, FEB. 10

A true cruiser, with no schedules to meet, would stay at least a week or more at Boquerón. But we still had a rendezvous looming soon in the Virgin Islands–just two weeks away. So after just a day and a half, we rolled out just part of the jib for a truly boisterous sail in strong easterly trades, to anchor off a delightfully lonely beach just a mile north of the great lighthouse at Cabo Rojo. All hands went ashore to beachcomb the fine white sand, swim in tepid waters,

A Cruiser's Tale

"No one thought Hurricane Mitch would hit here; then all of a sudden, here she came. We holed up in the mangrove swamp north of town with lines strung out to trees in five different directions. Ohhh-weee, didn't that wind howl. Over a hundred. Everything was flying. Then it all stopped, and you could look up and see this great circle of blue sky over us with just a wall of swirling angry clouds on all sides–the eye actually passed right over us. It gave us a chance to tighten up the lines, but most of all, run chain out to the trees in the direction the new wind would come from. You see, nylon stretches too much in tight quarters like the mangrove swamps so we used the chain and the wind ripped again and we never moved.

But oh, town was a mess and it was months before there was fresh water again."

and explore the palm lined beach.

"Pinch me," Mary Lou said, lying beside me on the warm sand. "I can't believe we've actually made it. I was so worried about being late to meet my dad. I feel like I can finally relax."

Kate wandered nearby looking for shells, and Matt walked north along the shore until he found a pick-up baseball game to join.

Mary Lou and I just lay on the sand, listening to the wash of the seas and the rush of the trade winds through the trees. Both of us thinking, "YES! We made it!"

Though we were still 150 miles from St. Thomas, the road ahead was all short passages along friendly shores. The islands ahead were for the most part well-populated. If we broke down, or someone got really sick, there would be a possibility of getting help or spare parts. It's a worry being so far out on the edge, among uninhabited or so thinly inhabited shores.

Where the path is not so thorny: Mary Lou at the beach at Punta Aguila. These were the warm waters of the true Caribbean Sea. For the first time we could truly relax, knowing that the hardest part of the journey was behind us.

This corner of Puerto Rico was also the destination of many Haitians and Dominicans hoping to sneak across the Mona Passage to start a new life in the United States. Local scuttlebutt in Samaná had it that some folks were willing to pay $5,000 or more to be smuggled successfully to some secluded part of the Puerto Rican coast.

Even as we lay on that lonely beach, it was obvious that such people were not welcome. Moving slowly just off the beach, a powerful Border Patrol boat passed us to tie to an old dock, to wait with radar on and guns ready for whatever the night would bring. A half-mile inland and 500 feet up, a large tethered blimp scanned the waters with powerful infrared cameras.

Puerto Rico and the "Caribbean Two Step"

The trade winds blow strongly along the south coast, but here, at night and until late morning, a lee, or area of little wind, is created before the day's heat draws the trades in close to the land. By about noon or so, the strong trades create a steep choppy sea, known to frequent travelers as the "Caribbean Two Step."

So the prudent traveler along the south coast gets up early to motor sail in light airs, and finds his next harbor before the trade winds get their strength up.

GILLIGAN'S ISLAND, PUERTO RICO, FEB. 11

Woke last night to sound of motors and voices close by. Looked out to black, black night–moon not yet up and a haze over the stars. No lights visible anywhere–was it illegal immigrants in small boats?

In the pale predawn light, I made the coffee quietly, raised the anchor and motored, turning east at Cabo Rojo to parallel the south shore of Puerto Rico, a couple of miles offshore.

The coast of the Dominican Republic had been dark green, primeval, jungle hillsides rising into cloud shrouded tops. But Puerto Rico was a dry, busy land, with brown hills, and here and there the stacks and squat buildings of an industrial complex.

Just at 10 o'clock, the trade winds began kicking up the seas and we passed the old sugar mill town of Enseñada to anchor off Gilligan's Island, a territorial park, with Mary Lou cheerily singing the theme song for an hour before arriving.

Out came the schoolbooks for a few hours while the adults savored coffee in the stillness of a peaceful anchorage broken only by bird calls and the low beat of the sea on the reefs.

Ashore we found a sandy path through the mangroves to a fine snorkeling spot off the south end of the island–a shallow coral reef inhabited by dozens of species of multicolored fish. My favorite was one that was basically camouflaging itself as sand, and which only scooted away when I noticed its eyes looking up at me. The true delight of floating effortlessly over an incredible and ever-changing world can barely be described with words.

Our son, the hunter. "But dad, it *really* looked big underwater." After a few disappointments, he discovered that there is a certain magnifying effect on critters viewed under water. Besides the incredibly colorful variety of reef fishes, here and there lurked big, big fish — groupers and jewfish, up to 400 pounds. Years earlier perhaps, a snorkeler might have easily been able to snag a dinner of spiny lobster. But after years of predation by locals and traveling yachtsmen alike, the spiny lobsters of most of the populated areas of the Caribbean are very wary of divers.

Rewarmed by the hot sun, we explored the maze of channels that penetrated the mangroves. White sand bottoms, turquoise water three and four feet deep, we let the current carry us silently around the bends, startling schools of fish.

Back aboard, Matt got out the fish books to identify what we had seen, while Kate heated up some left-over pasta. Mary Lou and I left them chattering as we dinghied away to explore, and found a sleepy settlement and a tiny restaurant with garlic shrimp and beer overlooking the harbor and our boat.

On the beach, Isla Caja de Muertos, Puerto Rico.

Finally back to *Wanderer* to find the kids noisily playing Hearts below and the very last color fading in the sky around us.

Just this–this peaceful coming and going, this family time together with nothing on the agenda but exploring, with no phones, TV, or interruptions–was what we had come so far to find. And tonight, as I took a last turn around the deck, I found the sky filled with stars above the open forward hatch that revealed each child with a book, reading in the coziness of their bunks, and our lives seemed particularly full.

ISLA CAJA DE MUERTOS, PUERTO RICO, FEB. 12

But where were the other cruisers? Our route was beginning to seem more like the lonely path. Another morning of motoring without a boat in sight put us into Isla Caja de Muertos (literally "Box of the Dead", meaning coffin) where we hiked to the lighthouse and had a quick dip as a violent wall of thunderheads swept down on us from the heights of Puerto Rico just six miles north. The wind pricking on very strong and we just made it back aboard as the first gusts of 30 knots swept the anchorage with furious driving rain. But by dusk the wind had moderated to light.

QUEEN ANGELFISH–a large–to 12 inches–and brilliantly marked coral reef fish. Look for black spot on forehead surrounded by dark blue.

FEB. 13, SALINAS, PUERTO RICO

"Yo, Matt and Kate, check this out…!" It was around ten in the morning and a forest of masts had just appeared above the low tops of the mangrove forest as we approached Salinas.

"Wow, Dad, this is like George Town," Kate said excitedly. "I bet there's kids."

But there was something odd about this fleet–no bathing suits or towels fluttered from the life–lines and their rigging was disheveled, broken, and loose.

Then I could see that the marina's docks and finger piers we had counted on for fuel and water were broken and askew, more casualties of Hurricane Mitch. The fleet we had mistaken for cruisers must have been moved from the docks after the hurricane.

We anchored off what was left of the marina, and rowed ashore past shattered docks and wrecked boats. But found a real laundromat and gave our kids lunch money and told them to shuttle water out to the boat with the water jugs while Mary Lou and I hiked off in search of the elusive grocery store.

Upon our return two weary kids awaited us back at the marina: "Dad, we'll never let the water run when we brush our teeth again . . . never!" Shuttling the heavy water jugs from the shore to the dinghy, and up over *Wanderer's* rail–12 trips, two jugs a trip–had been a wake-up call to the preciousness of water among these islands.

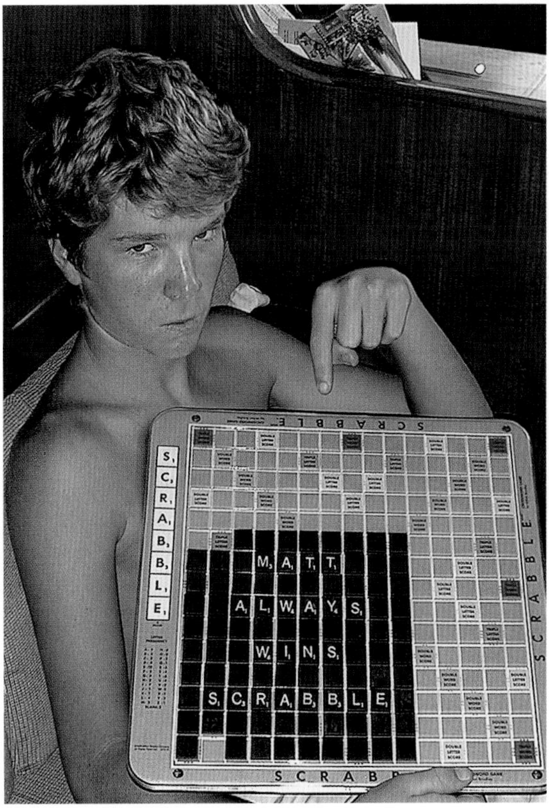

With no TV or VCR and box of movies, we spent a lot of evenings playing board games, reading or writing in our journals.

Matt's Journal: Salinas is an awesome town nestled up a mangrove creek. Many boats in the harbor are damaged from the hurricane that passed this spring, destroying the marina's docks.

The first night we went out to an awesome little Argentinian restaurant that's located at the corner of a little intersection. The tables are outside so you can watch all the cars and people go by. The food was delicious and our waiter was hilarious. He was an old painter that lived up in the hills but was filling in as waiter for his friend, the owner's wife. He joked that people liked him except that "They say I'm so ugly compared to the other waitress." The price was right too; we all ate for probably under twenty bucks.

The next day, while walking to get groceries in town, my parents were offered a ride by a doctor. He was soooo nice to them and even insisted on picking them up after they bought groceries because there was "no publico" back to the harbor. (That's a bus.) On the way back he found out that it was our first time in Puerto Rico, then said "Oh you must come to my party that is tomorrow." My parents didn't want to be a burden but he insisted and said he'd be offended if we weren't there. So the next day we all went. It was great–his entire family was there, his sons, grandchildren, and so on. Everyone was so nice and talked to us like we were long lost cousins. Their kindness and hospitality was really amazing. It's experiences like that that really make the trip memorable.

Glitzy, glitzy, on the canals at Palmas del Mar. Except for teams of carpenters repairing hurricane damage, the resort was quiet, with few of the fancy condos and houses occupied.

PALMAS DEL MAR, PUERTO RICO, FEB. 15 - 16

From four miles south we could see large pastel apartment buildings on the hillside. We slid into the very narrow entrance, then into a small basin almost totally surrounded by pastel condos and apartments. After so many miles with little recreational development, it was a big surprise.

We had hoped to tie right up at the fuel dock at the marina for fuel and water–silly us–Hurricane Mitch, as in Salinas, had also basically smooshed the marina. Front & center was a sad looking Peterson 44 with holes patched and rigging hanging loose. We had a great stroll around, exploring the huge compound, and followed music to a poolside open house for prospective buyers and found the free rum punches.

"I could do this," said Mary Lou. And we did.

Appearing as we approached like a medieval walled city, the opulence of the resort was stunning after our travels along the much more modest settlements along Puerto Rico's south coast.

CULEBRA, PUERTO RICO , FEB. 18 - 21

Bagels, in a laundromat? This ain't the third world any longer. Dakity, on the island of Culebra in the so–called, 'Spanish Virgin Islands,' was a regular stop for cruisers on The Thorny Path.

"KIDS!" exclaimed Matt, using the binoculars to study the other boats as we approached the anchorage. I told Matt and Kate they had to finish their schoolwork before they could have visitors and then Mary Lou and I headed for town in the dinghy.

When we returned, someone's dinghy was tied to our stern, and as we climbed aboard, we could hear excited voices down below, chatting loudly. The kids had a new friend, Lindsey, their first since George Town, *five weeks ago!*

So began four great days at Culebra, with wonderful snorkeling and another cruising family to visit with.

Once when I came back from a town errand, Mary Lou was waiting for me. "Wait until you hear this." But before I could even get aboard a dolphin surfaced very close and when Matt saw it, he instantly dove overboard with the cry, "Swimming with dolphins!" Of course the dolphin split. Then the news: while I was in town, Matt had called the high school on the cell phone and gotten his grades–all As and Bs, including a B in math and an A- in Spanish, both of which he had been having a hard time with early in the semester. He was very excited– Mary Lou said that he had barely been able to contain himself!

Motored carefully on the 21st through a pass in the reefs into the little harbor on Culebrita. All hands ashore for tricky hike over big boulders to "The Jacuzzis"–a big tidepool with a cliff on one side, and several narrow entrances to the sea through which rushed white water as the rollers pounded on the outside. I hung out on the top of the cliff for a while–getting totally great pictures

Kate: Today I met Lindsey who is in the picture to the right. She is 12 years-old and we have a lot in common! I am so excited to have a girl around! We are going to go snorkeling and maybe go into town together. Their boat has a TV/VCR and she wants me to spend tomorrow night and we would watch *Scream 2*. I am so excited–I haven't had a night away from my parents in so long! Way too long! I want to have Dad take an underwater picture of the two of us underwater! Got to go, I want to get ready to do something!

The "Jacuzzi"–a tide pool on the north side of Culebrita Island, about 20 miles west of St Thomas. As the surf beat on the outside, the water surged in and out of the big pool, making for exciting swimming.
***Below**: Wanderer* **at Ensenada Darby, sheltered by coral reefs. A perfect anchorage... except for the "whump" of bombs hitting the naval practice area at nearby Vieques Island. Note propane grill mounted on the stern rail–an essential piece of the Caribbean cruiser's equipment.**

and watching the whole scene. Then Kate and Lindsey swam through a narrow entrance to another smaller pool, and shortly after they were there, a sea very much larger than the ones before hit the outside, throwing spray thirty feet in the air and creating a true maelstrom in the pool where they were. They all had to cling to one another to avoid getting sucked into it. Joined them for some terrific swimming and just watching–the little crabs, for instance, were just watching the surf, almost getting swept away–what were they trying to get?

A little more snorkeling on the way back, the hunter gatherer gets his first fish (it looked really big underwater . . .) then back aboard for a hot sun shower, a little shark jigging, and then over to Lindsey's parents' boat for a really fun evening of visiting and a game of "Gestures". Back aboard with the stars bright above, just the two of us in the anchorage–how can it get any better?

The big and the small. *Grand Princess* and *Wanderer* at Charlotte Amalie, the capital of the US Virgin Islands.

SAINT THOMAS, US VIRGIN ISLANDS, FEB. 23

Wow! Hundreds of yachts, half a dozen huge cruise ships, such an incredible change from Culebra, just 20 miles away. Caught up with *Columbine* friends and heard about their offshore trip–gales, ripped sails; think we did the right thing by staying on The Thorny Path.

It's all a little much; when we pick up my father-in-law and his new wife we will be sliding away to somewhere quieter . . .

CHRISTMAS COVE, US VIRGIN ISLANDS, FEB. 24

Kate's Journal: Beautiful little island. Things are going smoothly with Grandpa and Brenda. The snorkeling wasn't that great along the anchorage and I got really freaked out because first, out of the corner of my eyes, I see a huge ray all of a sudden dig into the bottom. It's a really cool process actually: they dig in and then flap their wings in order to settle the sand around them. They look really sinister just laying there on the bottom looking up at you. I was really freaked out by that; then, lo and behold there were two sharks about five-feet long swimming underneath the boat. I egg-beatered up, grabbed the rail and pulled myself out of the water so quickly I bruised my stomach on the side of the boat. Sharks aren't anything to fool around with.

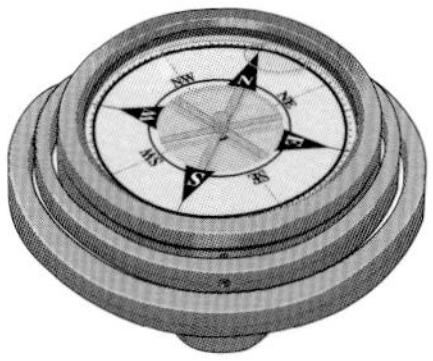

After so long among the undeveloped islands, we had a big list when we finally got to St. Thomas and its well stocked marine hardware stores.

This is why the Virgin Islands are so popular with sailors–good strong trade winds, generally deep waters and many islands, close together. The big sailboat is laying off Jost Van Dyke, in the British Virgin Islands, with the north side of St. Thomas behind it.

JOST VAN DYKE, BRITISH VIRGIN ISLANDS, FEB. 25

This small and very laid back island is one of the most popular stops for the many charter boats that operate both in the American and British Virgin Islands. We arrived in the late afternoon, and had trouble finding a place to anchor as there were many other boats there already. Finally anchored on the outer edge of the fleet, but when we dinghied ashore to go through customs, there was no one in the office. We found the customs guy playing dominoes in the shade with his buddies, who told me he'd be open in the morning at 8:30. When I asked if we could come ashore that night even if we hadn't cleared customs he replied, "Sure mon, have a good time, but stay out of trouble!!"

With a small church, and a couple of dozen modest homes set along the beach, Jost Van Dyke was life on Island Time. However on the east end of the beach was Foxy's, a beach bar and restaurant that was well known all over the Caribbean for its excellent music and big crowds. As evening fell, dozens of small dinghies made their way from the anchored fleet to Foxy's dock and Raggae music wafted out from the palm trees.

With so many boats in the Virgin Islands, the trick is to get to your evening anchorage in mid-afternoon, so as to get a spot without having to anchor in very deep water.

Kate's Journal: Matt caught a blowfish the other day and since we couldn't use it, we put it back in the water. Since it was all blown up it wouldn't go down. We also almost caught a sand shark! But after I found out what was in that water there was no way that I was going to get in that water. I'm here on the boat listening to Twist and Shout! Since the rough sailing is all behind us, I'm having a blast!

The dock at Cooper Island in the BVI. On the horizon is St. John, in the US Virgin Islands. For someone visiting and chartering one of the many available sailboats, the geography is perfect: all of the many anchorages are all within a few miles of each other. You can get up, have a relaxed breakfast and a swim, sail for a couple of hours, have another swim or beachcomb, then sail another hour or so to your anchorage for the night. Plus there are a number of restaurants in the various islands.

If there is a downside to the Virgin Islands, it's the crowds. Numerous fleets of charter sailboats and big marketing budgets ensure that the passages and anchorages are full. Since most of the anchorages are shelves of shallow water that slope off into the deeps, the smart sailor gets to his evening anchorage early if he wants to get a good spot.

We observed that some of the sailors on the chartered sailboats weren't fully aware of the need to set their anchor after they had dropped it. This was the process of putting your boat in reverse after dropping your anchor to make sure it got a good "bite" on the bottom. We had found out the hard way early in our sailing careers that it was far better to set your anchor right the first time than be surprised in the middle of the night by bumping into somone else's boat or worse, bumping on the bottom as you drifted into shallower water.

For our family, who had learned our cruising skills in the cold and darker waters of Washington State and British Columbia, perhaps the most remarkable thing was to be able to look down from the bow of our boat and see our anchor, sometimes even as deep as 50 feet down. When the water was shallow, say less than 25 feet, we got into the habit of diving down to do a close visual check to make sure the anchor was well dug in and secure for the night.

Most of the bottoms of the harbors in the Caribbean are sand, with an occasional coral outcropping. While offering good enough anchoring in most conditions, hurricane winds would often cause anchors set in sand to drag or break free.

To make their harbors secure in hurricanes back in colonial

When we jumped into the water near the Treasure Caves on Norman's Island, we found ourselves totally surrounded by these exquisite sergeant major fish. Then we saw why–another snorkeler was in the water feeding the fish with frozen peas out of a plastic bag. These striped fish are common throughout the Caribbean.

days, a number of harbors had so called "Hurricane Chains" stretched across the harbor from strong points on shore. Anchors that broke free or dragged, would fetch up on these chains and keep those boats from being swept ashore by the violent wind.

NORMAN ISLAND, BRITISH VIRGIN ISLANDS, FEB. 27

What would Robert Louis Stevenson have thought? This is the spot where he was supposed to have camped on the beach while he was writing part of *Treasure Island.* This cove and the caves around the point were the setting for part of his novel. Now it's one of the most popular anchorages in the BVI, due to the great snorkeling in and around The Caves, and two raucous bar/restaurants, including the well-known "*Willie T*", a replica schooner anchored 60 yards from us.

With whoops and shouts and jumpers off the top deck into the water below, quaint and elegant it was not; but the food was really great and the people watching even better. We

In the pirate spirit, the replica schooner *William Thornton* offers great seafood and strong drinks for sailors looking for an evening out.

Dining area at Marina Cay in the British Virgin Islands. On the top of the island is The Sunset Bar with almost a 360 degree view around the eastern Virgin Islands. American author Robb White moved here in 1936 and popularized the island with his book, *Our Virgin Island.*

watched one family arriving by skiff, with the mother and daughter in evening dresses, looking particularly uncomfortable as another family was pushing each other into the water! Then a party boat arrived from Road Town with about 40 aboard, and was greeted by a cherry bomb thrown by someone from the bar.

MARINA CAY, BRITISH VIRGIN ISLANDS, FEB. 28

Wow–what a totally great day! Underway at 8:30 from Norman Island, and sails up at 9 o'clock for a really exciting beat to windward in perfect *Wanderer* conditions: 15 to 18 knots of wind. And didn't we leave the fleet in the dust! First a new Lagoon 46 cat, then a Beneteau 48, and then a big shiny 55-foot glass schooner–we out-footed and out-pointed all of them–really exciting.

Got to The Baths around one and picked up a mooring. A wonderful spot with a path winding over, among and between these huge boulders, with little grottos and hidden caverns revealed at each turn. An exquisite place to photograph.

Getting off wasn't quite so easy. In the early afternoon a sea began to build and after I saw a couple and their dinghy getting tumbled in the surf when they tried to land, I picked my moment and ran our dinghy out through the waves and anchored it outside the surf line. When it was time to go, I swam out and cruised the surf line with the dinghy, found a break and got Mary Lou's dad, Bill, and the kids OK. But by the time I got back from dropping them off, the surf had built and I couldn't go through it.

Finally Mary Lou and her stepmom, Brenda, had to pick their moment and swim out through the surf out to me. If we'd waited another half hour, it might have been too rough to swim through.

But all's well that ends well–finished off the day with great downwind sail to Marina Cay and its convenient laundromat.

THE BATHS VIRGIN GORDA, BRITISH VIRGIN ISLANDS

At the opposite end of the Virgin Islands from St. Thomas, The Baths, on Virgin Gorda, are one of the most popular day stops for cruising yachts. Here, a number of house-sized granite boulders, interlaced with passages and swimming channels, offers a remarkable experience. A considerable swell from the open sea runs into the anchorage, and landing a dinghy through the surf can be a challenge.

ON THE ANEGADA PASSAGE, MARCH 5

Dropped off Bill and Brenda in Tortola yesterday, then over to Coopers for mellow day. Kate and Mary Lou snorkeled while Matt, in pig heaven, met some kids on the beach with a fast outboard and persuaded them to take him wakeboarding. I got things squared away for a passage across open waters–windsurfer tied down, outboard put away and inflatable lashed down forward.

Underway at 3:00, motored for a bit to charge the batteries, then sails up at 4:00 in Round Island Passage. Sloppy at first with East Northeast winds at 20 knots and an 8 foot swell, but once we got off into the deep water the swells became smaller and the wind eased to 12 to 14 knots, and we slid easily along away from the lights and into the dark.

We were sailing alone on passage for the first time, so it was a bit of a new experience being out in the Atlantic without a light or land visible anywhere around the whole horizon.

The kids steered in the dark when we crossed the Mona, but I decided to take this one myself, and it was a delightful evening: the night cloudless; the stars bright and the Southern Cross just visible, low on the horizon.

While the boats in the Virgin Islands were primarily from charter companies, St. Martin was an introduction to large custom vessels from all over the world.

MARIGOT BAY, ST. MARTIN, FRENCH WEST INDIES, MARCH 10

Comes very dark, with only the tiniest light on the southeast horizon. Finally around 2:00 a.m., I got out the binoculars and went forward, safety line clipped in of course, and peered into the black. I saw the dramatic extinct volcano that was Saba, clearly silhouetted against the moon bright sky. What a treat–it truly

THE 'OHMYGODDA' PASSAGE

If it weren't for the Anegada Passage, some 60 miles across, between the eastern Virgin Islands and St. Martin, the first of the Leeward Islands, yachts would be able to make a pleasant jump, daylight hours only, from island to island from Puerto Rico almost to South America.

But when the trade winds romp, the Anegada can be a challenging overnight crossing. For eastbound sailors, like ourselves that March, the ideal is a dying cold front that slows the strong trades and bends them so that they blow from the north or, even more ideally, from the west.

Where the big boys go: a large, classic yacht at anchor, Marigot Bay, St. Martin. Each fall there is a migration of very large yachts from European waters to the Caribbean. The Antigua–St Martin–St. Barth area is a popular cruising ground for these very large yachts.

is a remote, almost forgotten and little-visited island.

Tacked north then, to keep clear of Saba Bank, a bad spot with no lights or buoys to warn the unwary mariner. But then we were truly vexed by the wind and current–not bad seas, but the wind had gone a little light, so we really weren't making much progress. We finally turned on the motor at 3:30, and made St. Martin around noon.

But big WOW! You should have seen all the boats–it was right in the middle of the Heineken Regatta, and the fleet was all there–from the really big maxiboats and 12 meters all the way down to dinghies. And our course took us right along the edge of the race, right past the downwind mark with the big boats bringing in their spinnakers and shaving it close–really exciting.

Anchor down in the corner of Marigot Bay very busy with yachts. Went ashore to an exquisite little town, with a craft market right on the shore, and a delightful French mingled with West Indian flavor. Some great shops–Mary Lou bought a really gor-

One of the great things about Marigot Bay in St. Martin is that the main anchorage for cruising yachts is right in the center of town with a big craft market right where you come in and tie your dinghy.

THE POWER OF A GOOD FORT

The colonial powers–Dutch, French and English–struggled for supremacy among the many small islands of the Caribbean. Communities were always vulnerable to passing ships that would often attack, shell and plunder. Settlers quickly learned that a few well-placed cannon in a strategic site could hold off substantial enemy forces.

Top: Looking west from Brimstone Hill on St Kitts, with St. Eustatius and Saba in the distance. Left and above: El Morro fort, San Juan, PR.

The view from Fort Louis, overlooking Marigot Bay and the lagoon, through which runs the St. Martin-Sint Maarten boundary. The building of a fort was a huge event in an island's history in colonial days.

geous metal fish sculpture, just like the fish we had been seeing snorkeling, and we wasted no time getting it up. Then we shopped every electronic store in town for a CD player, and finally got a really nice Sony water-resistant one, that came with the batteries and a CD. It was really exciting to get it back to the boat and have real music for a change, as ours had died in the Bahamas in the second week of our trip.

We even had time to sit down at a little waterfront café with Mary Lou and have a rum punch with the activity of the town and waterfront churning all around us!

MARIGOT BAY, ST. MARTIN, MARCH 7

The French are sooooo casual–everyone smokes, no one wears a helmet or a seat belt. We even saw some guys driving their motorcycle, child in their arms and cigarette in their mouth. Got to love it!

But what a wonderful spot–narrow streets, great shops and

Saint Martin and Sint Maarten

When the tides of empire ebbed and flooded through this part of the Caribbean, legend has it that the French and the Dutch chose a more civilized way to determine the ownership of the island rather than the more usual cannons and swords.

Armed with a bottle of wine, a Frenchman started walking from the north coast of the island and a Dutchman from the south, fortified with a flask of gin. Where they met was to be the boundary. As the story goes the Dutchman was slowed down more by the gin than the Frenchman by the wine, and so the French part of the island is a bit bigger.

Today the island is one of the top visitor destinations of the Caribbean. While the French side is a bit sleepier and without a true, deepwater port, the Dutch side makes up for its reduced area with Philipsburg, a major cruise ship stop with extensive shopping opportunities

restaurants. A good grocery store with a free shuttle for yachtsmen back to the harbor–it doesn't get much better than this.

Plus ... friends arrived! Our neighbors from Bainbridge Island, Washington State, USA, showed up in their chartered 42-foot sloop, so we let the good times begin.

Our friends really know their restaurants, and of course, wanted to take us out to one of the three four-star restaurants on the island–on the water overlooking the inner harbor.

Here, the owner came by to welcome us and to explain the menu. Then, with the dessert, the waitress approached to make sure we ate in the proper manner. We had chosen a ball of ice cream with a pastry baked around it and a dollop of hot chocolate sauce in the middle. Our waitress cautioned us to let it dissolve slowly in our mouths so as to fully appreciate the developing flavors. Was she ever right!!

Above the harbor was one of the ubiquitous forts that dot the Caribbean. But here a plaque told a powerful tale:

Before the construction of the fort, the settlers here were at the mercy of whatever warship happened to anchor in the harbor and plunder the villagers. Shortly after the fort was built and cannons laboriously hauled to the top, the English frigate *Wanderer* tried to attack it with a force some 220 men and marines.

There were only 29 defenders, but because of their impregnable position, they were able to totally defeat the attackers. There was only one minor injury among the defenders and they weren't troubled by the British navy again.

Friends!! Few things were as thrilling for our teenagers as having friends visit. For a week, we cruised the St. Martin-St. Barts area with neighbors who had chartered another boat. Below: A perfect "Hurricane Hole." Port Lonvilliers, on St. Martin, offers a protected marina as well as a compete beach resort. There isn't room in the narrowest part of the entrance channel for two big boats to pass, so prudent yachtsmen sound their horn before entering!

WHEN HURRICANES COME CALLING

You don't have to look very far among these islands to see the effects of hurricanes. Each year from May through October tropical storms develop between South America and Africa to swirl westward with the trade winds toward the Caribbean basin. Some just bend the palm trees on the islands and bring steady, needed rain. But each year a few develop into immensely powerful hurricanes that cut a hard-to-predict swath of destruction.

Most susceptible are the low islands of the Bahamas, and the coast of Florida, where a storm surge–an extremely high tide–may allow high surf to roll over normally dry ground and batter waterfront buildings mercilessly.

During hurricane season, mariners in these waters travel knowing where the nearest "hurricane hole" is–typically a land-locked harbor or mangrove river–where small craft may seek protection, sometimes tied to trees on shore against the possibility that their anchors might drag.

Above: inter-island freighters thrown up on the shore of Road Bay in Anguilla show the power of a hurricane's storm surge. Right: The remains of a school bus in Dominica after a baobab tree smashed into it during a hurricane. Fortunately, there were no children in the bus when it happened.

ROAD BAY, ANGUILLA MARCH 9,

Sailed 12 miles from busy Marigot Bay yesterday afternoon to drop the hook off this sleepy settlement–just a few dozen small houses off a white sand beach with a little dock. Such a contrast to St. Martin. The Anguillans realized that their greatest resource was their abundant marine life and established a national park that covers most of their waters. Spear fishing and the collection of coral or live shells are prohibited, and anchoring is restricted in certain places as well.

After a lazy beach walk, we sailed with friends to nearby Sandy Cay where we anchored off a small coral reef, complete with beach bar and grill. Island is just a half-acre sliver of sand; food and drinks come over by outboard from Road Bay each morning.

Wonderful snorkeling; the youngest son of our friends was a little uneasy with all the marine life, and so I "buddy snorkeled" with him–he was never more than two feet away, not taking any chances!

Road Bay, Anguilla. While housing in St. Martin and nearby St. Barthéleme is among the priciest in the whole Caribbean, sleepy Anguilla, just a few miles to the north, has escaped many of the development pressures. Another difference: nude bathing is prohibited in Anguilla.

BASSETERRE, SAINT KITTS, MARCH 16

All ready and underway at 8:15 this morning from Gustavia, St. Barts. Motored until 10:00 to get to windward a bit and charge batteries, then it was up sails for a nice tight 25- mile reach to the west end of St. Kitts, with the steep-sided shapes of Saba and St. Eustatius looming to the west. While St. Barthéleme and St. Martin are among the most visited of the whole Caribbean, these three islands, on the horizon to the south, are entirely off most travelers' radar screens for a single reason: many fewer good beaches, as compared with the multitude of white sand beaches on the islands to the north.

Fishermen hauling a purse seine net west of St. Kitts. Set in a circle around surface-schooling fish, a line running through rings at the bottom of the net is pulled from both ends, transforming the circular wall of net into a basket or "purse" and trapping the fish within.

Island Fisheries: Living from the Sea

In 1982, I was sent to St. Kitts and Nevis as part of a United Nations team to develop the fisheries of these islands. My job was to work with the local fishermen to experience their fishing methods and catches, and to suggest ways that modern equipment, better boats, etc., might improve their operations.

For a period of several weeks, I traveled around the harbors–mostly open beaches–of these two islands, getting to know the local fishermen and traveling in their small open outboard-powered boats to fish.

What I found wasn't what we had expected. We fully anticipated finding an underexploited resource that could yield substantially higher catches with modern fishing gear and electronic navigational equipment.

Instead, we found that the local fleet was already harvesting the resource at close to the maximum sustainable level. By trial and error fishermen had found the place on the steep

Typically catches of Caribbean native fishermen consist of many species of generally small, and often very colorful fish. In St. Kitts, fishermen usually sold their fish on the beach in the mornings when they returned. The smallest fish were often saved to be given to individuals too poor to purchase fish.

underwater slopes around the island where their fish pots would tumble down into the depths below, taking buoys with them. They then fished their pots up to the very edge.

Instead of sophisticated electronic navigational units, they used "ranges" - lining up features on shore with each other and crossing them with other ranges to get a precise "fix" or position, so as to be able to place their pots in the most productive places, even though they were working miles from shore.

Fishermen hauling a typical Caribbean fish pot from a boat built in a local boat shop on Nevis. Made of sticks and chicken wire, and hauled by hand, this is probably the most commonly used commercial fishing method in the Caribbean.

Where sugar cane still rules: old sugar mill on the western end of St. Kitts. The volcanic dots that are St. Eustatius and Saba, are sticking out of the ocean in the background. This is what many of the islands of the Caribbean used to look like before tourism replaced sugar as the economic engine. Today most of the old small sugar mills around the islands are just ruins with an old chimney standing stark above the sugar cane fields, and the cane is taken by train to a large sugar mill near the capital of Basseterre.

BASSETERRE, SAINT KITTS, MARCH 16

All ready and underway at 8:15 this morning from Gustavia, St. Barts. Motored until 10:00 to get to windward a bit and charge batteries, then it was up sails for a nice tight 25- mile reach to the west end of St. Kitts, with the steep-sided shapes of Saba and St. Eustatius looming to the west. While St. Barthéleme and St. Martin are among the most visited of the whole Caribbean, these three islands, on the horizon to the south, are entirely off most travelers' radar screens for a single reason: many fewer good beaches, as compared with the multitude of white sand beaches on the islands to the north.

While the coast of St. Martin would be dotted with expensive condos or oceanside villas, here the shore was steep, with the only beaches rocky and accessed by narrow winding paths. Here and there were very modest villages, whose residents disposed of their trash by heaving it onto the shore below.

Before 1995 few yachts bothered to stop at Basseterre, the capital, as there was no real protection from ocean swells. Few things discourage yachtsmen more than an anchorage where it is difficult to sleep because of their boat's motion.

In our cruising guide was a full page ad for the new port facilities at Basseterre: "a brand new port facility of twenty-five beautifully landscaped acres of land, reclaimed from the sea, where you will find duty free shops, spacious plazas, elegant restaurants, a hotel and casino and a wonderful marina."

Instead what we found was a stark concrete basin with rickety pilings to tie up to, and a grand rococo building alone on an empty wasteland of dusty streets and vacant lots facing the pilings of the cruise ship dock destroyed by the latest hurricane. While marinas in most of the rest of the Caribbean were frequently full, we had just one neighbor, a small steel sailboat from Holland.

I asked the man who took our money for the dockage when the dock might be rebuilt.

"Just in time for the next hurricane, mon," was his reply.

As we had learned in our trip throughout the Bahamas and Caribbean, hurricanes affected everyone in the islands.

Anchored just off the marina was one of the most famous yachts of the western world–the four-masted *Sea Cloud*, one of the few true square riggers still in commercial service. Built for Marjorie Meriweather Post in 1931, craftsmen spared no effort to create a truly exquisite interior of rich paneling, the best of carpets and crystal.

In recent years, *Sea Cloud* has become available for charter, and may be seen almost anywhere in the temperate parts of the world's oceans.

The volcanic origin of these islands is evident at a glance. All are cone-shaped, rising to rainforest-like tops lost in the clouds, and from which the numerous streams run down the lower slopes into the sea. In the case of St. Kitts and Nevis, the lower slopes are level enough to be perfect for sugar cane.

"Uptown" we found a world as different from St. Martin and St. Thomas as night is from day. Modest stores spread out from a little plaza. Brightly dressed women shopped and visited with their neighbors. Drawn up on the shore were a number of fishing skiffs, selling their catch right out of the hold.

In the evening our Dutch neighbors, skipper Michiel Scholtes, his wife Catherine Dumont de Chassart, and their friend, Jan Kooiman, visited.

Michiel taught navigation and boat handling at a Dutch school, and sailed the little *Eelhorn* across the Atlantic by himself and the others flew out to meet him. After they'd toured our boat, Catherine said that their total living space for the three of them was probably about the size of our aft cabin.

The legendary *Sea Cloud*, anchored off Basseterre, St. Kitts. Launched in Kiel, Germany, in 1931 for Wall Street tycoon E.F. Hutton, and his wife, cereal heiress Marjorie Meriweather Post, *Sea Cloud* is one of the most elegant ships afloat. In the distance is the four-masted schooner *Polynesia*, which was built as a cod schooner, sailing out of Portugal to the Grand Banks, where her crew would work for weeks to catch, clean and fill her holds with salt cod. Today she has a much easier life–taking passengers among the smaller islands of the Caribbean.

Tame monkeys at Turtle Bay would come right up to Matt and Kate and take grapes out of their hands.

BASSETERRE, ST. KITTS, MARCH 17

Rented a car today for drive along the new highway to the southern peninsula of St. Kitts. Wow–what a road–very steep and curvy with great views. It was almost totally unsettled and unspoiled with many, many cattle in the road. This road was built with an eye to opening up the spectacular but remote southern part of St. Kitts to tourism.

Stopped at Turtle Bay, a very modest beach bar and the only tourist facility on the extensive waterfront served by the new road. As soon as we walked near the restaurant, we were almost assaulted by many monkeys, who had become quite tame. One of the restaurant owners brought over a little bucket of grapes for Matt and Kate to offer to the eager animals who seemed to come from all directions at once.

Kate's Journal: We saw a momma and baby monkey together, but when we got close the momma would hop away with the baby underneath, holding onto her stomach still trying to nurse. It was so cute! Then we got some grapes from the owner of the restaurant, and we could stand there while the monkeys came over to eat the grapes right out of our hands. It was really fun!

The beach had a dramatic view over to Nevis across the channel. Didn't really expect too much snorkeling, but then went quite a ways out, and found some coral outcrops with the usual wonderful array of brightly colored fish.

Saw a spotted trunkfish among others and then on the way back we saw a really big southern ray. At least I think it was. But we're talking BIG–this guy was probably at least four feet across, just laying there on the bottom underneath us, looking very sinister. As soon as Mary Lou saw it, she pushed Katie aside to swim away.

Then, out to find an inexpensive place for dinner and began to think that we were too late for most places in town. Then found this small, but very clean Chinese place with a very genial owner. About four minutes after ordering the table was literally covered with big steaming plates and I was thinking, "Oh, oh, we'll never be able to finish all this." And about ten minutes later it was all gone!

The ubiquitous **MOORISH IDOL** is the classic coral reef fish. Typically travel in pairs or small schools, they are found from Africa to Hawaii.

WHITE HOUSE BAY, SOUTH ST. KITTS, MARCH 18

A day of exploring the island in the little rented Suzuki. We stopped at the Caribelle batik factory at the Romney Manor old sugar plantation up in the rain forest. It was a really gorgeous setting and spectacular grounds with all the colorful batiks drying outside.

We kept on going, hoping to catch a glimpse of the sugar cane train, as it was harvest season. Sugar cane fields stretched from the lower reaches of the rain forest right down to the water's edge in most places. And always in the distance, the ocean: white–capped, stretching endlessly to the horizon. To the north we could see the shape of Saint Barth, and to the west was dramatic "Statia," as St. Eustatius is known locally, and Saba, but mostly, there was only the ocean, always a reminder of how small their little island world was.

The lines were off at five, and we motored over to the very peaceful anchorage at White House Bay. This was the first time since Big Sand Cay that there haven't been lights on shore near our anchorage.

A quick round of cards and all hands to bed early!

White House Bay, South St. Kitts. Drier than the rest of the island, the shores of these remote bays are only populated by a few wandering cattle and the occasional passing yacht.

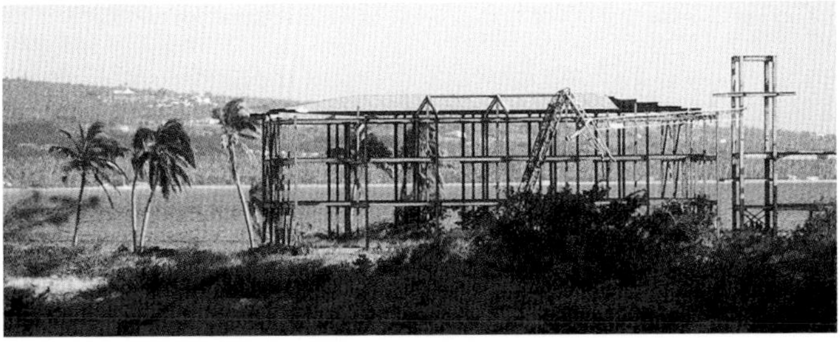

Abandoned hotel, South Saint Kitts. Out of the tourism mainstream, battered by hurricanes, too dependent on sugar cane, the economy of this small two-island nation still struggles.

Wanderer, anchored off Pinney's Beach, Nevis. The volcanic origin of the island may be clearly seen. Now and again as we lay here, a faint sulphur smell wafted across the anchorage –from the active volcano at Montserrat, 17 miles east.

PINNEY'S BEACH, NEVIS: FURTHEST SOUTH! MARCH 19

An easy sail to the east of us lay the Caribbean version of the Spice Islands–exotic Martinique and unspoiled Dominica. We had wanted to see the rest of the islands, as far as the coast of South America, but contrary weather along The Thorny Path, and the upcoming hurricane season–our insurance policy required us out of the Caribbean by June 1–made us decide to make Nevis our turnaround point, and save the other islands for another voyage.

A perfect day: woke this morning at White Horse Bay, St. Kitts. It was too breezy to varnish teak on deck, one of the constant maintenance projects boat owners work on, so Mary Lou and I had a good long walk to a beach across the peninsula, where a sad little abandoned drink and lounge chair rental stand was someone's tourist dream that didn't quite work out. There were lots of very healthy looking cattle wandering freely.

Back to the boat and while Kate did a little sanding to prepare the teak for varnishing for when the right conditions did happen, I put on snorkel gear and cleaned the port side of the bottom with a school of about 20 small fish following my every move. Then it was up anchor, roll out the jib for a boisterous sail over to Nevis–wow didn't we just boil along. It was too boisterous, actually; we had to roll in a bit of jib to keep our decks dry!

We dropped the anchor at 2 p.m. at Pinney's Beach with lots

of overhanging palms and the big volcano brooding over all. Like many anchorages that are exposed to waves and swells, there was a low surf rolling into the beach. We motored slowly in the dingy just outside the edge of the surf, waiting for a small wave and then motored in just behind it. Even so, the dingy spun sideways just as Mary Lou was getting out and she banged her leg. Getting ashore in such spots is always tricky.

We walked to town, past much hurricane evidence along the shore–homes and a modest waterfront hotel with windows and doors broken and fallen trees through roofs. "Town" was a few streets wide, along the harbor with a single small dock extending past the surf line. It was a Friday afternoon, and the streets were full with happy workers celebrating the end of the work week, and many of the little shops had boom boxes out on the sidewalk with blaring music making for a party atmosphere.

Church on the eastern side of Nevis. In the distance is the island of Montserrat, which began erupting in 1995. Today, what was once the main town, Plymouth, is abandoned, and lava is forming new land on the southeast side of the island. Though many of the residents have left and many businesses closed, a number of islanders are returning, hoping the volcano won't erupt again.

Nevis, the uneasy partner in a two-island federation with St. Kitts, is pretty much a mix between the old Caribbean–sugar cane, fishing and subsistence farming–plus a few older sugar plantations converted into exquisite guest lodges. The biggest employer on the island is the Four Seasons Resort, a mile or so west of our anchorage, which employs 600 local workers!

But the kids found free internet service at the local library, and there, 5,000 miles and four time zones from their friends, spent many hours busily catching up on the news from home.

Another cruising family was in the anchorage with their Freedom 40, *Running Free*–Carl and Joyce Berdie with their teen daughters Amber and Zoe. They also had a parrot that was much enamored of nautical expressions, such as, "Land ho, Carl."

Carl spoke of the last leg of their trip:

> "We passed by Plymouth, on Montserrat on the way to Nevis. The volcano was quiet, just blowing out a few whiffs of smoke, but it was eerie–the whole town was abandoned and we sailed by close enough to see the buildings half-buried in ash."

Our favorite spot to anchor in the whole Caribbean, was this bay, Anse du Colombier. It is on the NW tip of St. Barthélemy, just 4 miles and a world away from the narrow streets and ritzy shops of the only port, Gustavia. Not only was there wonderful snorkeling and a great white sand beach, but a trail led high over the headland to a little village with small shops and a great body-surfing beach.

ANSE DU COLOMBIER, ST. BARTH, MARCH 22

Our last goodbyes to our friends aboard *Running Free* this morning, then anchor up at 9:30 and away, away for the 48-mile run to St. Barthélemy. And didn't *Wanderer* seem to want to fly: 7, 8, even 9 knots a few times, the sheets pulling her onward. What a treat to ease the sheets and let her run, free on the wind, for truly the first passage this trip. But bittersweet as well, this turning around, and the crew seems in a contemplative mood today. I had been worried about getting in after dark, but we just ate up the miles and made it to our favorite anchorage in the whole Caribbean, Anse du Colombier, by 5:00. The rum came out as Mary Lou and I sat and looked out to where Sint Maarten could just be seen in the fading light.

Mary Lou had made up a big dinner for all hands and we quizzed each other about turning homeward.

"What did you miss on the trip?"

"I really missed my friends," said Kate.

"I can't wait to start playing water polo again," answered Matt.

"I really miss our little neighborhood and our house," said Mary Lou.

Then it came to me, and I had to think for a long while.

"I don't miss anything," I said. "I could just keep sailing."

ANSE DU COLOMBIER, ST. BARTH, MARCH 23

Fine relaxed morning with the kids doing school work, Mary Lou and I a bit of boat waxing. We then dinghied over to the northern shore with the kids for some great snorkeling along a steep wall with big groupers hiding in the cracks.

Then all hands ashore for that wonderful walk around the headland with the coral reefs laid out below us in the emerald water. The trail leads to a little village where we purchased quiche, coffee and Orangina, before hitting the white sand beach to body surf, and then just lay with the sun on our faces and the roar of the surf in our ears.

Ahead lie many long days between us and the coast of New England where we will spend the summer. We'll have to push hard, and I'm sure we'll be chafing. So for now, it's just right to

have a few relaxed days before the long push begins.

The trade winds were gusty and stronger than yesterday. Will this mean a difficult time when we cross the Anegada Passage?

The rented villa of a friend at St. Barths', with Sint Maartens in the distance.

ANSE DU COLOMBIER, ST. BARTH, MARCH 24

Can you tell we like this spot? Today's plan was to hit Gustavia for a little shopping and then the dusty trail to Saint Martin. But we were delayed a little in town so here we are again. I took the family for lunch at Le Select, which Jimmy Buffet sang about in "Cheeseburger in Paradise." Then a little shopping, naturally. This town is truly exquisite, but expensive.

As we were running a bit late to leave for St. Martins, we just went back to our usual spot and dropped the hook, and Kate read on the boat, Matt wind surfed among the anchored fleet, and Mary Lou and I had a great walk on a new trail, way high above the cove.

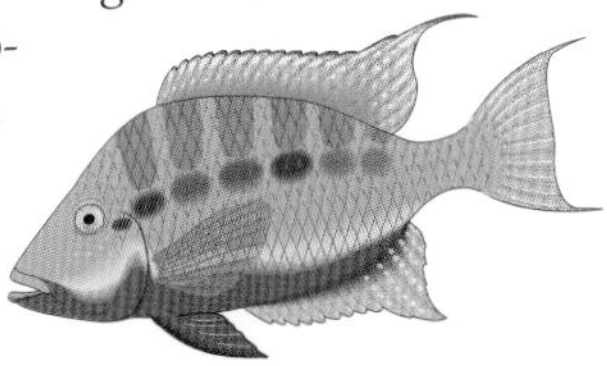

At this beach, there was a steep coral wall along the north shore with excellent snorkeling. The most spectacular fish would hide out in the holes and crevices peeking out at us.

Then in that wonderful relaxed way that cruisers become quick friends, Mary Lou stopped to ask a passing woman on the beach about her "San Juan Islands" t-shirt, and pretty soon it was drinks and smoked salmon with Clive and Karen aboard their boat, *Scott Free,* while their two girls and Matt and Kate were busy playing card games below and making their own plans for tomorrow.

Kate and her friend Allison windsurf together at Lemeseur Bay. It was the ideal place to mellow out before we began our long push to get to New England waters for the summer. Below: Scrabble with friends after a day on the beach - does it get any better than this?

LEMESEUR BAY, APRIL 4 - 6

THE FORGOTTEN VIRGIN ISLAND

LEMESEUR BAY, ST. JOHN, US VIRGIN IS., APRIL 4 - 6

Sailed in here on the morning of the 4th, on the off chance of finding a mooring. This quiet bay is part of the Virgin Islands National Park and no anchoring is permitted. To our great good fortune, a boat was leaving, so we spent three delightful days in a secluded harbor with just two other boats, and they were on the other side of the bay. No houses on shore, no lights but ours at night, and just the ruins of an old rum distillery and a terrific beach.

Another family with their two children had flown into St. Thomas to be with us, and the boat was a bit crowded. So this was perfect. We launched the windsurfer, inflated the other dinghy, and everyone could do what they wanted, be it windsurfing, beachcombing, or swimming. And the snorkeling was spectacular–fifty yards away was a point with some good caves and drop offs and a lot of fish we hadn't seen much of before.

Hard to believe that just across the mountain from us are the crowded harbors and busy waterways of the Virgin Islands. This bay and the whole park is a real tribute to Laurence Rockefeller, who donated the land, and the US Park Service, for so limiting the number of moorings.

PUERTO ESCONDIDO, DOMINICAN REPUBLIC, APRIL 13

We're on the long road back to the USA. After an uncomfortable overnight passage from Puerto Rico, we approached the harbor at Escondido, on the northeast corner of the Dominican Republic. The anchorage was lonely and the beach had steep jungle cliffs on either side. Three thatched huts slept beneath the palm trees with three dugout canoes in front.

"Dad, this looks just like where they filmed *Jurassic Park*," our son remarked comfortingly.

The night came early, moonless and very dark. The stars were hidden beneath thick clouds and only the faintest flicker of kerosene lamps or cook fires showed from the shore.

I was dead tired. We ate quickly, played a game of Backgammon, and I was ready to turn in.

"Hey, Joe," Mary Lou said. " No one knows where we are tonight. We couldn't get through. Remember?"

She was right. Usually when we took an offshore passage, we contacted friends on another boat or family back in the States by shortwave radio, phone, or e-mail, so that if something happened, someone would know where we had gone if we were overdue. But on this leg of our voyage, we had been out of radio contact with friends and unable to find a phone before we left Puerto Rico.

"Anything could happen here." Mary Lou said, clearly uncomfortable with the gloomy, almost ominious aspect of the land around us. "And if something did happen, no one knows where we are."

In the morning this local fisherman rowed out an official to check our papers. We learned that it was uncommon for yachts to visit this remote village.

"Hey, Dad," Matt observed as we listened to the chatter of birds in the dark and brooding rain forest as we approached Puerto Escondido, "this looks just like where they filmed *Jurassic Park*."

Tight quarters, you say? Getting fuel can be a problem on The Thorny Path. In the Turks and Caicos Islands, our only choice was a tiny man made harbor accessed by this narrow entrance. When we tried to get in, we bounced heavily on the bottom, and had to give it up until high water the following day, when the tide would be higher.

I tried to play down any danger. But Mary Lou was cautious, sleeping fitfully up in the cockpit, with a big mean-looking fish gaff at her side in case of intruders.

The night came incredibly black, thickly clouded and moonless. But it was uneventful, and in the morning a local fisherman rowed out a local offical who wanted to see our papers. We invited them for breakfast, and as the kids practised their Spanish with our visitors, we learned that few yachts ever visited this remote settlement.

BETSY BAY, MAYAGUANA ISLAND, APRIL 18

Night came early and found us closing with the land at Abrahams Bay, Mayaguana Island. We could see two other cruisers in there, safe and secure, but in the darkness I didn't feel comfortable attempting the dogleg passage between the coral heads, so we decided to keep going, trusting our radar and GPS to guide us safely to another anchorage with no reefs around it.

It was suppertime and very dark so Matt grilled the steaks with a flashlight, and then Mary Lou handed my dinner up to me in the cockpit. "The rice is at ten o'clock, the broccoli at two o'clock," . . but it was all delicious and we all participated in the mystery of nighttime navigation. The boat was totally dark but for the radar screen, our navigation lights and the dimly lit instruments. Closer and closer we approached the anchorage, and finally the bottom shallowed to anchoring depth. We dropped the hook, and stopped the engine to discover a delightful still and totally calm anchorage, with the sky full of stars above us–what a treat!

The Place No One Knew

West Plana Cay, Bahamas

Our own desert island. When we arrived, we walked for miles along the beach without seeing any tracks but our own.

WEST PLANA CAY, BAHAMAS, APRIL 20

We were underway at nine o'clock yesterday to sail 35 miles in light trade winds to West Plana Cay, an uninhabited dot.

But it had miles and miles of a really stunning white flour sand beach with wonderfully textured rocks and great beachcombing. The kids wanted to stay aboard working on their projects–Kate cleaning and Matt filing down the point of his spear for his Hawaiian sling. So Mary Lou and I hit the beach to explore, seeing no footprints but our own on the mile or two of white sand.

Sunset and dinner without a light or boat in any direction.

Up this morning with Mary Lou for a long beach walk while the kids were doing schoolwork. The sun on our backs, the soft sand under our feet, the sound of a few sea birds, and the faintly sweet smell of some plant on our own deserted island were all we found.

After lunch everyone piled into the dinghy for snorkeling on the isolated coral heads here and there around the anchorage, each with about eight feet of water over it, and each its own separate ecosystem–the little reef fish that swam about each one like a cloud probably spent their entire lives around that one coral head.

Then we landed, and walked the beach and beachcombed and swam for a bit, just savoring that moment and place as a family.

At four, three boats came around the southern point, one after another and two boats appeared out of the north. That spell we had so enjoyed was broken.

Of course Matt, our friendship ambassador, had to go out and talk to them, especially one Canadian boat that we had seen earlier in Nassau, traveling with a dog. He was eager to get news of the boats still at George Town, to find out if any of his many friends were still there. He learned there were many families with teens still there, and was eager to finally be with friends again.

STOPLIGHT PARROTFISH– these brilliantly colored fish use their beak-like teeth to scrape algae from coral and rocks, making quite a loud noise in the process. Abundant from Bermuda throughout the Bahamas and Caribbean to as far south as Brazil.

Nothing like a little competition between spouses–when Mary Lou and I discovered a bed of sand dollars in ten-feet of water near the Columbus anchorage, we tussled with each other underwater to get the best ones!

SAMANA CAY, BAHAMAS, APRIL 21

Sailed off the anchor this morning at eight for perfect downwind ride to the Columbus Anchorage at Samana Cay. This is the island, many scholars feel, that was Columbus' first discovery in the new world.

Snorkeled two big coral heads just inshore of where we anchored. Rising out of 15-feet of water, and extending almost to the surface and surrounded by white sandy bottom in all directions, it was a rich and diverse ecosystem of brightly colored fish and plants. And a huge Nassau Grouper! It must have been over 200 pounds with those thick spotted lips and big eyes lazily checking us out as he nosed out of a tunnel in the coral and as quickly disappeared into another. We dove down again and again to look for him, but only glimpsed those big eyes watching us from deep within the cavities in the live coral.

We saw no sail nor another boat all day anywhere on the horizon. Tonight the sea and the shore are lightless and inky black. But this is our last desert island on this cruise–ahead lies the populated islands of the Exumas and after that, the busy US East Coast. So we soaked up the silence and the darkness; it would be years before we would be this way again.

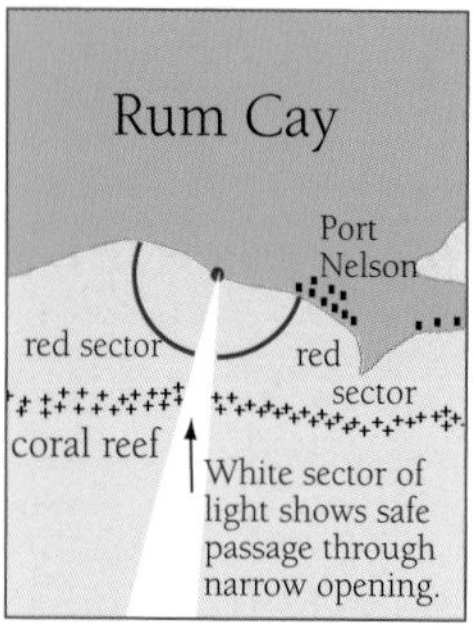

At Rum Cay a sector light indicated the safe path through the coral heads for the rare boat that arrived after dark.

RUM CAY, BAHAMAS, APRIL 22

A long day of sailing hard–underway at 5:45 a.m. with just enough light to pick our way through the coral heads. Trade wind sailing–12-15 SE–but had to tack downwind to keep speed up. We raced the night to get in through the reefs to the anchorage at Rum Cay, but the darkness caught us just at the entrance. Very fortunately, Rum Cay is one of the few places with a sector light to lead someone in at night. Still, I was uneasy to proceed without local knowledge. A big sea was running and an encounter with a coral head would be disaster. Fortunately Bobby at the Port Nelson hotel/bar had his radio on and gave us the OK.

We picked our way in very carefully, with Matt up on the bow, and Mary Lou with a flashlight on the depth finder. But it was almost 8 p.m. before we were safely anchored; thank you, Bobby!

It was a mean night out there and we were glad to anchor, and get a great new chicken recipe from the cracker box on the table! This is the last of the frozen chicken with the Russian writing on the package, rescued from a Russian freighter with refrigeration trouble.

Hold on tight boys! The Family Islands Regatta is held in George Town each April. What was especially exciting was that the course took all the boats close past our anchorage at Volleyball Beach.

GEORGE TOWN, BAHAMAS, APRIL 23-27

The anchor wasn't even down at our old Volleyball Beach anchorage before both kids had dived overboard and were swimming eagerly for the shore where they could see all their friends hanging out. After two weeks of hard traveling from St. Thomas, they're dying to get away from us and be with other kids.

So for five relaxed days–the kids body- and board surfing each afternoon with their friends on the beach on the back side of the island. Once Mary Lou and I hiked the winding trail over the hill to walk that beach and saw them all in the surf, like a bunch of happy seals, laughing and calling out to each other.

At night there was always a movie in someone else's boat or a board game in ours, and it was hard for Mary Lou and me to stay awake late enough to hear their radio call when they were finally headed back to *Wanderer*.

For Mary Lou and me there were old friends to catch up with over conch fritters and beers at the Chat n' Chill beach bar. Some we had met earlier, and while we had pushed hard to get to the southern islands, and pushed harder to get back, they had just stayed those ten weeks in mellow sleepy George Town. Now most families were getting ready to push back towards Florida and other East Coast destinations.

And as darkness fell each night, I looked off to the south and the door to that lonely southern highway, The Thorny Path. I knew that many boats had preferred the easy living of George Town over the challenges of that difficult road. But then I'd see our kids, strong and confident after their adventures and realized how much The Thorny Path had given us to grow as a family as well.

The rare four-point starfish. Actually, they only come naturally in the five–pointed version. Most likely this guy lost two arms to a predator, but for some reason was only able to regenerate one.

And it was such a nice quiet anchorage! Some of the very large yachts are available for charter when their owners aren't aboard. The word "on the street" was that for just $20,000 a week, you could have this rig plus crew, pilot, and chopper. . .

The big Family Islands Regatta on the 24th was the big event of the spring, and also marked when most of the families who had spent the winter here started saying goodby to old and new friends, and preparing their boats for the journey back to the States. While Matt and Kate were eager to get back too, these were also bittersweet days as they said goodby to friends with whom they had shared some remarkable experiences. And the weather, which had been delightfully warm turned chill on the 27th as we too, picked up our anchor off Volleyball Beach for the last time and headed north.

NORMANS CAY, APRIL 30

We had odd weather as a violent squall moved across the anchorage at Staniel Cay last night, with 40-knot winds and violent rains.

And today came with very strong breezes. *Wanderer* first hitting seven steady and then eight and even hitting nine knots once–really exciting! There was a threatening wall of clouds to the north, and just as we were about to make the turn to the NE at Elbow Cay, here came the black clouds and wind, so it was drop sails just as the squall hit with driving rains and 30-knot winds building some ugly looking seas right on the nose. We motored slowly into it until the wind eased, then rolled out the jib and sailed briskly for the narrow cut into the harbor at Normans Cay. Made it to within about three-quarters of a mile from the entrance when another squall was upon us with the

While reportedly on its way into Normans Cay airport with a load of Colombian drugs, this DC-3 developed engine trouble and ditched in the harbor.

driving rain hiding everything. As there were reefs on both sides of us, we dropped the anchor instead of jogging in a little gutter of deeper water between sand banks and coral heads.

Twenty minutes later it was a fine sunny afternoon, and we picked our way cautiously, bumping over the sand ridges in the entrance channel–gorgeous anchorage–little white sand cay nearby with long sand bars and a single picture perfect palm tree.

And who greets us as we drop our anchor but Mr. Really Big Barracuda? He was very interested in us until we took a swing at him with an oar.

And here was *Shannachie II* and Kevin and Ann, whom we'd last seen in Luperón, in February, and we had a lot to catch up on.

Entertainment in the anchorage was provided by the big mega yacht *Star Ship*, with a chopper giving rides to the guests. The noise, in that previously quiet anchorage, was more than a little annoying.

Eerie–a few hundred yards northeast of where we anchored, the tail and fuselage of a DC-3 stuck up out of the shallows.

Sloop riding out squall with slashing rain at Staniel Cay. Note the wind generator, busily spinning away. Many long distance cruisers have solar panels and wind generators.

Wanderer anchored off another lonely strip of sand surrounded by turquoise water and exquisite sea life. We're going to miss these islands.

This was a sobering reminder of the days when Normans Cay was the northern base of operations of Colombian drug king Carlos Leder.

Leder and his men are gone, but his legacy remains: a runway long enough to land a 737, and a large lodge and deck overlooking the harbor, but in rotting disrepair.

But north of the airport was a little beach development and a great little bar, MacDuffs, where Mary Lou bought me a beer and we hung out with the locals. On the way back we took a short cut past the dump where land crabs the size of cats were busily going through the trash!

MAY 2, NASSAU, BAHAMAS

A long thrash to windward across the Exumas Bank to Nassau.

The wind was a boisterous 15-20 nor'westerly with a two to four-foot chop. We started behind and to leeward of *Shannachie II*, with a reefed main and three-quarter jib. Kevin had some of his family aboard and was eager to show them how well his much newer boat would do against the older *Wanderer*. But his boat was built for easy coastal cruising, and the deeper draft *Wanderer* for ocean passages. In the fresh breeze and sloppy conditions *Wanderer* ate up the miles!

Leaving the Bahamas and heading up the east coast to New England meant a sad end to our almost daily ritual of putting on our snorkel gear, slipping over the side and looking to see what delightful sea life was around that day.

This was an upwind passage so we were tacking back and forth, sometimes almost losing sight of each other over the horizon when we tacked apart, then tacking together and coming closer and closer, until each time we would pass a little further ahead when we crossed.

Finally Kevin called on the radio a bit chagrined, "Well we'll just have to concede that *Wanderer* can point higher and go faster than *Shannachie*."

Blackjack lessons from a master. Kevin teaches us some basic strategy before we head over to the new Atlantis Casino to try and make a few extra dollars for the long trip up to New England waters.

But it was a bit tricky crossing Yellow Bank on the bottom of the tide with a swell going as there were supposed to be some six foot spots as well as coral heads. Kevin was a good two feet shallower than us so he didn't have to worry. But we kept a good watch, dodged the coral, and found deeper water than expected.

A few anxious hours at the very last, picking our way around the coral heads and shallow spots in the approach to Nassau in very bad glaring light.

The funds in the cruising kitty were now getting very low, so rather than spend the forty dollars for an extra night in a marina, we elected to anchor in the lee of the palm trees and big resorts of Paradise Island just as the sun went over the horizon.

MAY 3, NASSAU, BAHAMAS

Up to a still, still, morning. Marina at eight, slid in right next to *Shannachie II*, and free, good water, for the first time since St. Kitts! All hands hit the showers and laundry! Boat work and errands for me, buying things I couldn't find before–like AA batteries and a stainless shackle– and changed oil to get ready for the looming push up the East Coast.

Mary Lou and the kids all walked over to the Atlantis Resort with Kevin and his family, and went on all the really cool water slides! This was really big–the kids were especially impressed that Mary Lou did the big slide–we're talking about a 30-foot almost vertical drop then an abrupt transition to horizontal and shooting through a glass tube at the bottom of a shark tank!

Then everyone, Kevin and Ann, plus son Greg, daughter Kate, and her friend, Shannon, for drinks, and dinner aboard *Wanderer*! Next was a big night out at the Atlantis Casino, trying to bolster our meager cash reserves and looking around in awe at the opulent surroundings.

Dawn, on the Grand Bahama Bank. Miles and miles of sailing with just two or three feet of water between our keel and the bottom.

FT. LAUDERDALE, USA!!! MAY 5

A stunning end to the southern leg of our journey. Motor sailed yesterday from Nassau in light airs, and had planned to anchor for the night near the Northwest Channel Light, on the edge of the Grand Bahama Bank. But, when we stopped the engine to drift and eat supper in silence, a light sailing breeze sprang up.

So we set watches and kept sailing for a magic evening– sliding along at 5 knots–a perfect reaching breeze along an area of coral and shallow water, 60 miles across.

But what was stunning was this: the starlight was bright enough to illuminate the bottom, and we could look down and see dark and light patches sliding by just under our keel.

Around nine, when Kate was on watch, she called us all up into the cockpit. At first she thought it was a ship on fire, but in a moment we recognized it for what it was: a rocket arching

Wanderer gets her wind. With a northerly approaching that would have made crossing the Gulf Stream hazardous, perhaps for as long as a week, we took advantage of a window of good weather, and got across without incident.

After the austere islands and very modest economies of the islands through which we passed, the opulence of Florida's Gold Coast was almost overwhelming.

into the sky from Cape Canaveral, 150 miles away–a satellite launch and the separation of the rocket stages was clearly visible: truly an amazing sight–good eyes, Kate!!

And the god of Wayward Mariners certainly had his eye on us last night. I had the watch after midnight, and around 3:30 a.m. spied a small light that appeared to be far ahead. I went down to the radar screen in the navigation station, but couldn't see a target, and called on the radio without getting an answer.

But when I returned to the cockpit and put the binoculars to my eyes again, my heart went to my throat. What I had assumed was a bright light far away, was a dim light very close and the image of an anchored sailboat filled the binoculars! By then it was only 200-feet away, and we slid by, missing by just 100-feet. Too close for me! Fortunately, I had altered course slightly as soon as I had seen it.

The cruising guide for these waters cautioned mariners to anchor at least a quarter of a mile off our course, the most commonly used path across the Banks.

It was an easy mistake to make–you're on the Banks with no one in sight, it's getting dark, so you drop the hook without giving a second thought.

But what you don't realize is that many big sportsfishing rigs bound from Florida to Nassau cross the Banks at night, on autopilot, perhaps taking a careless approach to keeping watch when a party is going on.

And with today's precise GPS navigation and many vessels traveling on autopilot, they each travel along the same exact line, so that unwary mariner so casually dropping anchor did so without realizing that he was essentially on an ocean freeway.

The dawn came with those same gentle airs, but with the sky blood red in the east, a warning that our safe window for crossing the Gulf Stream might be shorter than we had planned on.

So we dropped anchor briefly in the protection of Gun Cay on the very western edge of the Banks, to haul the dinghy aboard and square everything away for what could be a rough 50 miles.

But the weather gods smiled and blessed us with a fair southerly breeze and it was an easy passage across "The Stream."

Just after one, the tall highrise towers of Florida's Gold Coast poked their heads over the horizon from 20-miles away, and at five we passed the Fort Lauderdale jetties, and entered the shel-

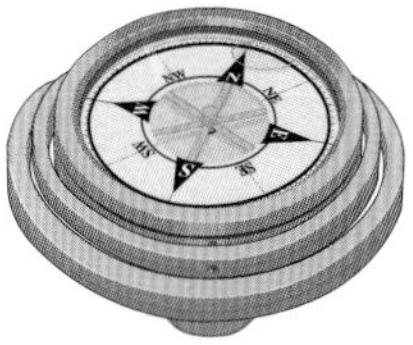

While there are scattered coral heads on the Banks, the precision of using GPS coupled to your auto pilot allows you to travel exact routes that have been traveled by many other boats.

Our phone is ringing!! Barely had we picked up the mooring buoy in Ft. Lauderdale, when our phone rang and we began to reconnect with friends and family after four months "down island." Once we were back in the USA, those lazy days on island time were a thing of the past and we missed them.

tered waters of the Intracoastal Waterway.

This was very, very different from the countries we had been visiting for the last four months. We passed sumptuous waterfront estates, with wide lawns down to the water where immaculate yachts were moored to handsome docks, and tall condominium buildings facing the open Atlantic. Our little family just stood up in the cockpit together, jaws open, just gaping at it all.

It was all very urban, with no place to anchor, and we knew it would be very expensive to tie up at a marina. Fortunately we spotted some municipal rental mooring buoys, which we knew were modestly priced, near a bridge, but then nudged the bottom as we approached. I had resigned myself to finding a marina, when a kindly Danish fellow from a moored sailboat buzzed over to us in his inflatable, and showed us the channel in to the buoy which we tied to.

In the warm dusk we walked the busy streets, found a 7-11 convenience store whose doors were emblazoned with brightly colored ads for the many products within. Inside my family and I wandered those brightly lit aisles in awe. In that one little store, which many Americans pass or enter without a second thought, was a greater selection of goods than in 99 percent of the stores we had been in on our entire four month trip through the Caribbean. Welcome to the USA, and the incredible marketing machine that makes it what it is, for better or worse.

Back aboard, with the rattle of cars across the bridge next to us and the noises of the city all around, our cell phone began to ring–friends and family reconnecting with the kids and us after many months away.

The miles ahead: up the winding passages that make up the Intracoastal Waterway, and finally to New England waters, would be very different. The phone would keep ringing and when school was out, the kids' friends would visit and travel with us. That tight family bond that we had forged on the lonely waters of The Thorny Path would change.

The simple goal for our trip had been this: for a brief time, before the kids plunged back into their busy high school lives and the wider world beyond, to have a time just for ourselves. To be challenged, all of us, to learn new skills together, and to create some indelible family memories.

And as I lay in my bunk that last night, as Kate kept watch by herself in the cockpit, tracking our progress confidently on the

chart as we slid across the Grand Bahama Bank, I knew that our goal had been achieved, but almost by a fluke.

If, as was our original plan, our boat had been delivered to Puerto Rico by friends, our trip would have been very different: one sunny, pleasant anchorage after another.

But instead we'd had to travel down The Thorny Path, waiting for weather, seeking out traveling partners, experiencing the very different communities of the less traveled Caribbean.

And I remembered something my son had written to one of his friends, from Luperón, on The Thorny Path.

> "The people here are all very poor. But they don't at all seem burdened by their poverty. I rode through some of the poorest neighborhoods where the houses were nothing but shacks held together by sticks. The little children would run after me giggling in Spanish. They were all barefoot, but dressed, and seemed to be healthy and well fed. Everyone smiled and said hello to me as I rode past. Most of the houses were run down and small but they were very clean and the people had pride in what little they had. It made me think about how materialistic we are and how we mostly base happiness on wealth. It was really sobering to see all these people who had almost nothing who were happy."

Somewhere on The Thorny Path, another lonely beach to explore. Leave only memories, take only photographs (and shells. . .) It was a big stretch to get a boat and take such a trip. We were very fortunate to have been able to take this little window of time as a family adventure before returning to the much busier pace of our lives back at home, school, and work.

CARIBBEAN
PORTS OF CALL

Premium beachfront properties on the narrow strip of beach that separates the waters of the ICW, or Intracoastal Waterway, from the Atlantic Ocean. In the background is the channel that your ship will transit to get out into the Atlantic Ocean. Here the fast moving Gulf Stream parallels the Florida coast just a few miles offshore.

Fort Lauderdale and Florida's Gold Coast

If your ship approaches Fort Lauderdale from the east–Bahamas or eastern Caribbean–get up early on embarcation day and look to the west. If the day is clear and the timing is right, you will see a remarkable sight–the pink light of dawn shining on the tall high rises of South Florida as they poke up over the horizon. What you are seeing is one of the more concentrated areas of wealth in the entire United States.

The Fort Lauderdale - Miami - Miami Beach area is known as the Gold Coast for the number of beachfront high–rise hotels and condominium buildings. In an ever changing process, old ones are sometimes torn down to make way for newer and better, where the larger oceanfront units can go for a million dollars and more. Some of the older hotels are American cultural icons, where families have returned generation after generation to enjoy the sun and the sand.

Behind the beach that stretches south to the Florida Keys, and north to the Georgia border are a series of channels–rivers, creeks and inlets–that have been dredged to create an inland passage. Known as the **Intracoastal Waterway**, it allows small craft to travel from southern Florida to Norfolk, Virginia, 1000 miles north, without having to go out into the ocean. Look carefully at the watercraft coming and going around your ship. If you see yachts laden with all sorts of equipment–surfboards, kayaks, outboard motors, strapped to their decks–they may be cruising families, headed or returning from the Bahamas or Caribbean, which are accessed through the nearby passage out

to the Atlantic Ocean.

Much of this part of Florida is sort of a tropical Venice with intricate waterways winding throughout the city to create as much waterfront land as possible. With some of the highest boat ownership per capita in the US, many homeowners along these canals are able to keep their yachts right in front.

But as you fly in or out of Florida, you may notice the stark dividing line between urban development and the Everglades that starts just a few miles west of the Atlantic. Wet, inhabited by alligators and an amazing abundance of birds and many insects, the **Everglades** are a vast swamp that covers much of the inland area of South Florida. The cross-Everglades highway is nicknamed "Alligator Alley." On any day dozens of the big critters can be seen, fortunately behind the fence!

The Ft. Lauderdale-Miami area is also the commercial center for much of the Bahamas and Turks and Caicos Islands. Many small island freighters will load their cargos here, bound for many of the more remote islands of the area.

The opulence of the Fort Lauderdale area is remarkable. Many of the glitziest residences are built along the Intracoastal Waterway or nearby channels. If you get a chance, take an excursion vessel along these waterways.

The Fate of the Manatee

As high-speed boating traffic increases in Florida–water skiers, sleek Cigarette style boats, jet boats and the like–more and more manatees are injured or killed in collisions. These large and placid mammals, weighing up to 2,000 pounds, are also known as dugongs or sea cows, and eat water plants.

To reduce injuries, speed limits have been widely established throughout many of Florida's urban areas. Unfortunately, many small craft operators choose to ignore these limits.

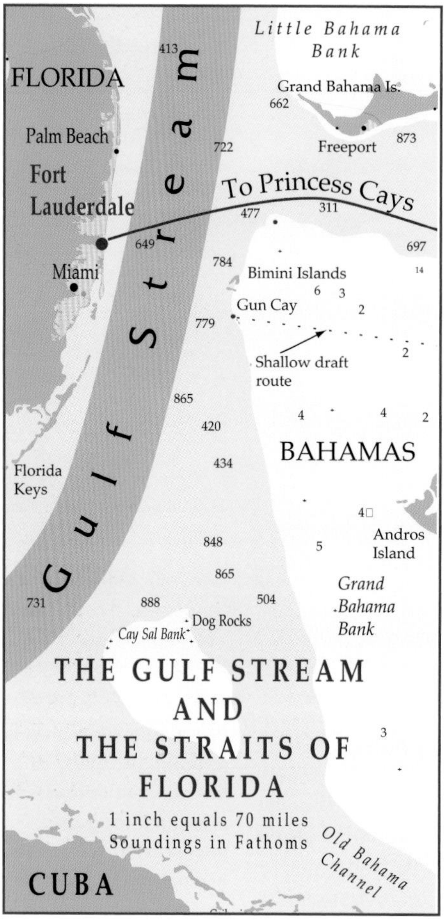

Crossing the Stream

The waterways of South Florida are jammed with boats. On busy days thousands of watercraft cruise the ocean and the region's intricate sheltered waterways.

Yet, just 55 miles away lie the Bahamas –hundreds of secluded islands, protected harbors, and stunning white beaches. But the majority of the small craft in south Florida never cross to the Bahamas. Why?

The answer is the Gulf Stream–a wide and deep river of warmer water that flows north out of the Caribbean. It is squeezed into the Straits of Florida, flows northward parallel to the US East Coast, swings east and creates a much milder climate in Iceland and Europe than their latitude would dictate.

Typically around 45 miles-wide opposite Fort Lauderdale, the Gulf Stream flows to the north at about three to four mph. In normal, fair weather with southerly winds, the "stream" presents no challenges to well equipped boats, say 20 feet and larger.

However, let the wind swing around into the north, as it sometimes does for days at a time in the winter, and it opposes the direction of the current. Crossing the "stream" with a strong southerly breeze of 20 knots poses no problems. But that same crossing, when the wind is 20 knots out of the North, would cause conditions that would challenge a 50-footer.

The effect is to create high, steep, and confused seas that can be hazardous even for medium-sized craft. For a vessel caught in these seas, there is no easy way out, and many South Florida boaters have tales of broken out windows or worse.

The prudent mariner waits for good weather to make a crossing. Unfortunately, in the winter, when cold fronts bringing north winds push all the way down into South Florida, the wait can sometimes go on for weeks.

Fortunately large cruise ships are little bothered by conditions in the Gulf Stream and make regular crossings without incident.

THE BAHAMAS

Seven hundred plus islands make up the Bahamas. Scattered over an area the size of Pennsylvania, many are little more than uninhabited dots of sand, coral, and scrub brush. When the Spanish discovered it, they called it the great shallow sea. Vast areas are less than four-feet deep. In places, such as the east coast of Andros, the largest island, it's swampy and hard to tell just where the land ends and the sea begins.

Most of the population is centered on two islands: Grand Bahama with its busy Freeport, and Providence Island, where the capital of Nassau with its major resort hotels is located. Life in these cities, with the bustle of commerce and the buzz of traffic, is what the visitor often sees.

Yet, there is a very different Bahamas–that of the so- called "Family Islands." On these islands, many without scheduled freight boat service, community electricity, or telephone, life is in the very slow lane with income from a combination of subsistence farming, fishing, and perhaps some visitor related activity.

A challenge for residents in the smaller islands is to provide work for youths as they are ready to enter the work force. It is not uncommon for young people to leave the smaller islands, spend a while in the very different world of Nassau and Freeport,

Shallow and lonely are the hallmarks of many of the cays in the Bahamas. Marine life, however, is abundant, the water is warm and clear as glass, so the snorkeling is a delight. Below: abandoned building shows hurricane damage, unfortunately not uncommon in this region.

Marching band at George Town, in the southern Bahamas.

Below: Marcher in Nassau's Christmas night Jukunu Parade.

most likely working in the tourism industry, and then decide to return to their home islands with their much slower, but comfortable life styles.

Some islands have small hotels catering to guests who seek a more peaceful experience than that available in the more "sun and sand" spots of the Caribbean islands, 400 miles further south and east.

A number of the smaller cays have been purchased by wealthy foreigners, who set up little private enclaves, ranging from modest bungalows to private resorts with their own landing strips.

The ubiquitous conch is used throughout the islands, for food, to mark paths through the underbrush, and even as a decorative building material. If you get a chance, stop at a conch salad stand, but be careful how spicy you want your salad – some of those peppers are incredibly hot!

Were it not for two weather phenomenon, the Bahamas would be immensely more popular and more built-up as a vacation paradise.

The "Dreaded Norther" is the nickname for the same strong cold fronts that bring snow to the Carolinas and occasional frost to South Florida. They lose much of their force over the warm waters of the Gulf Stream, but nevertheless bring cloudy weather and temperatures in

Reconstructed Mayan pyramid? No, this is the waterslide at the Atlantis Resort in "The Other Bahamas"–Nassau. The structures under the water are tunnels through which visitors riding the water slide pass after shooting down the face of the pyramid. The tunnels are made of thick plastic, so as you shoot along you can look out and see large sharks! The resort, in addition to the water slide and elegant casino, also contains an aquarium with a wide array of fish. There is also a plexiglass tunnel under one of the ponds allowing visitors to walk amongst the many fish!

the 50's to the Bahamas. Over the years vacationers have learned that if they want warm and sunny weather every day, it's probably worth it to fly at least as far south as the Turks and Caicos, an island group between the Bahamas and Puerto Rico.

The next is a problem throughout much of the Caribbean Basin–hurricanes. Every summer tropical storms breed in the warm Atlantic off Africa, and occasionally turn into full fledged hurricanes–some of the most dramatic shows of nature's power anyone is usually ever to see. Especially on the smaller islands, where rebuilding occurs slowly, evidence of the ravages of past hurricanes is very visible.

PRINCESS CAYS

Like many of the islands and small cays scattered around the Bahamas, Princess Cays have excellent beaches for sunning, swimming, and snorkeling.

An easy overnight steam from Florida, Princess Cays are several small islands connected by causeway to Eleuthera, one of the larger Bahamian islands.

What to expect: your ship will anchor about a half-mile from shore, and you will use the ship's lighters to travel to a small boat harbor in the middle of the compound. Although there are changing facilities, you will probably want to wear your bathing suit and bring your towel, as well as sunscreen and footwear.

Princess Cays have just about everything you could possibly want for a full day of fun in the sun. Snorkel the colorful reefs. Take a wild and crazy banana boat ride behind one of the speedboats or choose from a wide array of additional watersports.

Also available are snorkel gear, kayaks, sunfish sailboats, catamarans, banana boats, paddlewheelers, and more.

GLASSEYE SNAPPER –to 10 inches long, typically found near holes and crevices in coral reefs. Notice the big eyes–it likes to come out at night, though it is commonly seen in daytime as well.

Brought your kids? No problem–if you want to take a break and go out on your own, there is a special place for kids. The Pelican's Perch is fully supervised so you can relax, knowing they are in good hands.

There are beach barbecues plus full-service bars and a souvenir shop. Just like on the ship, pay for any extras like drinks with your cruise card and it will be added to your shipboard account.

Want a more private setting? The cays stretch for almost a mile and at the farther ends, you are apt to feel like you're on the island all by yourself!

But remember, especially if this is the first day of your cruise,

even on a cloudy day the Bahamian sun can be intense–so don't forget to put on sunscreen. You don't want to let a sunburn interfere with having a great time on the rest of your cruise.

You'll need some way to identify all the amazing fish you'll see, just a few feet below the surface here.

If you have never snorkeled before, Princess Cays are a truly excellent spot to learn this valuable skill. There will be an opportunity to snorkel at each of your other cruise stops.

First of all, relax! All you're really doing is just swimming along the surface, looking into a diverse and colorful undersea world. If you're worried about your ability to float, just partially inflate your life vest before you enter the water. The staff will show you how to use your mask and snorkel.

What's great about Princess Cays is that the bottom is shallow and gently sloping. You can snorkel along in a few feet of water, and just stand up if you feel uncomfortable or have a problem.

Bring a camera! Both one-time and rental waterproof cameras are available at Princess Cays. But read the directions carefully, underwater cameras usually have specific focus distances that you will need to be aware of.

You don't have to just swim on the surface. If you feel comfortable enough, try holding your breath, dive down, explore a bit, then surface. Still face down, and with a sharp exhale, blow the water out of your snorkel tube and then keep on snorkeling on the surface. As you develop your confidence, you may feel comfortable diving down to 15-20 feet and exploring as long as your breath holds out.

Buy a fish identification card or book. The variety of sea life here is absolutely amazing! A book will allow you to identify what you have seen and learn more about their habits.

Chalk Sound on Providenciales Island is becoming popular among Europeans for second homes. As a British Crown Colony, these islands are more visible to English and European travelers. Most Americans, unless they are divers, are unfamiliar with these islands.

Off the Beaten Path: Turks and Caicos Islands

Some historians feel Columbus first landed here. These islands were uninhabited then and essentially disappeared into the mists of time for over a hundred years. Entrepreneurs from Bermuda arrived here in the 1700's, importing slave labor to take advantage of the shallow lagoons that could be used as salt pans.

To create salt the lagoons were blocked off and after the water evaporated the salt was raked and bagged. This labor-intensive process was an economic mainstay in a number of places throughout the Caribbean as late as the mid 1960's.

Initially considered part of the Bahamas, these islands received a burst of settlement after American Independence in 1776. English settlers ousted from their lands in Georgia and the Carolinas came here to try cotton cultivation, receiving British Crown land grants. The islands were annexed to Jamaica in 1873, but after that island became independent in 1964, Turks representatives lobbied successfully to have their island declared a British Crown Colony.

Some 40 islands and smaller cays make up the Turks, but its 8,000 residents are just concentrated on eight. The islands surround Caicos Bank, a vast shallow area about the size of the state of Rhode Island. Even today much of the area is a maze of uncharted shallows and coral heads; yachts that elect to cross the "banks," rather than go the long way around, need to exercise extreme caution and keep a sharp lookout.

Life here was very sleepy indeed, with making salt and fishing the main occupations; few outsiders had heard of the place until the 1960's. Then Club Med built a resort on the excellent beach on the north shore of Providenciales Island, or just **Provo**.

AT A GLANCE

- 166 square miles.
- Eight large, many small islands, surrounding large shallow bank.
- Dry and barren.
- British Commonwealth.
- 8,000 residents.
- Some resorts; very popular with divers.

Around the same time, the spreading use of scuba gear, invented by Frenchmen Jacques Cousteau and Emile Gagnan in 1946, allowed visitors to explore the truly remarkable undersea world that surrounds these islands.

Wisely, Turks and Caicos authorities realized that one of their greatest resources was their rich undersea life, and they established a series of National Marine Parks to conserve it. The diving community responded, and today a number of operators offer dive tours here. The islands are known for their boat tours–week-long trips around the islands, living aboard a dive boat with good accommodations. For the more hard core divers, these trips offer extensive opportunities to dive in all sorts of environments, including night dives.

Divers from all over the world come to explore these islands.
PG photo

Below: Will the rusting machines ever start up again? Silent draglines and earthmoving machinery on the south coast of Provo mark a development that ran out of money.

Most hotels also offer diving packages; some of the most exciting are near **Grand Turk**, the easternmost island, and the last bastion of the salt trade before it collapsed.

Favorite dives here include the Black Forest with its dramatic live black coral formations, and the edge of the Columbus Passage, where the water drops from the shallows into 7,000-foot depths!

This and Mouchoir Bank further east are also excellent places to view humpback whales as they swim through on their way to their breeding grounds near the Dominican Republic.

Provo is the busiest and most developed of the islands. However, with almost no commercial settlement along the sheltered side of the island, and no dock or even easy access for cruise ships, life on Provo is still pretty much on "island time."

SAN JUAN, PUERTO RICO

If Spain is still bitter about losing Puerto Rico in the Spanish-American War (1898), it should be–this island was the jewel in their Caribbean crown.

Columbus discovered the island on his second voyage in 1493. The Spaniards were quick to enslave the 30,000 or so local natives to work in the gold mines.

However, after the gold played out around 1600, the Spanish essentially lost interest in the island until 1765, when plantations were built harvesting sugar cane, tobacco, and coffee, all for export.

Taking a walking tour of Old San Juan is an excellent way to see some wonderful old colonial architecture.

During the 1800's Puerto Rico was an increasingly wealthy agricultural colony. Ironically, just when Puerto Rico gained its autonomy, the Spanish-American War broke out and the island became a US territory.

Islanders became US citizens in 1917. However a proposal to initiate the process towards statehood was defeated in Puerto Rico in 1998, and today it remains a commonwealth–a murky condition somewhere between a colony and a state. The issue of statehood is still very much a topic of discussion.

As islanders were quick to see, being affiliated with the US had its benefits. Just 70 miles to the west is the Dominican Republic with very similar geography and natural resources. The constant stream of Dominicans and Haitians, trying to sneak across the Mona Passage and into Puerto Rico, speaks of the vibrant economy which characterizes life here.

With substantial investments from US companies and easy access to US markets, many Puerto Ricans enjoy a standard of life that is a lot higher than much of Latin America.

AT A GLANCE

- 3,500 square miles.
- US Commonwealth.
- Much industry & agriculture.
- 3,500,000 residents.
- Spanish and English.

Puerto Rico is very different from the Bahamas. The central range of mountains, 4,300 feet, is high enough to scrape moisture out of the passing clouds. This creates a rain forest on the upper slopes, surrounded by a drier coastal plain, and by the deep and breezy Atlantic.

Your ship will usually tie up near **Old San Juan.** Almost entirely surrounded by six miles of fortress walls, it's a good example of the value a good fort had to a town in those days of constantly passing hostile ships. Many islands in the Caribbean changed hands a number of times until a fort strong enough to ward off marauders was constructed.

Today, Old San Juan is the vibrant city core full of shops, restaurants and businesses. There is some great shopping here, so take advantage of it. A great place for crafts is the **Arts and Crafts Center** on Cristo Street in the southwest part of the old city. When you plan your cruise, assume that your ship will begin disembarking around nine, so allow time for a city tour ending up at the airport.

If you just want to explore on your own, consider the **Old San Juan Walk**, about a two-mile loop through the heart of the old city. Not to be missed stops on this loop are the **Convento de los Dominicos** and the **Cathedral de San Juan.**

The latter is a truly elegant

El Morro is one of the great forts of the Caribbean.

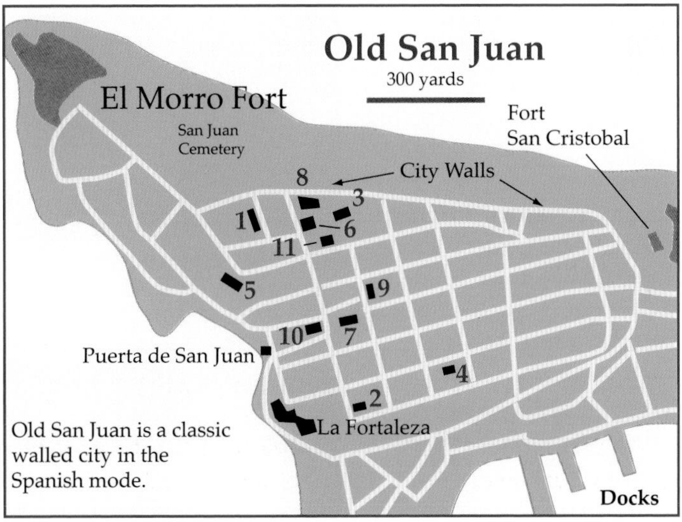

Old San Juan is a classic walled city in the Spanish mode.

Map Key:
1 Américas Museum
2 Arts & Crafts Center
3 Art & History Mus.
4 Butterfly People
5 Casa Blanca
6 Church of San Jose
7 Cathedral de San Juan
8 Convento de los Dominicos
9 Museo del Indio
10 Museo del Niño
11 Pablo Casals Mus.

A hammock maker sets up on a sleepy street in Boquerón, in the dry southwest corner of the Island. This is a popular stop for families traveling in their small yachts along the so-called "Thorny Path" between Florida and the Caribbean. A number of northern sailors make this community their winter home, perhaps living on their boats and working on shore to get away from cold Canadian and New England winters. Puerto Rico, like the rest of the Caribbean islands, has a richly varied local crafts community.

structure, a symbol of the enormous power of the Catholic Church all throughout Latin America, and the former, built in the early 1500's, is now the home of the Puerto Rico Institute of Culture.

Don't miss going through one of the forts. **El Morro** is the largest of these on the very northeast tip of the peninsula that comprises the old city. Construction started in 1540 and continued in fits and spurts over many generations until it reached its present state some 250 years later.

Want one last beach break? Just a mile or two east of Old San Juan are some great beaches. You want "balnearios." These are public, government-operated beaches that have changing areas, lifeguards, etc. The closest of these are **Escambron Beach** and **Isla Verde Beach.**

Got a Few Extra Days?

Consider taking a few extra days to explore Puerto Rico–there's a lot to see, most folks speak a bit of English, and prices are moderate

For a short visit, think about renting a car or taking a tour to **Eastern Puerto Rico.** One of the most unique places in the region is the **Caribbean National Forest**, but known locally as **El Yunque.** It's a 28,000 acre reserve where you can see high waterfalls, the rich diversity of flowering tropical plants, as well as richly varied bird life. Just 25 miles from San Juan, the center is

A number of luxury communities are near the southeast corner of Puerto Rico. This is Palmas del Mar, which, approached from the water, looks a bit like a medieval walled city. Roof workers here were particularly busy after hurricanes in the late 1990's stripped the roof tiles off of hundreds of units.

the **El Portal Tropical Forest Center**, which has a fascinating entry via an elevated walkway through the rain forest canopy.

On the very northeast tip of the island is **Las Cabezas de San Juan Nature Preserve.** This is a small preserve (just 316 acres) on the ocean with a wide range of ecological niches including Laguna Grande, one of Puerto Rico's bioluminescent lagoons, where the water glows dramatically upon being disturbed.

If you're interested in architecture and history, consider a visit to **Ponce**, Puerto Rico's second largest city, which dates back to 1662. Filled with many historic buildings, what's exciting is that many of the buildings were restored in the early 1990's as part of the Columbus quincentennial celebration.

The southwest corner of Puerto Rico, including Boquerón and Ponce, is the driest part of the island, but with some great beaches and popular resorts, including **La Parguera**, which is also known for the dramatic bioluminescence of a nearby lagoon.

If you have any interest at all in caves, **Río Camuy Cave Park**, in northwest Puerto Rico, is a must see. Here a river has carved its way through the limestone heart of the land, creating an unusual series of sinkholes and caverns. There's even a motorized tram that takes visitors safely deep into the cave system. The main cavern is some 200 feet high and side pathways lead to some huge sinkholes, one of which, **Sumidero Tres Pueblos** (Three Towns Sinkhole) is 400 feet deep and six acres big!

The limestone landscape in this area also allowed workers to carve out a 20-acre antenna in a natural crater to create the **Arecibo Observatory**, which was featured in the movie *Contact*. Contrary to popular impressions, only a small part of the center's work is searching for extra-terrestrial contact.

Guesthouse in quiet Dewey, along a narrow canal that slices through the middle of the island. Below: Brain coral on the beach at Culebrita, a smaller, uninhabited island NE of Culebra and facing the Virgin Islands.

Culebra and Vieques: Off the Beaten Path

Every weekend dozens of fancy yachts blast out from the huge marina at Puerto del Rey in eastern Puerto Rico for the busy anchorages and towns of the Virgin Islands. But if it's quiet they're looking for, they're shooting past Puerto Rico's secret hideaways, Culebra and Vieques.

Also known as the **Spanish Virgin Islands**, they are off the radar screen of most travelers because of the more publicized attractions of the islands on either side.

Vieques is best known as a controversial bombing range used by the US Navy. Many ships test their guns here before heading out on deployment, and the sound of gunfire and bombs exploding is common.

But Vieques has some truly excellent beaches as well as another of Puerto Rico's bioluminescent bays. Vieques is accessed by ferries from **Farjado** to **Isabel Segunda**, the main town.

Culebra is a lot quieter. Much of the island and surrounding islets are part of the **Culebra National Wildlife Refuge.** Many species of wild birds make their nests here, as well as **leatherback turtles**.

Dewey is the only town on Culebra and in recent years has become a center for folks seeking good beaches, great snorkeling, and modest prices.

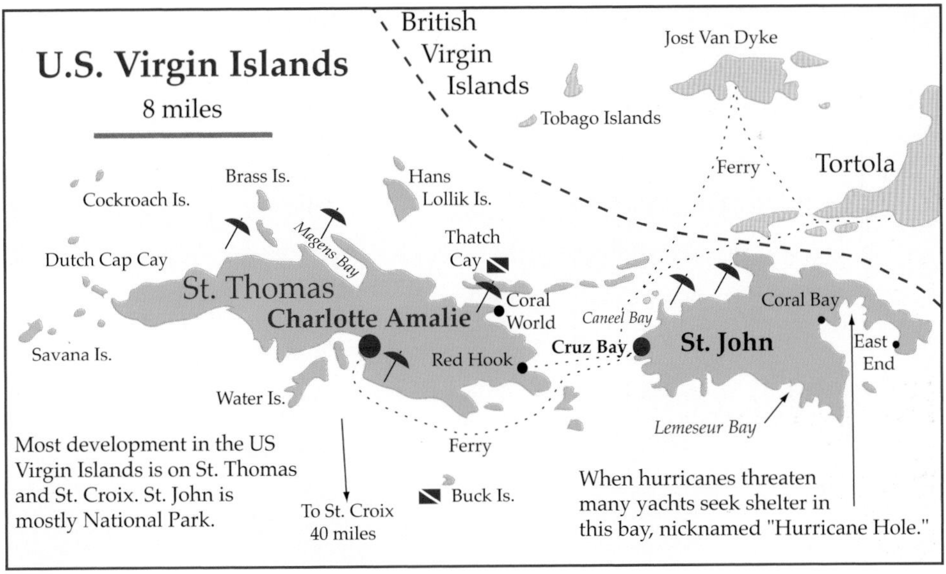

Virgin Islands

St. Thomas

The Cuba effect? When Fidel Castro took over Cuba in 1959, he closed the door on what had been many Americans' easy access to sun and fun in the Caribbean, and indirectly began the transformation of the US Virgin Islands.

Before this time, St. Thomas, St. John, and St. Croix–the main islands in the US Virgin Islands–enjoyed a sleepy and somewhat forgotten existence.

First settled by the Danes in 1671, St. Thomas was first a slave trading and trans-shipment center, as well as a convenient port for pirates (if only Blackbeard could see it now) who preyed

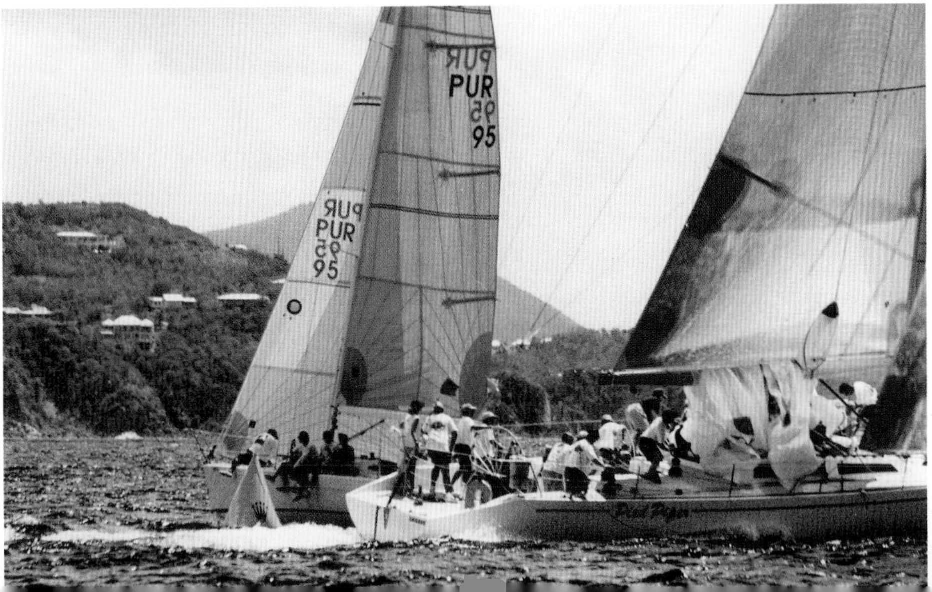

Fast action during the Rolex Cup, a racing series held each April. In the background are hillside villas on the southeastern end of St. Thomas.

on nearby trade routes.

When sugar, molasses and rum were king, these islands were a profitable center for Danish entrepreneurs.

But when the US, worried that Germany might seize the islands for a submarine base and threaten the Panama Canal, offered the Danes 25 million dollars for their holdings in 1917, they sold quickly. The collapse of the sugar market–Europe started making sugar from beets in the 1800's –had hit the islands hard.

Your ship will anchor or berth at St. Thomas' main town, **Charlotte Amalie**, named for a Danish queen.

In many minds St. Thomas is synonymous with duty-free shopping, but there's a lot more here than just crowded streets and shops.

Snorkeling and diving here are as good as anywhere in the Caribbean. Nearby **Buck Island** is an excellent site, where the ubiquitous **Atlantis Submarine** operates frequently.

On the east end of the island is **Coral World**, with an unusual underwater reef observatory and glass bottom style boats that offer visitors an excellent opportunity to see marine life. Next door is great swimming at **Coki Beach**, which also has a rental center for dive and snorkel gear.

If you're looking for a great beach, head for **Magens Bay**, a few miles out of town on the north side of the Island. You'll have to pay a small fee to get in, but it's been called one of the ten best beaches in the world.

Charlotte Amalie's shopping district is spread along the waterfront across from where most ships usually tie up. Below: distinctive Fort Christian, built by the Danes in the 1670's, has served many purposes since, including as a jail, and presently, a museum. Left: harbor view, Charlotte Amalie

AT A GLANCE

- 132 sq. miles; three main & several smaller islands.
- US Territory.
- Major visitor destination.
- 114,000 residents.
- Language: English.
- Very popular destination for yachtsmen.

The beaches on the north side of St. John offer excellent snorkeling, and even an underwater snorkeling trail. Below: local fishermen here still fish in their traditional ways. Here are some stick and chicken wire fish pots in a locally made skiff.

St. John: A World Apart

When Laurence Rockefeller donated a huge chunk of his land here to the US Park Service in 1956, he was doing more than cannily protecting his exclusive Caneel Bay Resort. He was creating an unspoiled natural environment that continues today.

St. John is a great contrast to St. Thomas. Two thirds of the island is the **Virgin Islands National Park**, and much of the rest is undeveloped forest. Savvy travelers have discovered that camping at the park service campground on the beach here is one of the best travel values in the whole Caribbean. Watch out, however, for the wild donkeys that can cruise the campground looking for treats–they'll root around inside your tent if they think there is food there!

Passenger ferries from St. Thomas disembark passengers in **Cruz Bay**, St. John's only town. From **Charlotte Amalie**, a ferry ride takes about 45 minutes and costs around $7 and usually operates every hour or two. Occasionally smaller cruise ships will anchor off and send in passengers by small boats or lighters here as well.

The best way to get around the island is in one of the open- air safari-style buses that operate out of Cruz Bay, near where the foot ferries tie up. There is also a visitor center near the ferry dock.

Beaches here are apt to be uncrowded and truly exquisite. **Cinnamon Bay** and **Trunk Bay**, both part of the park, have to be some of

Lemeseur Bay, on the southern side of St. John, offers seclusion for those lucky enough to find an empty mooring.

the most spectacular beaches in the whole Caribbean. They have places to eat as well as to rent snorkel and watersports gear. A well-known underwater snorkeling trail is at Trunk Bay. Keep your eye out for **Hawksbill turtles** which are common here. With their wide flippers, they are unusually graceful underwater.

As any sailor who travels these waters can tell you, the harbors and anchorages of the Virgin Islands are crowded for most of the winter sailing season with the boats of the many charter fleets, as well as the many private vessels that visit here. By establishing a no anchoring policy in most of the bays in the park, and by putting in a very limited number of mooring buoys, park service managers have created a wonderful situation for those boats lucky enough to find an empty mooring buoy–almost your own private bay.

St. Croix: The Forgotten Virgin

While St. Thomas is viewed as a "must" stop by many cruise lines, some ships are electing the quieter atmosphere of St. Croix, about 40 miles south. With flatter terrain, this was a major sugar cane island in Danish days, though today the biggest employer is an oil refinery out near the airport. Danish architectural influence is very strong both in the capital, **Christiansted**, and at **Frederiksted**, where there is a cruise ship dock. Each town has the usual forts to visit and there is excellent snorkeling and diving, especially at **Buck Island National Monument**.

AT A GLANCE

- Much of St. John is the Virgin Islands National Park.
- Very rural.
- Exquisite beaches on north side.
- Regular ferry service from St. Thomas.

Stardust

VIRGIN ISLANDS SCRAPBOOK

Left: Catamaran entering anchorage at Peter Island, BVI. Above: A crewed charter yacht at Christmas Cove. In the background is a large cruise ship, just leaving Charlotte Amalie harbor. Right: Dock at Marina Cay, BVI.

Dining room at Marina Cay, an island of just a few acres off the east end of Tortola. Below: Church on Jost Van Dyke, a small island three miles north of Tortola.

The British Virgin Islands

While the Americans got the big islands, the British got a delightful archipelago that is unique in the Caribbean. The biggest island, **Tortola**, is almost the size of St. Thomas, while the smaller islands, like Salt Island or Scrub Island, are little more than dots with a bit of beach and a few palm trees.

But it is the layout that makes the BVI so unique–for the most part the islands surround **Sir Francis Drake Passage**, about 12 miles- long by three wide. These are hilly islands, creating a fascinating landscape of dark green hills rising from white sand beaches, surrounded by turquoise water.

Though Tortola was first settled by Dutch settlers in the 1640's, the British quickly saw the value of these islands and seized them in 1742 and held onto them until independence. The early economy was based on cotton and sugar cane, but the challenging terrain led many of the plantations to fail and some owners abandoned their slaves to their own devices and left the islands. Turning to subsistence agriculture and fishing, these ex-slaves

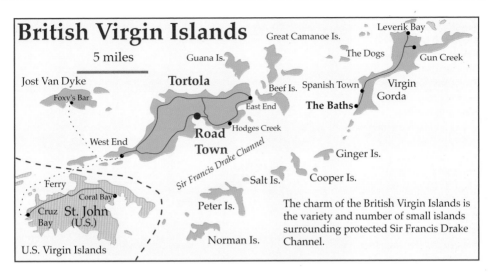

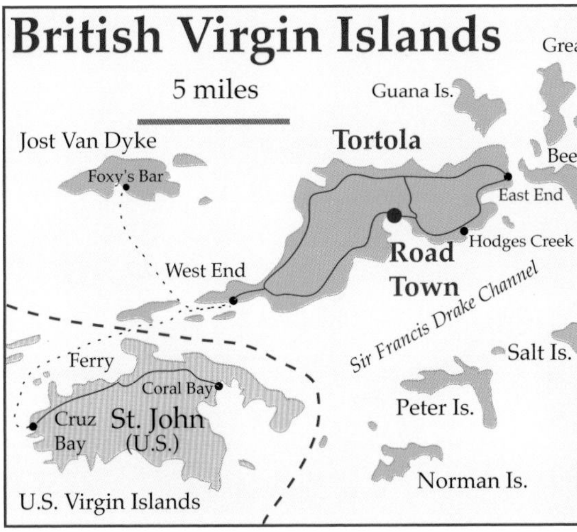

The charm of the British Virgin Islands is the variety and number of small islands surrounding protected Sir Francis Drake Channel.

formed the bulk of the population in the BVI. Yachtsmen and English travelers began to popularize the islands in the 1940's, and today they have become a destination for visitors seeking a quieter Caribbean experience than that available on the nearby American islands.

Don't expect crowded streets and side-by-side diamond and gold merchants in **Tortola**. What you'll find is a modest

The harbor at Soper's Hole, at the very west end of Tortola. This is also a major port for charter sailboat operators.

Cooper Island is typical of the low key resorts on some of the smaller BVI. Particularly popular with visiting yachtsmen and charter boats, visitors ashore will find a beach bar and restaurant, dive shop and waterfront cabins. There is excellent snorkeling off the rocky island located off the south end of the beach. *Below*: charter group working to raise the sail on a catamaran. *Right*: The Baths, a jumble of huge rocks set on a white sand beach is a popular attraction on Virgin Gorda.

community, **Road Town**, the capital of the BVI, built around a harbor very busy with charter boats, yachts, and small freighters. The hills around town are very steep and dotted with substantial vacation homes with impressive views out to the islands across Sir Francis Drake Channel.

But don't miss an opportunity to take a drive over the high central ridge on the island to the beach communities on the north side. As on most of the islands in this part of the Caribbean, the northern and eastern coasts are the most exposed to the swells of the Atlantic. **Apple Bay** is a favorite for surfers, though some of the breaks are over sharp coral, and **Cane Garden Bay** has a good selection of restaurants and water sports rentals. .

On top of the ridge is the **Mt. Sage National Park**, a rain forest setting with stunning views out to the surrounding islands. Before it was developed, much of Tortola was covered

Life in the slow lane. Downtown Jost Van Dyke is a popular stop on the yachting circuit. Below: The many secluded coves of the Virgin Islands are very popular with boaters.

with rain forest like you will find here.

On the west end of the island is **Soper's Hole**, a sweet little harbor tucked into the hills and the center for a couple of fleets of charter yachts and ferries over to the US Virgin Islands, as well. **Pusser's Landing** offers a selection of shops and places to eat in a nifty harbor front setting.

A favorite spot for boaters here is **Jost Van Dyke**, where life is definitely on "Island Time" and hikers often mix with goat herds on the narrow island roads. This small island, just four miles across the channel from Tortola, is a favorite spot for folks coming over for some beach time. Scattered along the shore is a modest community with water sports rentals and a couple of beach bars including **Foxy's**, which has gained the reputation as the place to be on New Year's Eve. Ferries to Jost Van Dyke operate out of Soper's Hole

Norman Island, south of Tortola, is supposed to be the place that Robert Louis Stevenson wrote about in Treasure Island. Today, instead of treasure, the caves are a spot for snorkelers to swim into seaside caverns set into the rocky shore. With both a floating restaurant and one on shore, the harbor is particularly popular with charter boat users wanting to avoid cooking on board.

Northeast of Norman is **Peter**

Island with its exclusive Peter Island Resort. It's a pretty nifty spot, and excursions to the resort are available from Roadtown.

The wreck of the **Royal Mail Ship *Rhone*** is probably the most popular dive around the BVI. Trying to find shelter from a violent hurricane in 1867, the ship sank near Salt Island with the unfortunate loss of 300 souls. Lying in water depths between 30 and 80 feet, it is an exciting experience for snorkelers as well as scuba divers.

Little visited **Anegada** is off by itself 12 miles northeast of Tortola. Very different–almost totally flat, but surrounded by an exquisite coral reef–it is popular with divers and is the site of many, many shipwrecks that occurred before accurate electronic navigation became so affordable.

If you really like what you see here, consider returning and chartering a sailboat, if you are a sailor. If you are not, consider a crewed charter, which range from the ultra-luxurious to your basic 40-footer with a local to show you the ropes and keep you off the reefs.

Snorkeling off Norman Island. The caves in the background are supposed to be the cache for the booty in R.L. Stevenson's *Treasure Island*. Snorkelers may swim in and out of some of these.

NASSAU GROUPER

These can be big–up to 3 feet plus–and like to hang out around coral heads and reefs, and have the ability to change color quite rapidly to dark. Range: throughout Caribbean.

AT A GLANCE

- 25 square miles, some 60 islands, many small and uninhabited.
- 18,000 residents.
- Much more rural and laid back than US Virgin Islands.
- British Dependency.
- With steady winds, and many anchorages close to each other, it is some of the best sailing in the Caribbean and very busy with charter yachts.

Looking from Fort Louis toward the harbor of Marigot, with Simson's Lagoon in the distance. On the horizon is Saba, rising from the ocean and obviously an extinct volcano.

Below: For the very well-heeled: a gas dock at Simson Lagoon, which divides the Dutch and French parts of the island.

SAINT MARTIN - SINT MAARTEN

When the ebb and flow of European colonialism washed over this island, France and the Netherlands, according to legend, came up with a unique solution to the problem of how to share the land. A Frenchman, fortified with a bottle of wine, and a Dutchman with his rum, agreed to start walking around the island in different directions, from a common starting point. Wherever they met would determine the border between the two nations on this island. The Dutchman, as the story goes, was slowed down by the strong rum and so made less progress than his French counterpart.

The result is a divided island. The northern part is considered a province of France, while the southern, and slightly smaller section, is a Dutch possession.

AT A GLANCE

- 37 square miles.
- Uniquely divided between France and Netherlands.
- Busy and popular.
- Excellent beaches, especially on west and northwest coasts.

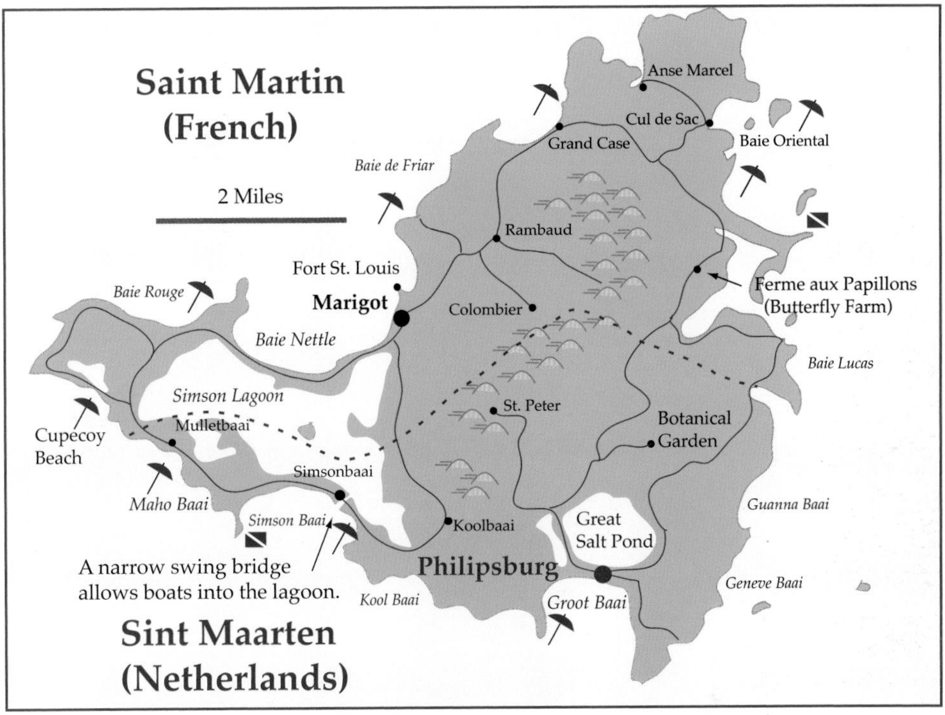

As many residents live in one country and shop and work in another, a casual arrangement has evolved.There are no real border crossings or immigration controls, and the two cultures mix more or less seamlessly with one another.

Philipsburg, on the southeast side of the island, is the major cruise port. With limited docking facilities, most ships anchor off here and passengers go ashore by tender. While sheltered from the east, the harbor is somewhat exposed to the southwest and in the occasional strong winds, your ship may elect to stop at a secondary port, such as nearby St. Barthélemy or St. Kitts.

It's no secret what brings most folks here–the many beaches on St. Martin and its French neighbor to the south, St. Barts, have something for everyone.

What's unique about Philipsburg is its location–on a narrow spit of land–just five streets wide, between the Great Baai (the harbor) and Great Salt Pond, a shallow lagoon. The alleys between the streets are called *steeges* and are full of hidden little shops as well as places to eat.

You'll come ashore at **de Ruyderplain**, or Watley Square. If you're looking for local crafts, try the street market down the street, to the right of the courthouse. Sint Maarten Museum has an excellent overview of local history, including a sobering video of Hurricane Luis in 1995.

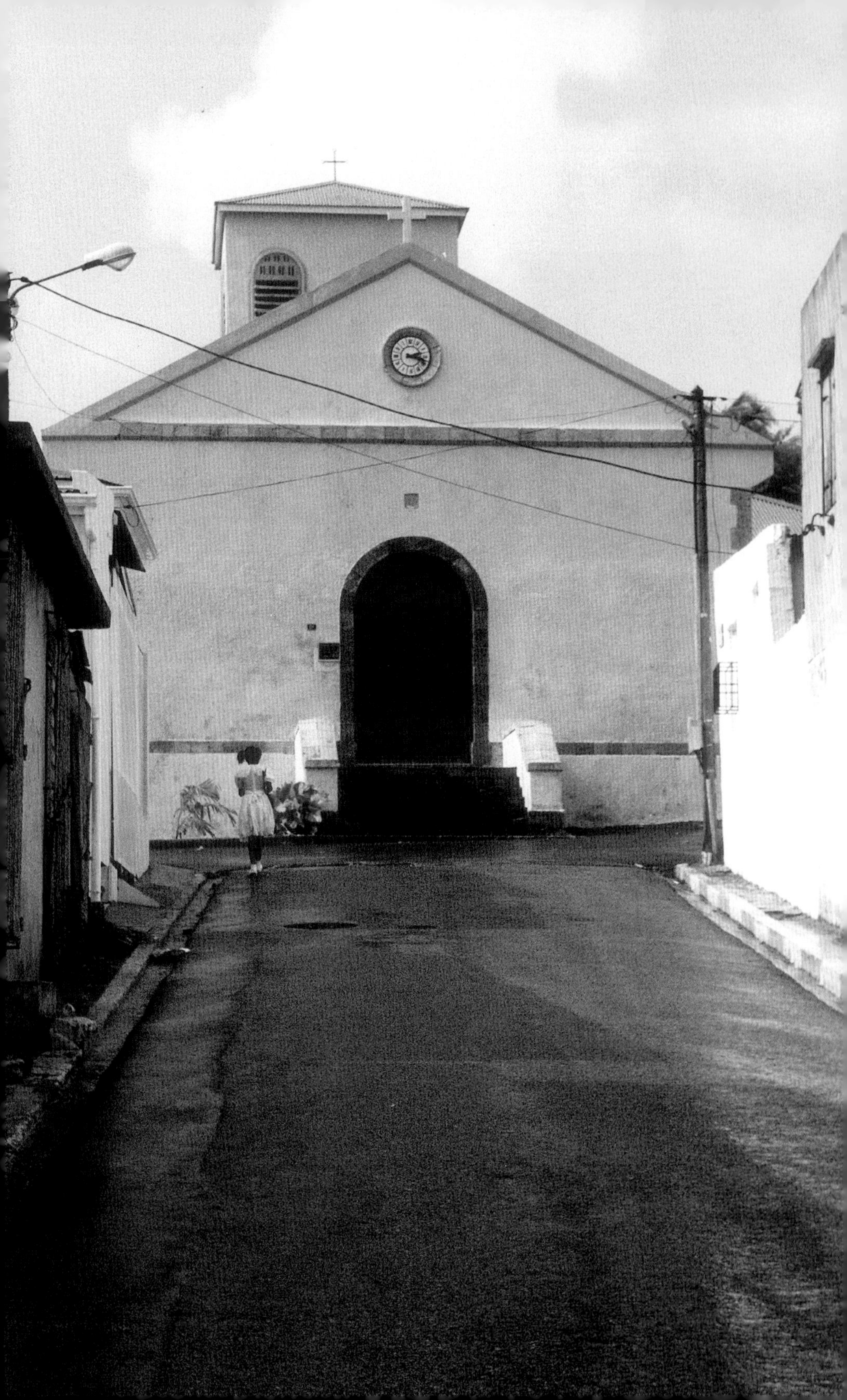

Overlooking the harbor is **Bobby's Marina**, with a couple of good restaurants. This is also the place where ferries leave for Marigot Bay, as well as the nearby islands of Saba and St. Barts. There are also buses for Marigot Bay leaving from Front Street.

Anse Marcel is tucked into a hideaway bay on the northern tip of the island. Below: Philipsburg, like most Caribbean ports, has ample shopping opportunities. Left: church in Marigot Bay.

While Philipsburg is known for its shopping, don't miss an opportunity to take a tour around the island. With its two cultures, this island is unique in the Caribbean.

Beaches are why many folks come here. Try **Simson Baai Beach**, just three miles west of town, for great windsurfing, though there is a bit of airport noise. If you want something quieter or want to work on that all-over tan, **Cupecoy Beach**, a mile further west, is for you.

Minibuses run regularly from Philipsburg to **Marigot**, on the western side. This town is is very French, with many boulangeries, pasteleries, restaurants and shops–it could be straight out of the French Mediterranean. Don't miss the part of town that wraps around **Marina Port La Royale** at the head of Simson's Lagoon. Here you've got shops, restaurants, and craft sellers with a strolling path around the yacht-filled harbor. The town's early history is centered around **Fort Louis**, a worthwhile walk up the hill overlooking the harbor. If it's a clear day, look to the south. That obvious volcano sticking up from the ocean is Saba, almost entirely isolated before an airport was hacked out of the rugged hillside. Saba and its neighbor to the east, St. Eustatius, nicknamed Statia, are part of the Netherlands Antilles, and popular with divers and those seeking a very low-key Caribbean vacation.

Anguilla is a combination of modest West Indian settlements and elegant beachfront restaurants and hotels.

Off the Beaten Path: Anguilla

Just a 40-minute boat ride from downtown Marigot Bay is a very different world. For such a small island, tiny Anguilla, with wonderful beaches and a huge number of restaurants–70 –has become a favorite retreat for those seeking sand and sun, but without the glitz of the larger islands. A local t-shirt says it all: "Life's a beach, then you dine."

First settled by farmers from St. Kitts around 1650, Anguillans eventually grew tired of being governed by St. Kitts when the tide of independence swept across the Caribbean. After a sort of "mouse that roared" conflict in 1967, Anguilla became a sleepy but very contented British possession.

Exquisite is the word for these beaches–some with sand so fine you almost have to wade through them and others, at the base of steep cliffs, only for the hardy–but all with wonderful snorkeling offshore.

The Anguillan government

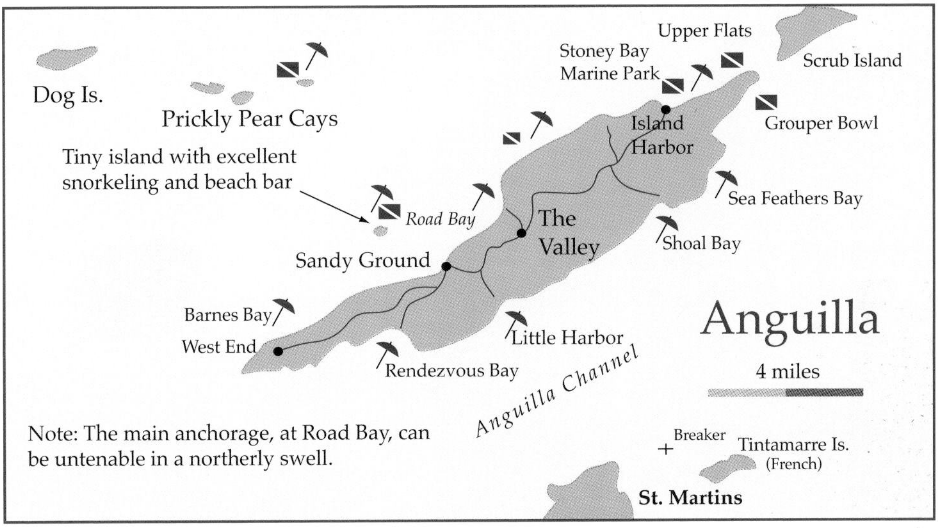

–it's still an English possession –was wise enough to realize that the best use of its fisheries resource was as a visitor attraction, and created a series of marine parks that encompass much of the island's waters, and banned jet skis as well.

Just three miles wide by 16 long, low key developments, hotels and private homes are scattered around the island.

Two tiny islands, **Sandy Island** and gorgeous **Scilly Cay**, offer palm-thatched beach bars surrounded by excellent snorkeling on the nearby reefs.

Their island too dry for good farming, many Anguillans turned to the sea, earning a living as fishermen or boatbuilders.

Saint Barthélemy

When Jimmy Buffett sat in a St. Barts (or St.-Barth in French) café and wrote his signature song, "Cheeseburger in Paradise," he was getting it just right. Long favored by the wealthy as an exclusive winter retreat, this island with its exquisite harbor at **Gustavia** is truly a special place in the Caribbean.

To get here travelers must brave one of the most challenging airports in the entire region. Pilots have to swoop low over the mountain ridge that rises sharply over the west end of the runway and manage to put their wheels on the ground soon enough to stop before skidding into the ocean. But the good part is that the ride in thins out the crowds–there are few large hotel developments on the island, and instead the island is a pleasant combination of sleepy beachfront communities and elegant homes tucked in the hills.

Above: a tropical corner of old France. A resident takes his rest by the side of the municipal library at Anse du Flamands on the north coast. Right: at a private villa with a view off to St. Maarten and Anguilla in the distance.

The island is French to its roots–technically a province rather than a colony, and its residents are proud of that fact.

Too dry and rugged for sugar cane, residents in its early days made a living by piracy, attacking passing ships. Colonized by 60 French-descent settlers from nearby St. Kitts, France traded this tiny and "unimportant" island to Sweden for Baltic trade routes in 1748.

As a free port in the early days of American independence,

AT A GLANCE

- Eight Sq. miles.
- Hilly and dry.
- Very French.
- Just 3,000 residents.
- Low key development.
- Very expensive.
- Wonderful beaches.

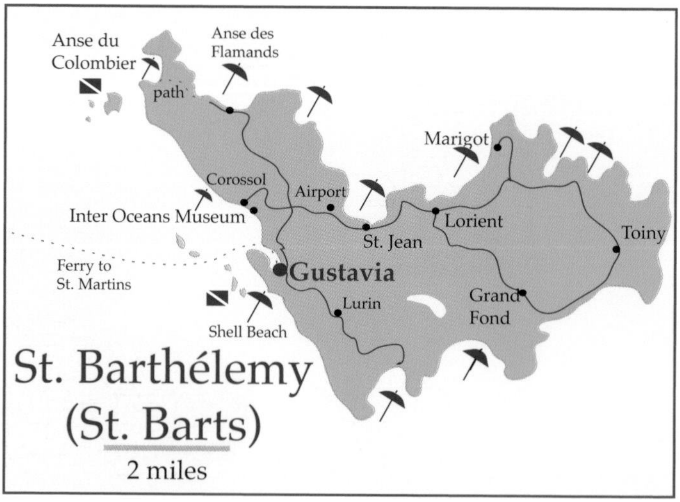

Gustavia, with its wonderful harbor protected by four forts, prospered. But when business tapered off after the American Civil War, France, for some curious reason, repurchased its old possession, and many stolid settlers from Normandy and Brittany came to carve out new lives in this forgotten corner of the French Antilles.

But word of its spectacular white sand beaches and the attractiveness of Gustavia spread. By the 1980's St. Barts had become one of the spots to be seen in for the wealthy set that frequented the French Riviera

This isn't a community that caters to the $100 a day vacation crowd. It takes serious money to own or rent a house here, and nothing on the island is inexpensive except the sun and the sand. And don't expect a busy night life; this isn't St. Thomas.

There's always a private corner of beach here. Below: Look for the rich and famous and their yachts in Gustavia's small harbor and its four forts.

Downtown **Gustavia**, just a few streets that front the narrow harbor, is an eclectic collection of boulangeries that would be at home in a modest French farm town, and haute culture boutiques, jewelry shops and galleries, where serious money changes hands. Don't be fooled by the modest facade of some of the restaurants here; Gustavia has more four-star restaurants than any other such small city in the Caribbean.

A walk over the steep hill just north of Gustavia along the waterfront brings you to the small fishing village of **Corossol**.

And a short walk around the harbor and over the hill to the south brings you to **Shell Beach**, hemmed in by steep hills, with gentle surf and great shelling.

If your ship stops here, consider yourself lucky. Because of the limited space, narrow streets, and geography that requires large ships to anchor some distance off, most big ships don't stop here unless stormy conditions preclude a stop at nearby St. Maarten.

But if you do stop here, spend some time in Gustavia. Then rent a car or take a bus tour around the island. The road runs along the top of the ridge that planes must skim to land and offers spectacular views out to nearby St. Maarten to the northwest and St. Kitts and Nevis to the south as it winds up to the island's heights to get from beach to beach.

The other major community is **St. Jean** with its excellent beach and a low-key row of shops, hotels and restaurants.

If you want white sand and seclusion, try **Anse du Grand Saline or Anse du Governeur**, both undeveloped and on the south coast.

Stark reminder of life on "Hurricane Alley:" a hotel on Anse des Flamands on the north coast shattered by Hurricane Hugo ('95). Below: the surfer's center on the beach at unpretentious St. Jean.

The waterfront of Basseterre witrh sugar cane growing on the slopes above town. Below: Fishermen, with St. Eustatius in the distance.

The Old Caribbean: St. Kitts and Nevis

Just 22 miles south of elegant St. Barts lies a very different world–a pair of sugar cane islands–struggling to gain a foothold with tourism, but still very much the Old Caribbean.

What makes these islands so different, especially St. Kitts (properly known as St. Christopher), is simple–fewer of the kind of dreamy white sand beaches that make St. Barts such a mecca for vacationers.

Instead, much of **St. Kitts** is essentially a volcano sticking out of the water with small settlements typically set on steep and rugged shores.

A sugar cane train circles the island to bring the cut sugar cane to the mill that looms over the main town of **Basseterre**. Many of the population of native Caribbean islanders scratch out a modest living working seasonally in the cane fields and maintaining good gardens, though more jobs are being provided by a resort hotel complex on the

AT A GLANCE

- Two volcanic islands, 100 sq. miles total.
- Independent.
- 35,000 residents on St. Kitts, 9,000 on Nevis.
- Sugar cane still important.
- Some old sugar plantations now are upscale inns.
- Little development.

Batiks strung up to dry at Caribelle Batiks, east of Basseterre. Set in an old sugar plantation, it is a worthwhile stop on any island tour.

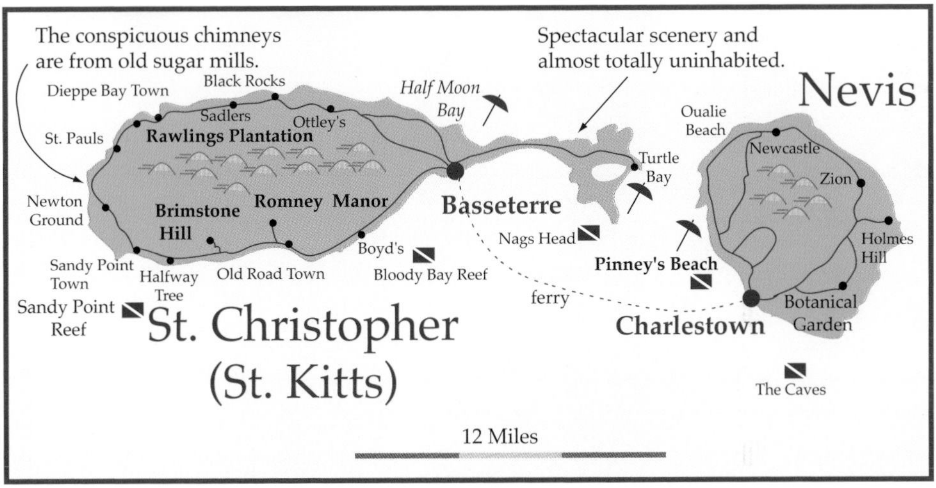

Locally built fishing boats on Nevis. Below: A St. Kitts boy demonstrates his agility at climbing a coconut palm.

beaches to the north of Basseterre.

First settled by the French, the British took over in the early 1600's, and used this base to colonize Antigua and Tortola, giving St. Kitts the nickname of the **Mother Colony.** Sugar cane immediately became the economic focus here and remains a major employer. Many of the old plantation **great houses**, however, have been refurbished as elegant inns, serving well-heeled travelers seeking elegance in a secluded tropical setting.

A stroll through downtown Basseterre is a trip back in time compared to many Caribbean capitals. Local fishermen sell their catch right on the beach, roadside vendors offer sugar cane and local produce, and the local dialect is a rich twangy English that must be heard to be appreciated.

A new cruise ship facility was built in the 1990's on filled land south of Basseterre, but a passing hurricane in 1997 wiped out the dock. The dock has since been rebuilt, but only dust swirls through the empty lots that were to have held shops, restaurants and a big casino. Unfortunately, such is life in the hurricane belt.

Consider a drive or tour around the island if you have time, and make sure you stop at

Brimstone Hill Fort, as well as **Caribelle Batiks** in an old sugar mill. Local taxis can often arrange a round-the-island tour combined with a lunch stop at one of the plantations.

If you have time get driven on the road down the south peninsula, at least as far enough to see the stunning views.

Anglican church near Tabernacle on the north coast of St. Kitts. On most days the French resort island of St. Barts may be clearly seen on the horizon.

St. Kitts, along with nearby Nevis, form an independent country. However, this has always been a bit of an uneasy marriage, with **Nevis** regularly threatening to secede. Though a lot smaller, Nevis has managed to create a more active economy based on low key tourism and offshore banking, and is increasingly restless with St. Kitts. Can such a small island (36 square miles) successfully become a country? Stay tuned.

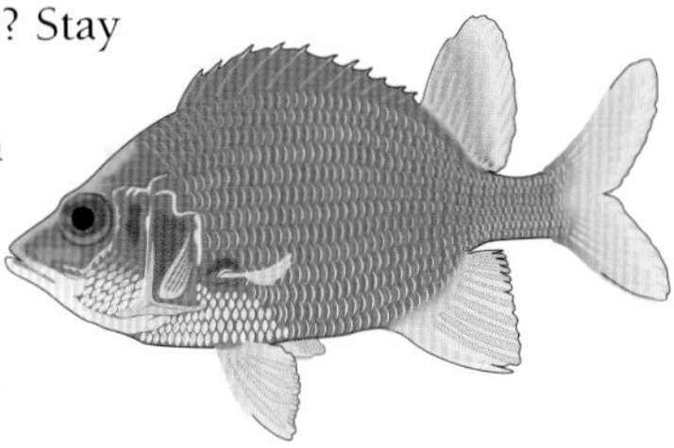

Ferries leave regularly from downtown Basseterre to **Charlestown**, the capital of Nevis. Life here is about as laid back as a Caribbean capital can get. With little for dock or harbor facilities, getting ashore when a big swell is running can also be a bit of an adventure.

A short walk north of town is four-mile-long Pinney Beach, also the site of the **Four Seasons Resort**, the only really big resort and the island's largest employer. Guidebooks often preface their description of it with "If it's open. . . " Set close to the beach, it is a natural target for passing hurricanes. All beaches on St. Kitts and Nevis are free and open to the public.

The best way to see the island is just to grab a cab and ask him to drive you around the 20-mile island loop. Allow three to four hours, as you'll be sharing the road with goats in places and the driver might want to show you the location of the best sugar cane and stop to cut you a sample.

The **SQUIRRELFISH**, and its similar kin, the soldierfish, like caves and holes in coral reefs. For this reason you are more apt to see them on cloudy days and at night when they leave the shelter and forage for small crustaceans.

Where the big boys race. Antigua is the sailing center for the NE Caribbean and the destination of many European yachts each winter.

ANTIGUA

There's no wonder why the annual Antigua Race Week is such a hit among the well-heeled sailors of the world. With some of the best harbors in the Caribbean, many wonderful white sand beaches, plus strong and regular trade winds, it's a yachtsman's paradise.

Needing sheltered harbors for their West Indies fleet, the English built forts to protect English and Falmouth Harbors, and the Spanish, French, and Dutch fleets learned to give this island a wide berth.

Like many other islands, Antigua's early fate mirrored the ups and downs of the sugar cane trade. In the glory days of the 1700's slaves worked at many plantations, and the island was dotted with windmills that crushed the cane to release the juice, which was boiled to extract the sugar.

But by the time slaves were emancipated by the British in 1834, much of Europe's sugar was produced by locally grown beets; the big Caribbean plantations were abandoned and most islanders were living very modestly on subsistence farms.

Antigua's beachfront resorts tend to be of the smaller secluded variety rather than the high-rise style, and many visitors come just for that flavor.

Most cruise ships visit **St. John's**, the capital, situated on a very protected harbor on the northwest corner of the island. On the waterfront is **Heritage Quay**, the glitzy shopping mall.

AT A GLANCE

- 108 square miles.
- Flat and dry.
- Independent ex-British colony.
- Population: 67,000.
- Yachting center.
- Excellent beaches, especially on west and northwest coasts.

Make sure you stop at **Redcliffe Quay** just south, an attractive area of cafés, shops, etc. Another place to go if you are in town on Fridays and Saturdays is the **public market** south of town — follow Market Street or ask a cabbie. You'll find a bit of the old Caribbean here where the locals go to shop for their food needs.

A good walk in St. John's is following Fort Road along the harbor north to **Fort James**. Then just keep following the shore and you'll come to a headland and then into **Dickinson Bay** where you can rent windsurfers, etc.

English Harbor, on the south side of the island, is where Horatio Nelson, later to become England's most famous naval hero, served as second in command of the English naval station. Abandoned in 1889, this facility began undergoing a decade-long rehabilitation in 1951.

The result, **Nelson's Dockyard**, sort of a Caribbean version of Williamsburg, is today one of Antigua's most popular attractions. You'll find places to eat as well as shops and hotels. If you have any interest in history, don't miss the **Admiral's House Museum** with a wonderful collection of models, paintings and other great artifacts.

Unfortunately hurricanes take their toll here, and some of Antigua's exquisite hotels got a little more waterfront than they wanted when Lenny and Floyd blasted through here in 1999. The wind didn't do the damage so much as the swells that

Heritage Quay, in downtown St. John's, is a distinctive place to shop, but don't miss visiting the local craft vendors as well. If you're a sailor, you may be able to rent a sailboat for a few hours to explore the harbor. DV Photo.

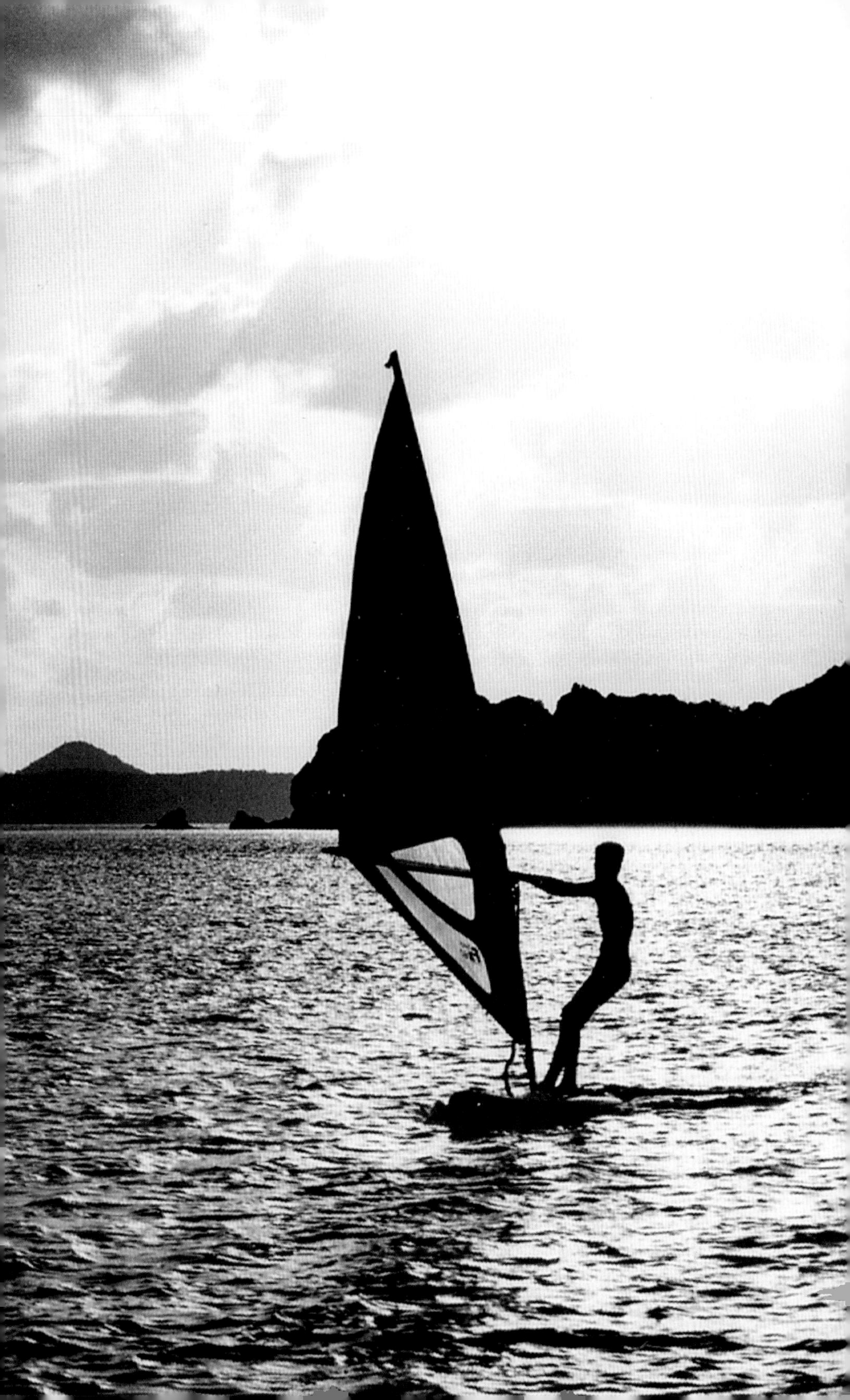

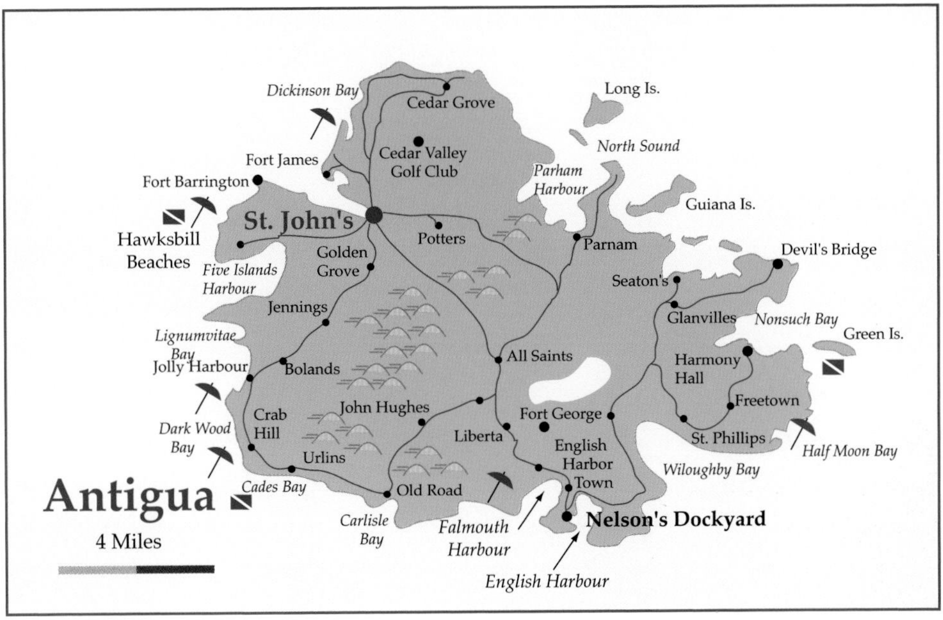

washed away wide swaths of beach. At English Harbor in one recent hurricane, the winds were so strong that they literally blew some of the artifacts of the museum through the roof!

If time allows and a trip to **Montserrat**, an island 21 miles to the southwest, is available–there is both ferry and helicopter service–you might consider it. **Soufrière Volcano** erupted in 1995, burying parts of the main town, Plymouth, in ash, and many residents fled. After the pace of volcanic activity slowed in 1999, people started coming back to their homes and to re-establish visitor attractions, but with a definite ecological slant. Another major ash eruption occurred in 2003.

High enough to create rain forest-like conditions on the mountain slopes–some have compared it to Ireland –it is totally different from Antigua. The devastation wrought by the volcano is vast and stark. If you do come, try and get to see Plymouth. It's a sobering sight to see buildings buried in ash; not your usual Caribbean experience at all. You can rent cars here, but remember you have to drive on the left, and make sure you check on which areas to avoid because of possible volcanic activity.

In the slow lane is **Barbuda**, administered by Antigua, but 28 miles north. Too dry for sugar cane, and almost totally surrounded by coral reefs, it's home to some pricey exclusive resorts and wonderful beaches, as well as excellent diving. Birders come to visit the **Frigate Bird Nature Reserve**, accessible by water only.

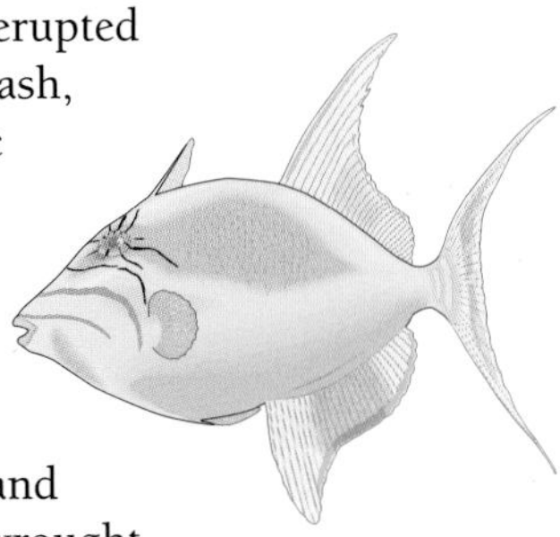

The **QUEEN TRIGGERFISH** is the most colorful triggerfish seen around coral reefs. Especially likes sea urchins, flipping them over and attacking their softer underside. Length to 20 inches. Look for bright blue lines on side of head and conspicuous dark lines around eyes.

Under the Sea

If you take a Caribbean cruise and don't get underwater to see some of the exciting sea life, you will be really missing something. Going under the surface, just floating slowly with a snorkel and looking down with a mask on your face opens up vistas to a totally different world. The sea life in the Caribbean is as colorful and diverse as anywhere else on Earth, and snorkeling especially is easy, even if you are an older traveler.

You may be also seeing something that is fast disappearing. The coral reefs of the world are in trouble. Biologists are uncertain as to the cause, though there are many suspects–global warming, pesticide runoff, and others. But in some places in the Caribbean, pristine reefs are dying for no clear reason. Fortunately many of the areas visited by your ship have healthy coral.

First timer? No worries–all the snorkeling excursions offered by Princess include a comprehensive demonstration of the techniques as well as equipment and safety orientation.

It's easy. Even if you can barely swim you can snorkel by using the life jacket included in all snorkel packages to keep you floating comfortably on the surface.

Beginners often start by just moving slowly along the surface–there's plenty to look at in these clear waters.

Reef Life. In some places you may find isolated coral heads, sticking up from the sandy sea floor. Consider this: many of the sea creatures in this little ecosystem will spend their entire lives here, unaware perhaps that another coral world of sea-life exists 20 or 30 yards away. This is a Sally Lightfoot crab. PG Photo. **Left: Cave diving. Some of the walls–areas where coral reefs drop off into deep water–have caves or passages through the coral. Unless you're a very experienced diver, be very careful about going into places where you can't swim straight up to the surface in an emergency.** PG Photo.

Left: The Red Hind, the most common grouper in the West Indies, grows to around two feet long. A popular food fish, look for it around coral reefs. PG Photo. **Right: coral is created by small, living creatures that form a hard exoskeleton that becomes the concrete-hard part of the coral reef. Soft corals are more plant-like, creating structures that are easily broken when disturbed.** PG Photo. **Below: A visit to Stingray City is one of the most popular excursions in Grand Cayman. On a shallow sand bar, large stingrays congregate to be fed and touched.** DV Photo.

But as your comfort level increases, you may find yourself taking a deep breath, and diving down to peek into hidden crevices in the rocks and reefs beneath you.

Don't forget that as you are floating along viewing the sea life below, your back is exposed to the hot sun. So, if you are untanned, consider wearing a t-shirt in the water or plenty of sunscreen. If the snorkel excursion you want is full, often there will be opportunities on shore to arrange a snorkeling trip, maybe just as close as the nearest beach with a water sports rental shop.

Scuba diving programs are available at different islands. Inexperienced divers may choose an escorted shallow dive in a resort program; certified divers will have a choice of open-water dives.

The
INFAMOUS
AUTHENTIC
CASUAL
Wear

DOMINICA

Waterfront, Soufrière, a small fishing village and site of some excellent diving and snorkeling.
Below: as in many British ex-colonies, the Dominicans take their cricket very seriously.

According to Caribbean old timers, Dominica is about the only place in the region that Columbus would recognize today. Known for its rain forests and wonderful diving and snorkeling, waterfalls and tiny settlements, it's a refreshing change from the commercialism of many island ports.

Today the charm of Dominica is that it is one of the few remaining sleepy Caribbean havens where much of the population still makes its living on small farms or making traditional crafts.

Hostile Carib natives resisted early settlers. Eventually many slaves were shipped from Africa to work the plantations here, and the races mixed to form today's population.

Your ship docks in **Roseau**, the capital. A block up from the water is **Dawbiney Square**, where newly arrived slaves were auctioned off. Today expect to find t-shirts displayed side by side with some excellent native crafts. As you look around town you'll see a combination of classic colonial buildings and sturdy hurricane damage replacements.

Trafalgar Falls is one of the signature attractions of the island. Situated near the **Morne Trois Pitons National Park**, a trip here allows visitors both a rain forest experience and also to see the typical small farms and garden plots, often on amazingly steep slopes,

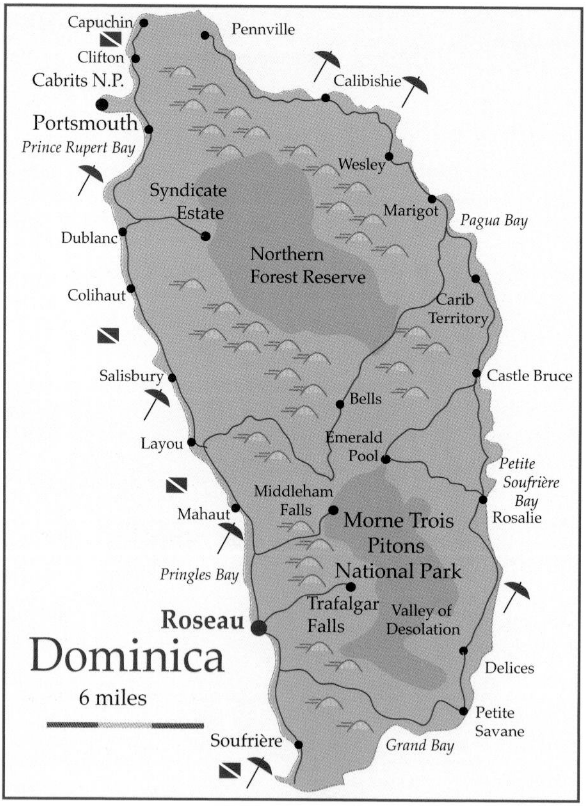

that sustain many island residents.

The feature that creates a rain forest on Dominica but only modest rainfall on some other islands is the height of the north-south mountains –almost a mile. They serve to scrape the rain out of the prevailing trade winds and fill the streams. **Middleham Falls** offers a more vigorous hiking experience for those wanting to get deeper into the rain forest: a 45-minute hike to this 400 foot cascade.

Boiling Lake, located deep within the park, is actually the flooded top of a small fumarole–sort of a tiny volcanic steam vent. Just 200 feet across, it is full of almost boiling water through which steam bubbles vigorously. The trail to the lake crosses **Desolation Valley**, sort of a moonscape where the fumes from sulphur springs have killed all but the hardiest vegetation.

Unfortunately, the lake and the valley are only accessed by a winding foot path. A lake round trip takes seven to eight hours, so only the fittest travelers should attempt this journey if they want to make it back aboard before the ship leaves!

A great excursion involves kayaking from Soufrière to Champagne, an excellent snorkeling site.

Soufrière is a small fishing village five miles south of Rosseau. Just the road alone is worth the trip. It winds through a number of small coastal towns, climbs very steep bluffs to plunge suddenly into Soufrière. It is the base for some remarkable diving opportunities. Dominica was hailed in several diving magazines as one of the ten best dive destinations in the world. What is really fascinating about a dive or snorkel excursion here is that not only do you get to see some really exquisite dive sites, but the dive base is located in an extremely scenic coastal fishing village.

Dominica is a volcanic island, and its beaches are mostly black sand. The best beaches are on the northeast side of the island, like **Hodges Beach**. But be aware–this is the windward side and surf and currents can be strong. Closer to town is **Picard Beach**, 20 miles up the west coast, and popular with both windsurfers and snorkelers.

A really nifty spot is **Champagne**, near Soufrière. Here a volcanic vent bubbles hot gas up through the shallow bottom. If the snorkel excursion is full, or you just have a few extra hours, consider renting some snorkel gear from your ship and ask a taxi driver to take you to the rocky beach just inshore of the bubbling area. It's a pretty unique experience to swim down and feel the warm gas bubbling up from the ocean floor!

AT A GLANCE

- 464 sq. miles.
- Rugged and mountainous.
- Independent ex-British colony.
- 75,000 residents.
- Rural,with less development than nearby islands.
- Becoming popular as an eco-tourism destination.
- Excellent diving.

Excursion catamaran at Bridgetown. This trip combines a few hours of trade winds sailing with a stop at an excellent snorkeling site.

Barbados

Set apart from its neighbors by 100 miles of water, Barbados is both the largest and most populated of the Lesser Antilles. Though discovered by the Portuguese in 1536, it wasn't settled until the British arrived in 1627. Spared the back and forth colonial ownership of smaller islands, Barbados remained continually under British rule until 1966, when it became an independent member of the British Commonwealth of Nations.

High enough to scrape rain out of the passing clouds, for centuries the business of Barbados was sugar cane. A plantation culture developed and thousands of slaves were brought over from Africa to work the fields. A major sugar producer, the economic and political power of Barbados was significant.

Today, like much of the Caribbean, the biggest resource is its white sand beaches and other visitor attractions.

English traditions run deep here. Most islanders belong to the Anglican church and are extremely well-spoken in the local version of the King's English. Cricket and afternoon tea are respected cultural traditions, and even dress here is apt to be more formal than islands that were former French or Dutch colonies.

The **Platinum Beach** is the nickname for the area along the west coast facing the Caribbean, and very popular with British visitors. Americans and Canadians prefer the faster lifestyle of the resorts, night clubs, and hotels along the south coast, while locals prefer to spend their vacations along the rugged east coast, facing the Atlantic Ocean.

AT A GLANCE

- 294 sq. miles.
- 100 miles east of other Caribbean islands.
- English, some French spoken.
- Currency: Barbados Dollar = .50 US $
- Population: about 260,000.
- Excellent beaches and strong tourism industry .

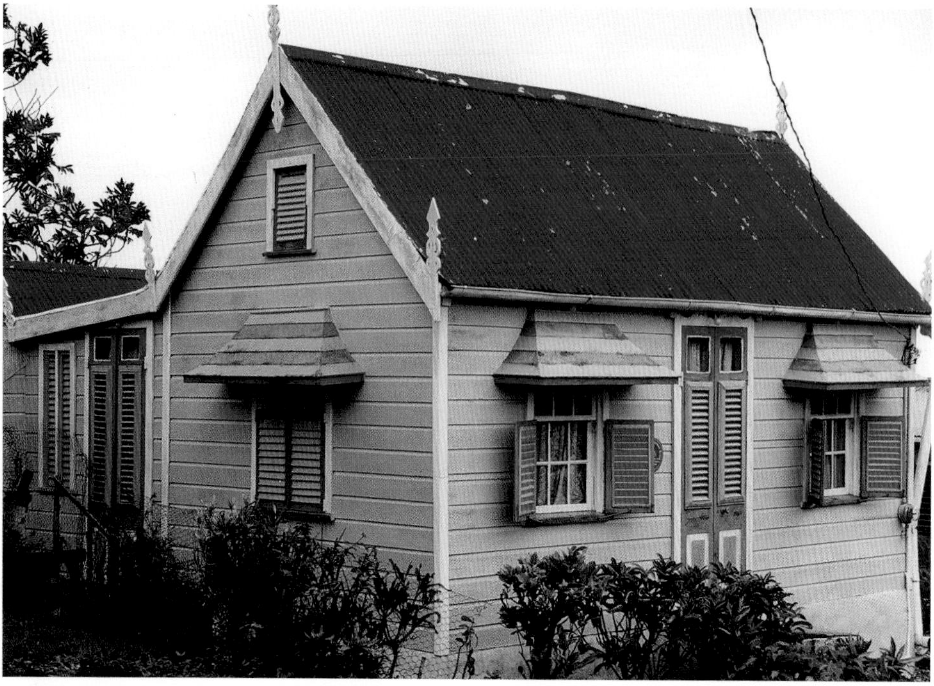

A so called chattel house, dating back to sugar cane days. Sort of a kit house, it was designed to be easily assembled. It's not uncommon for these to be taken apart, put on the back of a truck, and taken to a new location.

Your ship arrives in **Bridgetown** and ties up a short distance from the new cruise ship terminal. Bridgetown itself is about a mile from the terminal, a hot dusty walk, so you might want to consider a cab for around $5. The island is pretty big, so if you really want to get out and see something of the country, you're better off taking a tour or hiring a taxi for a few hours. Settle on price and specifics before you go.

Beaches on the west coast and south coast are about a 15-minute or $8 taxi ride away. Don't worry about private property; by law all beaches in Barbados are open to the public.

Windsurfers say Barbados is as good as Hawaii. Try **Casuarina Beach** and **Silver Sands Beach** on the south coast. Snorkelers favor glassy **Mullins Bay** on the west coast. Best surfing is on the east coast near **Bathsheba**.

Golf is available at **Sandy Lane Hotel.** A cab is about $13, but make a course reservation.

East of Bridgetown is an area of sugar cane fields, with **Francia** and **Sunbury Plantation Houses** open to the public. Nearby is the **Gun Hill Signal Station**, where sightings of approaching sailing ships were relayed to British naval forces.

The interior of central and northern Barbados is rugged and hilly, unsuitable for sugar culture. If gardening excites you, consider stops at **Welchman Hall Gully** and the nearby **Flower Forest.** Continuing east, you will come to the very rugged northeast coast, whose attractions include **Andromeda Gardens** and **St. Nicholas Abbey**, dating from 1650.

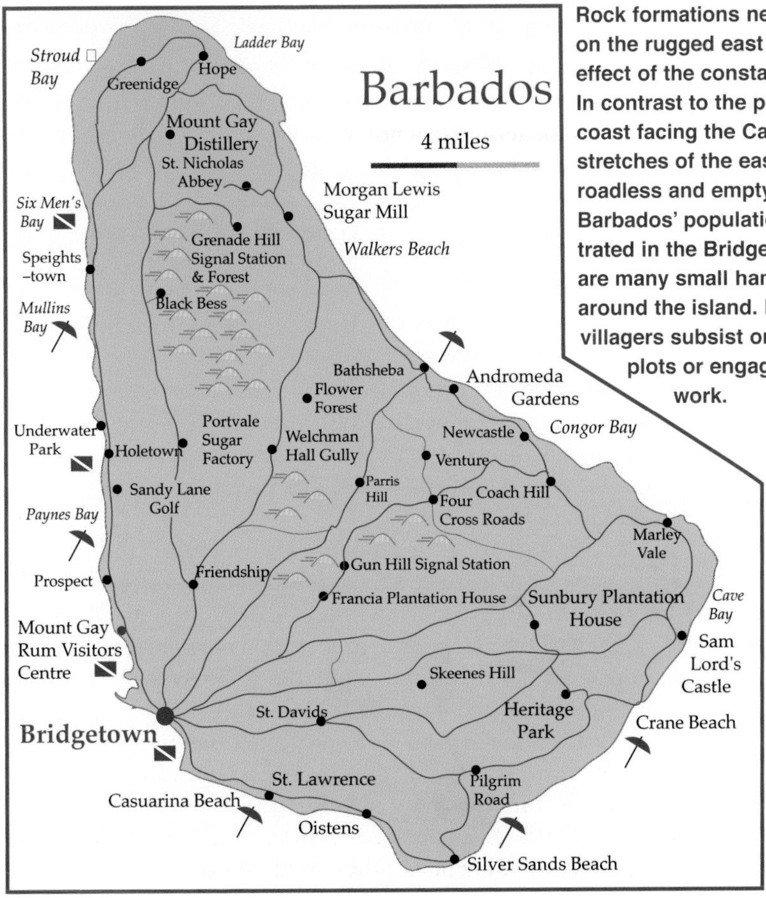

Rock formations near Newcastle on the rugged east coast show the effect of the constant Atlantic surf. In contrast to the populated west coast facing the Caribbean, stretches of the east coast are roadless and empty. While most of Barbados' population is concentrated in the Bridgetown area, there are many small hamlets scattered around the island. Many of these villagers subsist on small farm plots or engage in small craft work.

Above and right: Sheltered Marigot Bay was the place where a British admiral covered his ships with palm fronds to hide them from the French. Today you'll find good snorkeling plus lots of hotels and restaurants and yachts. DV Photos.

St. Lucia

It's probably a good thing that Columbus didn't land here or history might have been very different, for its fierce inhabitants killed or drove off two groups of English that tried to settle here in the early 1600's. Finally the French arrived in greater numbers and 1651 and stayed.

But the English hungered for this lush spot and regularly sent warships to capture it. Possession of St. Lucia changed hands 14 times before England finally captured it for good in 1814. This was the sugar cane era and the makeup of the population changed rapidly as slaves were imported from West Africa.

Large coal deposits were discovered in the 1860's at a time when steam was appearing on world trade routes, and St. Lucia quickly became an important coaling station. By around 1960, bananas, locally known as figs, had replaced sugar as the main cash crop.

Becoming an independent state within the British Commonwealth in 1979, St. Lucia still retains a strong French influence in island dialect or patois, cuisine, and place names.

The many hotels and inns are mostly located on the northern part of the island, while the southern part is mostly thick rain forest and banana plantations.

Most cruise ships arrive at protected **Castries**, the capital on the northeast coast. Unfortunately much of the fine colonial architecture that once stood here was lost to fire, but it's one of the Caribbean's busiest ports, with freighters as well as cruise ships coming and going, so there's lots of activity.

AT A GLANCE

- 30 x 12 Miles.
- Mountainous with much rain forest.
- Independent, in British Commonwealth.
- Language: English.
- Currency: E.C Dollar.
- Population: about 150,000.
- Major tourist destination with many luxury beachfront resorts.
- Excellent beaches, diving and snorkeling.
- Significant French influence.

Pointe Seraphine is the shopping facility created specifically for cruise ship passengers, a 20-minute walk north around the harbor from the center of town. Usually when passenger ships are in port there is a convenient launch shuttle service.

Don't miss the buildings downtown with the bright red roofs. These produce and craft markets are busy colorful places and are good spots to pick up locally produced spices, wood carvings or other excellent local crafts.

Derek Walcott Square in the center of town honors the island poet who won a Nobel prize in 1992. It's also the location of some of the few major colonial buildings that survived the fires.

Ft. Charlotte, built on steep Morne Fortune, was the place where the English and the French battled for control more than once. It's worth a trip, if just for the great views it affords.

Excellent beaches are nearby. All beaches on St. Lucia are open to the public. Most of the beaches on the west or Caribbean coast are also the site of hotels which may offer waters sports equipment rentals, restaurants, etc. If it's a secluded beach you're looking for, you're better off on the east or Atlantic coast, where, exposed to the steady trade winds, the surf often runs high.

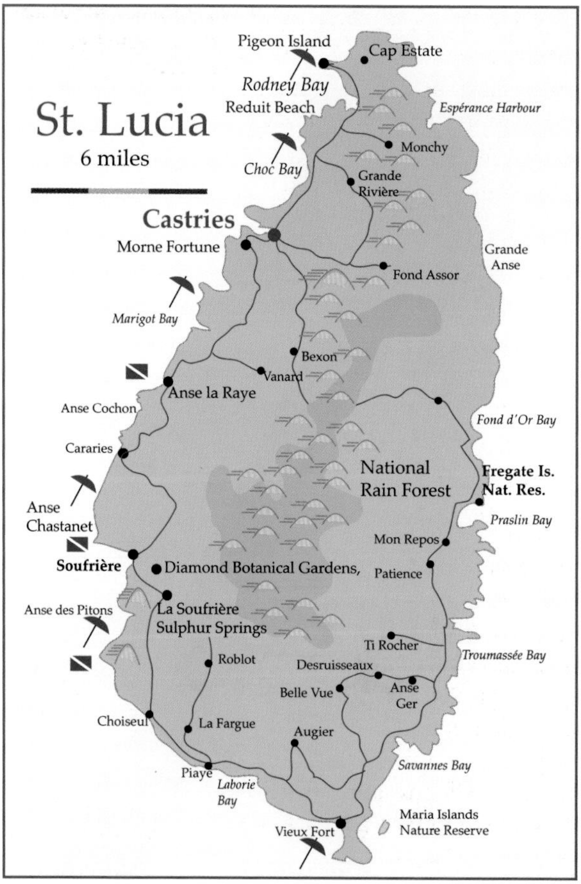

Several good beaches are located within a few miles of Castries. Popular choices are **Reduit Beach**, about 5 miles north, and nearby **Choc Beach**. The yachting center of St. Lucia, **Rodney Bay**, is just to the north. Glitzy and surrounded by restaurants and hotels, it really gets busy in December when the many yachts participating in the Atlantic Rally for Cruisers arrive in town from Europe.

Popular with families with children is **Pigeon Island**, just north of Rodney Bay. Connected by a causeway, this 44-acre island is a popular venue for concerts, as well as having calm beaches, a museum, and interpretive center.

Most sightseeing trips focus on the less developed south coast including a stop at **Soufrière**, a two-hour drive

south of Castries. Expect a small town (8,000 folks) with a strong French flavor, excellent colonial architecture and fishing boats on the beach. Occasionally cruise ships will stop here, mooring in the bay and sending passengers ashore by tender.

A number of good dive sites, including a wreck in 65 feet of water and several dramatic walls, are located off Soufrière.
PG Photo.

If the wind is right you'll get a whiff of **La Soufrière Volcano**, located four miles east of town. Nicknamed the "drive-in volcano," actually it's more like a sulphur spring where you can wander around the steaming pools. Pretty interesting, but the odor can be strong on a hot day.

Probably the best beach near Soufrière is **Anse Chastanet**, a volcanic, dark sand beach with great diving and snorkeling on the nearby reefs. A hotel south of town imported white sand to cover the dark at **Anse des Pitons**, another exquisite spot with great diving.

Diamond Botanical Gardens, near Soufriére, was the place where a bathhouse was constructed for French King Louis XVI's troops to soak and get away from the rigors of the steamy climate. Today you'll find lush gardens, a dramatic waterfall and mineral baths–bring your swimsuit and it's a fun place for kids as well.

If you're looking for wildlife and have a bit more time, consider a visit to either the **Fregate Island Nature Reserve** or the **Maria Islands Nature Reserve**. Both are on the east coast of the island and tours can be arranged through the St. Lucia National Trust. **The Pitons**, the visual icon for the island, rise steeply east of town. Ironically, the taller is Petit Piton, at 2,619 feet. If you're really in good shape, there's a climb up Gros Piton (2,461 feet), but you'll need permission from the Forest and Lands Department and a guide that will cost around $45. But check to make sure you'll have enough time to get back to your ship before departure.

With more uninhabited islands than almost anywhere else in the Caribbean, the Grenadines are the dream destination of many yacht owners.
DV Photo.

St. Vincent and The Grenadines

For decades the island chain that stretches like the tail of a kite for 45 miles southwest of St. Vincents was sort of a Shangri La for yachtsmen. They'd leave chilly New England or the provinces of Eastern Canada in the fall, working their way down the eastern seaboard and cross the Gulf Stream to the Bahamas. From there the larger boats would head offshore for Antigua or St. Thomas, and the smaller boats would begin their winding journey along The Thorny Path.

Arriving at the Grenadines–an archipelago of a dozen or so larger islands and smaller rocks and cays–was always a moment of celebration. With little development even now, life on these islands went on much as it had for generations.

The construction of a new cruise ship dock in **Kingston** is bringing more visitors here. But still for the most part, St. Vincent is primarily rain forest, growing bananas and other produce for export, and dominated by Soufriére, which reminded locals in 1979 that it is still considered an active volcano.

The island passed back and forth between the British and the French, including one embarrassing episode in 1779. When several French ships sailed into Kingston, the entire British fighting force was away, working on the governor's plantation, and no one in town could find the keys to the gun battery!

After the British regained the island in 1783, many French stayed, joining with slaves in a particularly nasty revolt. Some

AT A GLANCE

- 18 x 11 Miles.
- Mountainous with much rain forest.
- Independent, in British Commonwealth.
- Language: English.
- Currency: E.C Dollar
- Population: about 103,000 on St. Vincent, another 9,000 scattered among the Grenadines.
- Low key tourism and agriculture.

planters had the gruesome fate of being fed into their own cane-crushing machinery. To avoid further troubles, thousands of these slaves were deported to British Honduras.

Check out the waterfront in downtown **Kingston**; you'll find bustling produce markets offering some excellent local crafts as well. Like most of the Eastern Caribbean, vendors and shopkeepers are used to offering a fixed price and not dickering for discounts.

The waterfront is also the place where all the little local freighters, some sailing sloops, load their varied cargos to take to the small islands of the Grenadines. You'll see small craft from all over the Caribbean and South America.

There are two unusual churches in town, the pastel **St. Georges Anglican Cathedral**, and the somewhat odd-looking **St. Mary's Roman Catholic Church**, with its bizarre combination of classic and moorish stying.

The **Botanical Gardens** above downtown are certainly worth a visit. It was here that Captain Bligh's breadfruit tree, imported from Tahiti, was established as a food for slaves. Though the gardens are free, you might want to consider the services of one of the guides hanging out around the entrance –they'll liven up your visit with a lot of local color!

"Stick a pencil in the ground and it will grow." was how one observer described the verdant rain forest of St. Vincents.
DV Photo.

Local produce stacked on the Kingston docks is ready for shipment to the smaller islands of the Grenadines.

Being volcanic, most of the beaches on St. Vincents are black or brown sand. **Villa**, two miles south of Kingston, is the primary center for hotel based tourism. All beaches are public except, naturally, the one nice white sand beach, on Young Island just off Villa, which is private. As in almost every island in the Eastern Caribbean, the beaches on the west, or Caribbean side, are much calmer than on the east, or Atlantic side, where the steady trade winds create an almost constant rough surf.

On the eastern side of the bay at Kingston is **Fort Charlotte** on the top of a 600 foot-tall promontory. It's worth a hike up–the views are wonderful. And you'll notice something not seen much in Caribbean forts–the cannons face back into the island. When it was constructed, the threat was from unruly natives.

If you take a car there are a number of beaches and fishing villages along the coast road north of Kingston that are worth a visit.

You can hike up to the top of the **volcano** for some great views, both into the crater, and if it's not cloudy, up and down the Windward Islands. But don't underestimate it–you'll need stamina, water, and good shoes, as well as most of a day to make it. The best way to do it is to arrange for a guide through the St. Vincent Board of Tourism in Kingston and make sure there's enough time to get back to your ship before dpearture.

The Grenadines are the island chain that stretches south toward Grenada. Part of the charm of these islands, especial-

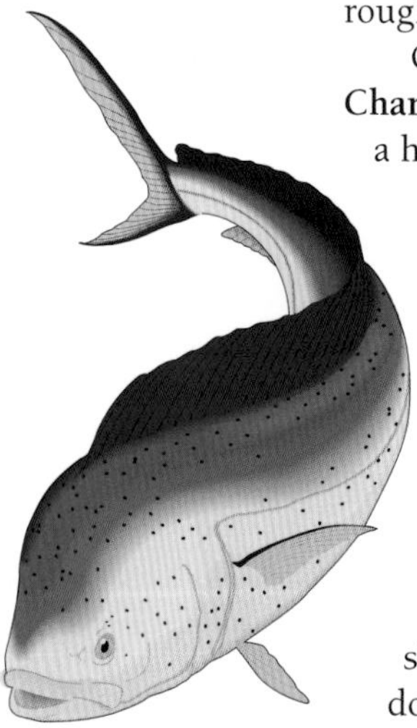

Brightly colored **DOLPHIN**, also known as mahi-mahi, are a popular menu item with sailors.

ly for yachtsmen, is that most of them are uninhabited, little sand and palm tree dots, the perfect Caribbean anchorage.

Bequia, just an hour's ferry ride from Kingston, is the largest of the Grenadines. The ferry docks at the quaint settlement of Port Elizabeth, where in addition to waterfront shops and restaurants, there are water taxis to nearby beaches. Further north along Front Street from the ferry dock are open air produce and craft markets. as well as a number of shops where model boat builders both create and feature their exquisite work.

Whaling was a tradition here for generations. Fishermen here are allowed to catch just three whales a year; however, few have been caught in recent years. A tiny whaling museum, operated by Athneal Olivierre, "last of Bequia's harpooners," is located at Paget Farm on the south coast. Just offshore is Petit Nevis, where the whales were once cut up.

Sleepy **Canouan**, located halfway down the Grenadines, is just beginning to welcome visitors to its white sand beaches. As one guidebook puts it, "Goat-herding is still a career choice here." Welcome to the forgotten Caribbean!

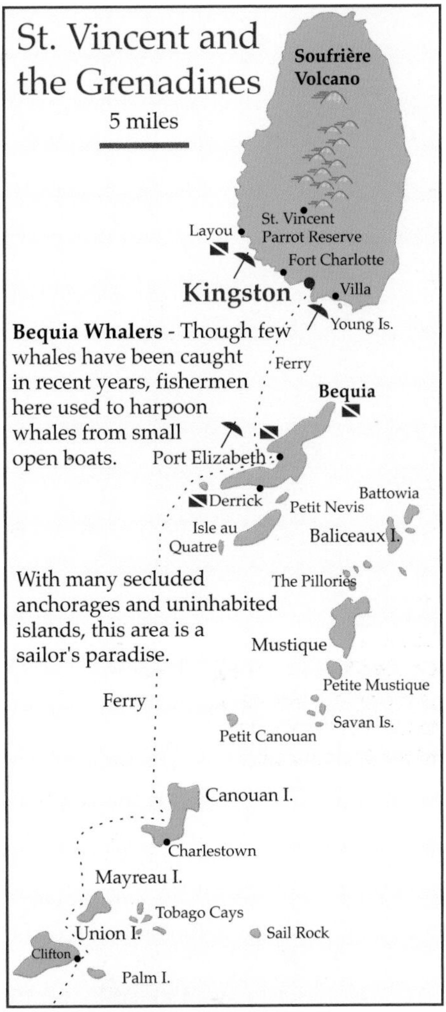

The beaches here are great, but a building ordinance that limits buildings to no higher than a palm tree means development remains low key.
DV Photos.

GRENADA

When your ship docks at **St. George's**, you'll be in one of the most picturesque ports in the entire region. The steep-sided harbor is actually the crater of an extinct volcano, complete with a tunnel bored through the side of the mountain to the other side of town.

Supposedly named by Spanish sailors for the hills of southern Spain that it reminded them of, the island, like many in the region, bounced back and forth between France and England until Britain came out on top in 1783.

The defining event in Grenada's economic history came around 1830 when according to local legend, a doctor arrived from the so called "Spice Islands" of the East Indies–Indonesia –carrying some nutmeg trees. Taking his leisure with a rum toddy, he noted that the taste lacked something. He plucked a nutmeg off a tree, grated it into the drink and lo, an industry was born!

It came at a fortuitous time–the local economy was at a low ebb; and raising and processing spices was well-suited for the land and natives. When disease struck the East Indies plantations where most of Europe's spices came from, the boom was on!

After becoming independent in 1974, Grenada pretty much cruised below much of the world's radar screen until it suddenly exploded onto front pages nine years later when the US, fearing a Marxist-Leninist takeover, sent in an invasion

AT A GLANCE

- 21 x 12 Miles.
- Mountainous with much rain forest.
- Independent.
- Language: English.
- Population: 90,000.
- A major spice producer, the only Caribbean "Spice Island."
- Excellent beaches, diving and snorkeling.
- Just 100 miles from South America.

force that stormed ashore, much to the surprise of startled vacationers. Today islanders remember the event as the "intervention," and generally regard it as a positive event.

You'll come ashore by tender in the **Careenage**, named for the old practice of hauling boats on their sides here to clean their bottoms. Today it's a busy waterfront with yachts as well as colorful local craft that take produce and freight to many of the smaller islands that form the **Grenadines**, stretching away to the north.

Don't miss going into the local markets right on the waterfront. The bustle of produce and craft vendors, the pungent aroma of local spices, the colors, the noise–all make for a powerful experience. While you can't bring fruit back to the US, spices are presently okay (check with your ship), and there are some great values here.

In the waterfront markets, vendors offer craft items, spices, and produce.

Near the ridge above the Careenage is the **Grenada National Museum**, and nearby the short (350-foot) Sendall Tunnel through the hilltop to the bay side of town, called the **Esplanade**. If you are here on a Saturday, ask your way to the market square where local spice and produce vendors will have their offerings spread out on the sidewalk. Many of the government buildings perch on the hillside above the Esplanade with excellent views.

Most of the resort development is along **Grande Anse**, a two-mile-long white sand beach south of town. In the next cove to the west is quiet **Mourne Rouge Beach**. If you're looking for a bit of fun, try the little bar-restaurant-water sports rental spot at the very end of **Tamarind Beach.** They have kayaks here as well as snorkel gear, etc.

If you rent a car, try going north of St. George's following the Caribbean. Take the sign to **Concord Falls**; you'll wind up going through spice and cocoa plantations to the first falls. From here there is a path through the forest to the two upper falls, each with a swimming pool.

Back on the coast road north, a great stop is the fishing village of **Gouyave**, where you'll find locally built boats drawn up on the beach and the **Grenada Nutmeg Cooperative**. It's a great place to experience spice production a little further.

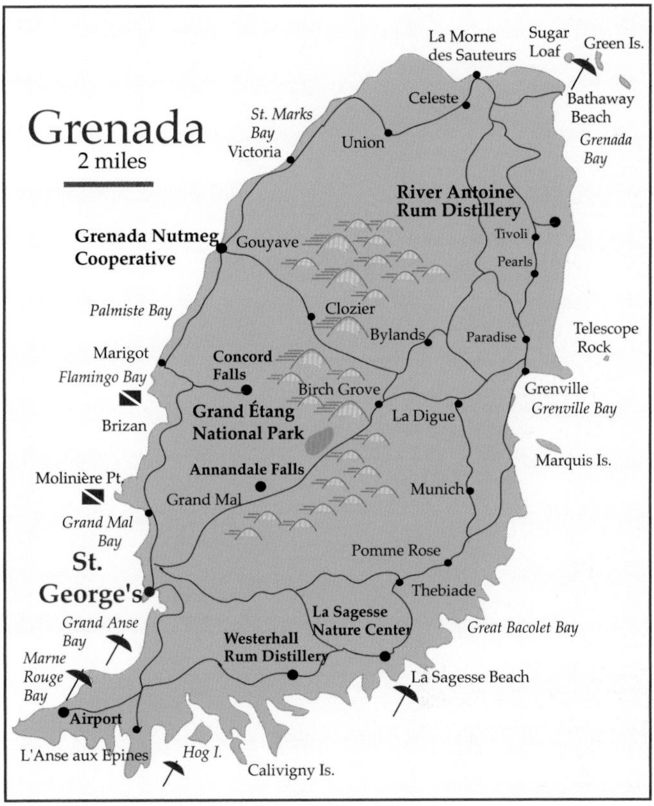

Continuing further, the road curves around the rugged north tip of the island and parallels the rough Atlantic, traveling inland through several picturesque villages. At Grenville take the cross island road east, climbing up into the rain forest, past **Annandale Falls** and **Grand Étang National Park.** There are a number of hiking trails here, including one up to a crater lake and a longer one that leads back to upper Concord Falls.

Fortunately for snorkelers, one of the best sites on Grenada, is Molinière Point, just north of St. George's. Divers especially like the wreck of the 600- foot cruise ship *Bianca C.*, which burned in 1961, and conveniently sank in around 100 feet of water, creating excellent habitat for many species.

Divers especially like the wreck of the Bianca C., conveniently located in 100 feet of water off St. George's. PG photo.

In the harbor at Oranjestad, you'll see glitzy yachts along with small inter-island freighters and fishing boats.

Right: At a hair braiding kiosk near the docks.

ARUBA

If only the Spaniards could have thought, "Beaches!" When they first passed this way in their search for gold and other riches, they dismissed this dry island just 15 miles off the coast of Venezuela as an "isla inutil" (useless island).

For a century or so, economics here centered around ranching and horse breeding. Gold was the next little boom after it was discovered in 1824, but the first real solid modern employment base began in 1924 with the construction of an oil refinery at Sint Nicholas, on the southern tip of the island. By then Aruba was part of the ABC islands of the Netherlands Antilles, B and C being Bonaire and Curaçao.

The refinery complex brought a new prosperity to the island At its peak in 1949, it employed over 8,000 people and attracted many immigrants to the island. The oil boom peaked in World War II as much of the refinery output went to fuel the Allied war effort. The oil wealth transformed Aruba with rapid growth and one of the highest standards of living in the Caribbean Basin. The refinery complex closed in 1985, though a smaller refinery opened a few years later, and the government and merchants of Aruba realized that their best choice for a prosperous future lay in encouraging tourism.

It was a wise move. Its beaches, especially on the northwest coast, were perfect for resort style hotel development and its clear warm waters with excellent visibility made it an inviting spot for snorkelers and scuba diving enthusiasts as well. Most

AT A GLANCE

- 20 x 6 Miles.
- Flat and dry.
- Independent.
- Language: Dutch, Spanish & English.
- Population: 72,000.
- Major tourist destination with many luxury beach resorts.
- Great beaches, diving and snorkeling.

Like most of the Caribbean, the old ways and the new are often side by side. Here a native sloop, used for freight and fishing, is hauled up on the beach for repair next to the waterfront casino and shopping complex.

of Aruba's hotels are concentrated in the area along **Eagle** and **Palm Beaches**, beginning about 4.5 miles west along the shore road from Oranjestad.

Cruise ships generally tie up at the big wharf in downtown **Oranjestad.** The craft markets and a big shopping complex are right across from the wharf. A short taxi ride along L.G. Smith Boulevard for about four miles to the west will take you past Druif Bay to excellent beaches and the main hotel and resort area.

The oldest building in Aruba is here. **Fort Zoutman** was originally built right on the water, but since it was built in 1796 the harbor in front was filled to create more land. Oranjestad also features three small, but very good museums: historical, numismatic, and archaeological.

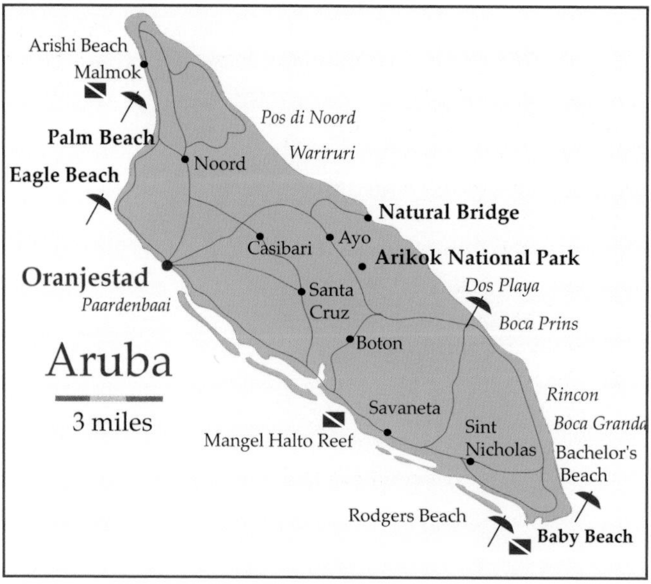

If you want to snorkel and excursions are full, there will be tour vendors on shore. A restored sailboat, the *Mi Dushi,* offers a popular four-hour snorkel and lunch cruise.

Schooner Harbor, right next to the cruise

ship wharf, is a great opportunity to have a look at the small craft that serve many of the islands. These small freighters, with their crews unloading produce by hand into pickup trucks, serve the less developed ports of the Caribbean. Many are from Venezuelan ports. You may also see local sailing schooners here, which are still used in the freight hauling trade all throughout the region.

Renting a jeep is a great way to see this roughly 20-mile-long island. If you don't rent through your ship, a number of car rental agencies are located close to the dock, along L.G. Smith Blvd. A good tour is your basic loop, following the island's perimeter roads.

The Dutch influence is very strong throughout all the ABC islands.

Eagle Beach was designated one of the ten best beaches in the world by *Travel and Leisure* magazine. Before time-share condominiums began to be built here, this was a sleepy corner of the island, a gorgeous almost deserted beach. Those days are gone.

If you want water sports, **Palm Beach**, the most northerly of the three, has the best offerings.

Some of the best dive sites, including the wreck of the ship *Antilla*, scuttled here in 1940, are along this coast.

Did you bring young children? **Baby Beach**, near the south end, is perfect: shallow and placid.

The east, or windward coast, exposed to the trade winds, is much less settled than the Caribbean or leeward side. If you want to swim here, exercise care–expect rough seas and strong currents. The **Natural Bridge** is where wind and waves have created a coral arch. There's a café here as well and it's a good chance to see how different the windward side of the island is.

When oil drove the Aruba economy, **Sint Nicolas** was a bustling port. Now it's undergoing a major facelift to make it an attractive stop for visitors. There are a lot of craft vendors' stalls on Main Street, and Charlie's Bar and Restaurant is a popular watering hole.

Take a ferry across the harbor to the Punda district–just like Amsterdam, only warmer.
***Right*: snorkelers at Knip Bay.**
DV photos

CURAÇAO

Squint when you come into the harbor of **Willemstad**, and you'll swear you are in Holland. The C of the ABC islands of the Dutch Antilles (Bonaire and Aruba are the others), Curaçao has the air of a place that had always been part of the same culture. Once the Dutch arrived here in 1634 (they did have to throw out a few Spaniards), they stayed. Quickly seeing the advantage of Willemstad's excellent harbor, they built a fortified town and created an economy based on free trade of sugar, gold, and other goods, as well as the largest slave market in the Caribbean. A few hardy landowners built plantations, but the dry climate made agriculture a challenging business.

The modern Curaçao economy began in 1918 with construction of the world's largest oil refinery drawing workers from all around the Caribbean and beyond, and creating a tolerant multi-ethnic culture. Today, sun, sand, and great diving and snorkeling attract the people to fuel a different economy.

Cruise ships arrive in the **Otrabanda quarter**. There is a new shopping complex along the waterfront near the docks, but don't miss the opportunity to cross the bridge or take a ferry across the harbor to the **Punda District** with the gorgeous row of brightly painted buildings and street cafés facing

AT A GLANCE

- 150 square miles.
- Flat and very dry.
- Dutch colony.
- Language: Dutch, English & Papamiento.
- Population: 55,000.
- Oil refinery-based economy slowly giving way to tourism.
- Very close to South America.
- Excellent diving.

Fishing boats at Lagun Beach, about 10 miles west of Willemstad. Locals feel this is some of the best snorkeling on the entire island. DV Photo.

the water. There's more shopping here, with two streets, Heerenstaat and Gomezplein, set up as pedestrian-only areas. Walking to the left along the waterfront will take you to a narrower channel that is the site of the **mercado flotante**, or floating market. Here you'll see dozens of native sailing schooners from Venezuela, as well as small inter-island freighters from all over the Caribbean. It's a colorful and frenetic place. The best action is early, but there's plenty going on all day long. Not to be missed!

Dominating the southwest corner of Punda is **Fort Amsterdam.** Once the center of the city, now it houses the governor's residence, offices and Fort Church. If you're interested in history, across the Wilhelmina drawbridge is the **Maritime Museum**, or the **Curaçao Museum**, west of the docks.

Curaçao is a great place to rent a car or jeep and head out for a beach and countryside tour. A nice place to start is **Daai Booi beach**, about 10 miles west of Willemstad. It's public, and has a snack bar plus rest rooms and pretty good snorkeling.

Ten miles further west is **Lagun Beach**, with good snorkeling and popular with locals. Two more miles takes you to **Knip Bay.** There are two really nice beaches here, but be cautious about getting under the trees for shade–they are manchineels, whose leaves exude a fluid that irritates the skin, so be careful. Once you go around the tip of the island and start down the north coast, you'll be in the trade winds where the beaches are generally too rough for good swimming. Follow signs to dramatic **Boka Tabla**, where the ocean has carved large grottos, some used by nesting birds.

While you're on the northeast end of the island, consider a visit to **Christoffel Park**. You'll find 4,500 acres of garden and wildlife preserve. It gets pretty warm here, so early is better.

Don't just be looking for big critters when you dive or snorkel–there's a lot going on at the macro level as well, like this small shrimp walking on a big starfish. PG Photo.

Four miles south of Willemstad is the **Curaçao Seaquarium**. This is a lot more than just another aquarium. Besides some 40-plus excellent specimen tanks, multi-media show, and glass-bottomed boats, they have something called the **Animal Encounters** section. It is a series of enclosed salt water ponds, where you can swim and even feed rays, toothless sharks and the like. There is a package price that includes diving instruction if you want, and it is definitely an exciting way to get down and close with sea life. Plus, right out front is one of the nicer beaches on the island, protected by a breakwater, and with a restaurant, water sports center, etc. You do, however, have to pay around $2.50 a person to get in.

A favorite place for divers and snorkelers is the excellent **Curaçao Underwater Marine Park**, which occupies about 10 miles on the southeast side of the island. Visibility is excellent and the water is quite warm.

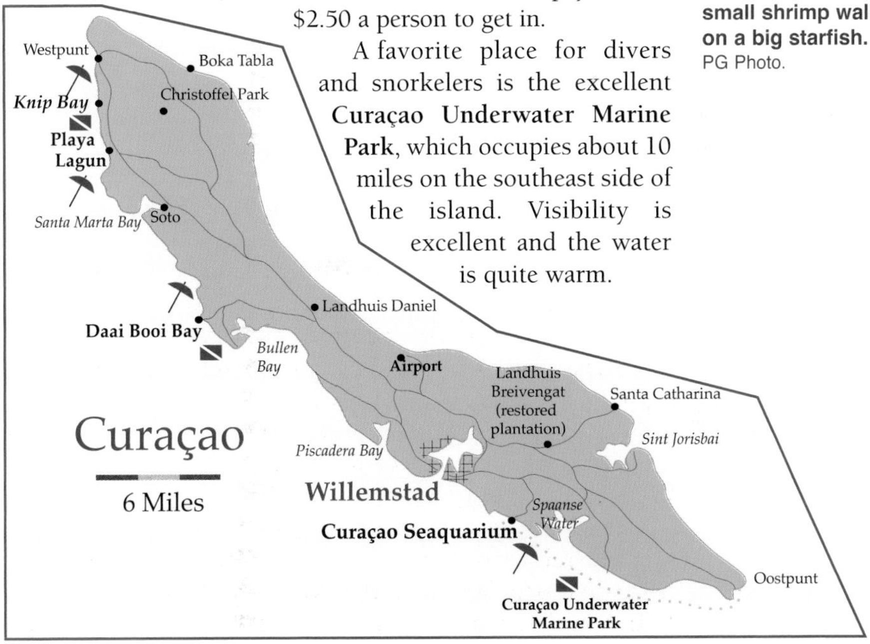

Churches dominate the skyline of the walled city that is the core of downtown Cartagena.
Right: a vendor in Las Bovedas carefully watches his wares.

CARTAGENA, COLOMBIA

Cartagena is South America in all its gritty, bustling glory: men with huge parrots or three-toed sloths on their shoulders looking to sell you an photo opportunity with their pet; vendors constantly plucking at your sleeve to buy a hat or a piece of carved or woven art; churches as grand as in Spain; a fortress-like walled city once built to protect Spanish treasure and the biggest African slave market in the Caribbean basin.

In its infancy, beginning in 1533, Cartagena was the only Spanish port on the South American mainland, and the port for all the gold and silver looted from the natives. This fact wasn't lost on English buccaneer Sir Francis Drake, who torched the city and 200 houses before taking over 100,000 gold coins and sailing off to England in 1586.

The walls that form the **Ciudad Amurallada** came next and today surround the oldest part of town. The newer parts of the city, with most of the high rises and restaurants, stretch southeast along the peninsula that forms the **Bocagrande** district.

Within a short distance from each other in the walled city are some excellent sites. The **Cathedral** with its huge gilded altar is a must see, as is the **Palacio de la Inquisición**, where infidels and doubters were stretched on racks, which are on display as well. **Plaza Santo Domingo** features a church dating to 1539 and gets extra busy after dark when all its restaurants and bars fill up.

A great fort that overlooks much of the city is the **Castillo**

AT A GLANCE

- Major bustling city.
- Rich colonial heritage.
- Core is walled city.
- Language: Spanish.
- Good local crafts.

Cartagena's colonial heritage is evident in its architecture. Below: the parrot's owner makes his living by offering it to travelers to have their photo taken with it.

de San Felipe de Barajas. If you haven't yet explored one of the old Spanish forts that rim the Caribbean basin, this is an excellent one, designed to still protect the defenders even if part of it was overrun.

Cerro de la Popa is one of the highest points in the city, topped by a monastery turned chapel. The views are terrific; fortunately a visit is included in most city tours.

Don't miss the area called **Las Bovedas** in the northern tip of the walled city. Here, a large number of craft vendors have set up shop in a row of what used to be storage vaults during colonial times. The hustle and bustle can be a little overwhelming, but it is definitely worth a visit just to see the rich variety of local crafts. If it's Colombian emeralds you're after, a good spot to stop is the area around Calle Panteón, next to the cathedral downtown.

There is something called a **Rumba en Chiva** that's pretty popular with the locals. It's a bus, complete with a band playing on its roof that cruises from bar to bar around town.

Looking for a quieter way to see the city? Usually there are a number of horse drawn carriages, or **coches**, that start at the Charleston Hotel or

the Hotel Caribe and take a loop around town. It's better at night when the streets are a bit quieter. . .

There are some beaches right in town that get pretty busy. If you are looking for something a little quieter, consider a 15- minute boat ride to **Playa Blanca**, or an hour trip to **Islas del Rosario.** Boats to both places leave from the Muelle de los Pegasos, the pier just outside the city walls with the big statues of flying horses.

Most city tours will include a stop at Las Bóvedas. Prepare to be amazed at the variety of local crafts on sale.

A "glass bottom" style boat. You walk down a set of stairs to an underwater viewing area.

GRAND CAYMAN

If you only do one dive or snorkel excursion on your cruise, Grand Cayman should be high on the list. Largest of three islands and nicknamed the "**Underwater Capital of the Caribbean**," here you will find large marine sanctuaries with a wide variety of sea life. Many divers come here to experience so called **wall dives.** The north shore drops off steeply into the 25,000-foot depths of the **Cayman Trench**, and exploring the rich life of the steep walls is a remarkable diving experience.

The landscape here is very different from the lush steep islands of the Leewards and Eastern Caribbean. Dry and flat, with no opportunity to grow lucrative sugar cane, the inhabitants here focused on the ocean for their livelihood from the earliest days when sailors frequently stopped here to capture abundant sea turtles. Columbus found so many turtles here that he named the islands Las Tortugas, or Turtle Islands.

Turtle fishing was a major business in the islands until ice and refrigeration was available on ships in the late 1800's. Turtles could be kept alive on board until chow time.

The island was governed by Jamaica until Jamaican independence in 1962, when the Caymans elected to remain as a British Crown Colony.

Well known as merchant seamen and boatbuilders throughout the region, a new era for the islands began in the 1960's when islanders prudently recognized that offshore banking was an excellent opportunity for isolated tropical places and passed appropriate laws.

AT A GLANCE

- 100 sq. miles.
- Flat and dry.
- British Crown colony.
- Highest per capita income in Caribbean due to offshore banking.
- Excellent beaches, diving and snorkeling.

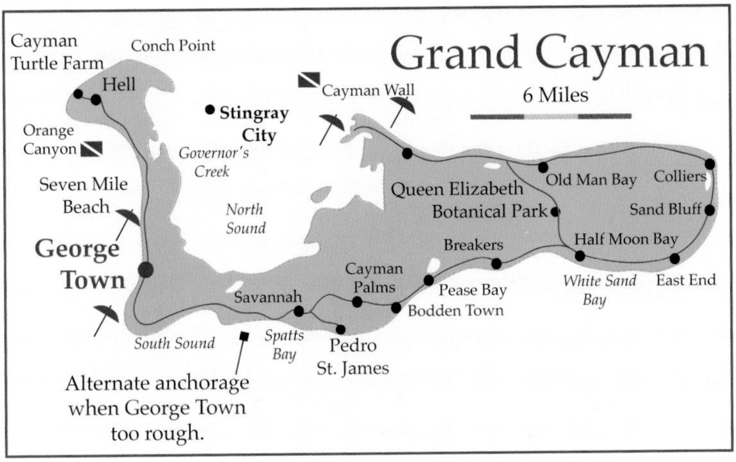

Stingray City is one of the island's most popular attractions. Its shallow water and sand bottom mean that even inexperienced swimmers can get a chance to get close to these big rays. Tip: take off any sharp jewelry –the rays' skin is very soft and easily cut or bruised. DV Photo.

For an unusual underwater experience, several operators offer trips in craft like these. Lowered by cable to depths of up to several hundred feet, viewers are able to observe sea life not seen near the surface.

Their vision was uncannily correct–today the Cayman islands has the highest per capita income of anywhere in the Caribbean, due to offshore banking. In George Town alone, hundreds of offshore banks contribute to a strong economy.

Cruise passengers arrive by tender in downtown **George Town**, where there are a number of small outfits offering dive and snorkel trips. One of the most popular is **Stingray City**, where tame sting rays loll about on a shallow sand bar, allowing visitors to touch them. In the shallower spots, it is only a few feet deep, meaning that it is accessible to snorkelers as well as scuba divers.

Seven Mile Beach, one of the most attractive in the Caribbean, begins just a couple of miles north of the docks. Though it has been developed substantially in recent years, zoning rules have kept hotel construction here below the height of the trees so as to avoid the Miami Beach look. Many passengers find it pleasant to just walk to the left from the downtown docks with their towels and hang out on the beach, doing a little shopping on the way back to the ship.

The **Cayman Turtle Farm** is a popular attraction for visitors. You can try out a turtle burger, but when you shop, be aware that the US and many other countries oppose the importation of turtle-shell products.

They're big but they just take little bites.... Growing to 20 feet long, these **WHALE SHARKS** are occasionally seen cruising the outer edges of the coral walls. They feed by straining plankton through filters like some whales.

LADY LUE
GRAND CAYMAN

The Mayan Riviera

The traditional "Mexican Riviera" began at Acapulco and then spread as a string of beach resorts was developed along the west coast of Mexico: Ixtapa-Zihuatanejo, Puerto Vallarta, Mazatlán, and Huatulco.

Then in the 1970's developers began to focus on the unspoiled beaches and jungle of the eastern side of the Yucatán Peninsula, creating a number of resorts–Isla Mujeres, Cancún, Cozumel, Playa del Carmen, and most recently Costa Maya. With initially cheaper land and lower air fares, especially for travelers from the US East Coast, this area has developed rapidly.

The predominant cultural theme in Yucatán is Mayan culture. Though this civilization was already in decline at the time of the arrival of the Spanish in the 1520's, many of the Mexican natives whom you will see in this area are of Mayan descent.

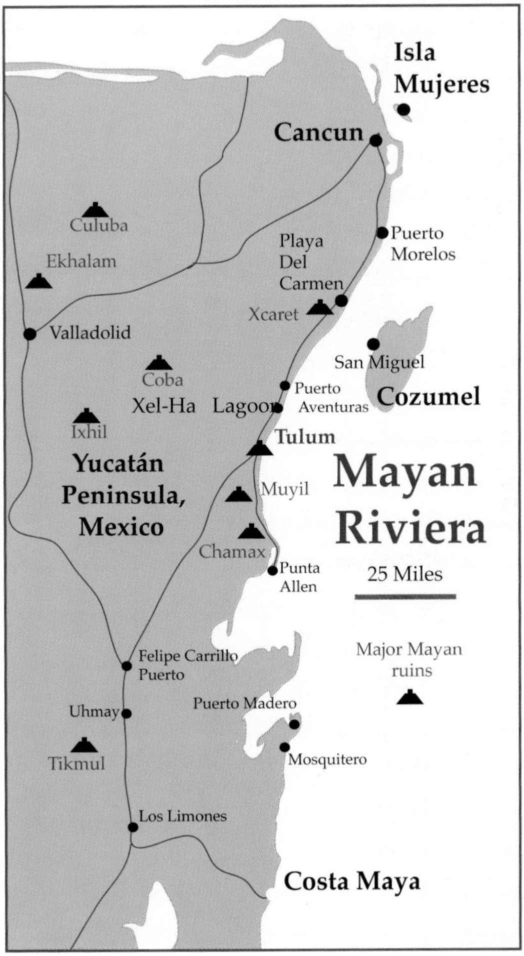

Below: the Mayan ruins at Tulúm, with the high rises of Playa del Carmen in the distance. Left: Maya greeter in Cozumel.

Cozumel

Note the clarity of the water. Cozumel is an excellent place for a dive or snorkel excursion.

Below: Into the caves; but maybe not on your very first dive. . .

As Mexico's largest cruise ship port, expect to find main street, Avenida Rafael Melgar, jammed with shops and street vendors, especially if several ships are in.

But there's much more to this island than the busy waterfront shopping district.

A Mayan sacred place, whose inhabitants were largely killed off by the Spaniards, the island was pretty much forgotten until 1843 when 20 Mexican families settled here. In the early 1900's a brisk trade in chicle–as in chewing gum–from the abundant zapote trees pumped up the local economy for a while, but the event that put Cozumel on the map was the 1961 visit by Jacques Cousteau.

On a personal mission to explore and publicize the world below the ocean's surface with the new scuba gear that he invented, Cousteau was stunned by the beauty of the coral and reef life here. The Mexicans prudently realized that their sea life was more valuable on the bottom than on the table, and created a series of excellent marine parks.

Cruise ships tie up at **San Miguel**, on the leeward side of the island. If you want to hit the beach, the protected, white sand beaches are on this side, while beaches on the eastern, or windward, side are apt to be smaller and rougher. Many passengers

AT A GLANCE

- 9 x 33 mi.
- Flat and dry.
- Part of Mexico.
- Major cruise ship port.
- Wonderful snorkeling and diving.
- Excellent Mexican crafts.

Cozumel is definitely a cruise ship port, with many vendors seeking the almighty American dollar!

travel to **Playa San Francisco**, 10 miles south of town, or **Playa San Juan**, three miles north of town. These beaches do tend to get a bit crowded if there are a lot of ships in town. For more privacy you'll need to go a bit further–the southeast corner of the island has some good beaches, including **Playa Paradiso.** Be extra careful on all these windward beaches, as dangerous undertow currents are common. If you want to hike to some really secluded beaches, there's a path south toward the Punta Celerain Lighthouse, which also goes by the Mayan ruins of **Tumba del Caracol**, but don't miss your ship!

Cozumel is a good place to rent a jeep to explore. But if four-wheeling is your thing, check out the insurance details pretty carefully because many car rental operators have policies denying coverage if you stray from

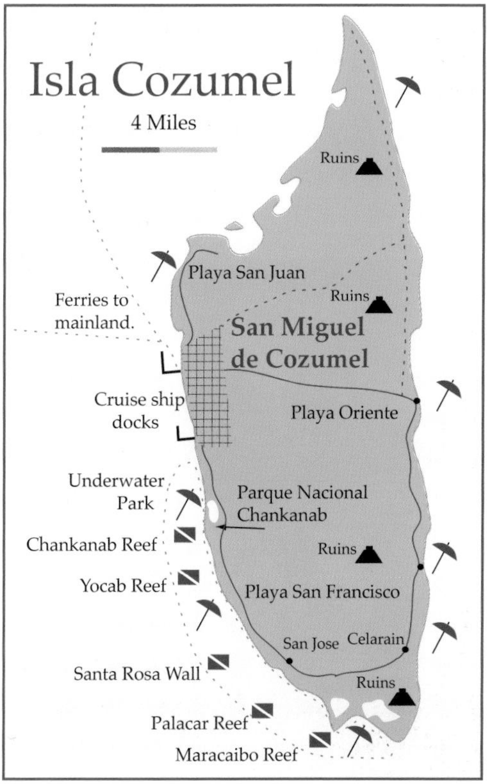

There's an excellent variety of local handicrafts in the waterfront shops here.
Below: Local fishermen land their catches right on the beach in front of downtown.

the pavement. A great loop–get a map –goes south from San Miguel along the shore to the south end of the island, then up the eastern or windward side of the island to **Playa Oriental** where you take the road back to San Miguel. Oriental is a good beach for sunbathing, albeit windy, and beachcombing, but it's not recommended for swimming because of rough surf and current.

This loop takes you past a number of attractions including **Parque Natural Chankanab**, a beach and saltwater lagoon with a number of attractions including an excellent botanical garden and archaeological displays. The beach here is also an excellent place to snorkel. There are a number of Mayan ruins along this loop. The coast road north of Playa Oriente goes to the Mayan ruins at **Castillo Real**, but the road is rugged. You might even see a boa constrictor, crocodile, or iguana sleeping on the nice warm road!

If you want to see some excellent Mayan ruins, consider an excursion to **Tulúm** on the mainland. A major site, overlooking the Caribbean, it is the most popular visitor attraction on the Yucatán Peninsula.

During Carnival in February, huge sculptures decorate the waterfront.

REEF DIVES

Some favorite dives are:

Chankanab Reef: Good drift diving just off of the park, 350 yards offshore, with a lot of caves full of fish. Typically, you will descend to around 40-50 feet, and just float with the current along the reef.

Palancar Reef: Cozumel's best known dive–a large reef about a mile offshore with a multiplicity of coral formations, canyons and zillons of fish. Excellent visibility.

Santa Rosa Wall: Experienced divers only: About 50 feet down there is a drop-off with tunnels and caves full of the usual suspects.

EXPLORING MAYAN RUINS

When the Spanish Conquistadores arrived in Mexico in 1521, the Mayas who dominated the Yucatán Peninsula had almost disappeared. But 500 years earlier they were living in a sophisticated culture with magnificent temple complexes and trading routes throughout the region, both on the land and along the coast and among the nearby islands. When their civilization declined, the thick jungle quickly covered and buried their pyramids and temples.

But archaeologists were suspicious about the unusual mounds on the otherwise flat landscape. Excavations revealed overgrown cities with huge temple complexes. The peninsula is still dotted with suspicious mounds waiting to be excavated and explored.

Top and right: Tulúm, on the Caribbean, 32 miles south of Playa del Carmen, is the most visited of all Maya sites. Left: Ruins near Costa Maya. This site, like many major Mayan ruins, used to be a mound of vegetation in the jungle until it attracted the curiosity of archaelogists.

Grand Princess approaching the pier at Costa Maya. Set in the middle of miles of totally undeveloped coast, you'll find sort of a Mayan theme shopping park with a wide variety of local craft items. There are plenty of water toys to go around here for kids and parents as well.

Costa Maya

Also known as **Majahual**, this port, situated between Cozumel and Belize, was created out of an undeveloped part of the Yucatán jungle specifically to serve cruise ships. As the cruise industry expanded rapidly in recent years, the Mexican government saw an opportunity to create the nucleus of a development that could eventually grow into something along the line of Cozumel or Isla Mujeres.

What you will find is a new pier leading to a sort of Mayan theme shopping park, complete with restaurants, pool, beach cabanas and many booths leased by vendors who would usually only open when a cruise ship was in port. At the time of my visit in early 2003, the shore on either side stretched away unbroken and undeveloped, much as it was in Mayan times. Many visitors here take a tour to Mayan ruins, or grab a cab to the nearby village of Majahual for a slice of traditional Mexican village life.

At a Glance

- Cruise ship facility hacked out from the jungle.
- Pools, restaurants and many craft vendors
- Cultural demonstrations.
- Nearby Mayan ruins.

Belize has the longest coral reefs of the Caribbean.
Right: Many excursions offer excellent opportunities to snorkel or scuba dive.

Belize and Its Reefs

Don't be one of the numerous passengers that come back from a short tender trip ashore to Belize City thinking there's nothing there but the duty-free, crafts, and souvenir shopping center.

Explore! You should consider Belize City as a gateway to some of the more interesting areas of this part of the coast.

Originally settled by the descendants of British pirates, it became the crown colony of British Honduras in 1862. The chief export in the early years was hardwood logs, and settlements grew up along rivers in the forest.

Today many fewer logs are exported, and the main cash crops are sugar, fruits and bananas.

Isolated from the rest of Central America by miles of thick jungle, Belize was in a unique position to establish itself as an ecotourism destination. With relatively few inhabitants – 220,000 in 8,900 square miles (Compare to El Salvador on the Pacific coast–smaller in size, but with 6 million!) Belize saw itself in a unique position to promote itself as a eco-tourism destination. Not only having the longest coral reef in the western hemisphere, it has the most accessible tropical wilderness as well, with a wonderfully diverse mix of birds and animals.

For a small country, it is also one of the most culturally diverse. While about a third of the residents are creoles descended from African slaves and British buccaneers, there are two other distinct groups. Most obvious are the Mennonites, easily recognizable by blond hair, fair skin, and very traditional clothes–long dresses for women and often denim overalls for men. Originally from the Netherlands, their arrival in Belize in 1958 marked the hoped-for end of a three-century odyssey that took them to Russia, Canada, and Mexico as they sought freedom from government interference in their affairs. Fortunately, Belize desperately needed people with agri-

AT A GLANCE

- 8,900 sq.. miles.
- Much thick jungle.
- Independent.
- Thinly populated: just 220,000 residents.
- Out of the way, but becoming known for ecotourism and diving.
- Longest coral reefs in Caribbean.

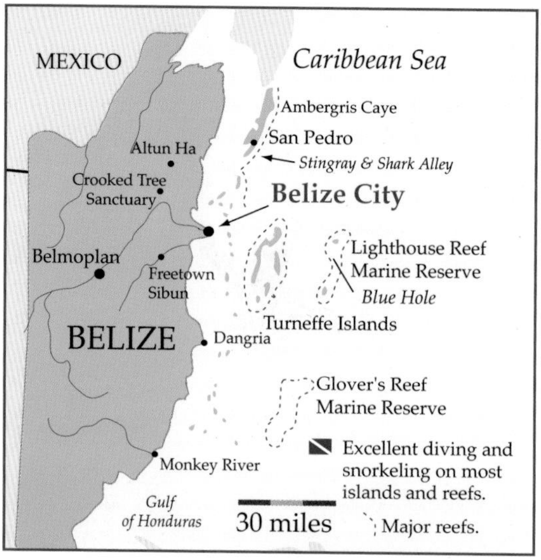

cultural skills, and they had them in abundance. Within a few decades, the Mennonites were producing much of the country's food as well as creating furniture and other craft businesses.

The south of Belize is largely populated by the Garinagu people, who descended from a group of 2,000 free islanders of African descent deported from St. Vincent around 1798. Their story began in 1635 when two slave ships wrecked on St. Vincent. The survivors mixed with the local Carib natives, but when British settlers began to import slaves for their plantations, the presence of a community of free slaves on the island, was at the least, an irritation. So the British shipped them to remote British Honduras.

Belize City used to be the capital, but after a direct bit by Hurricane Hattie in 1916, a new government center, **Belmoplan**, was carved out of the jungle 40 miles southeast.

Visitors with a bit more time might consider a trip to **Freetown Sibun**, about 22 miles east of town. Here you can often arrange river expeditions, or if you have more time, rent a houseboat or a cabin on the river.

The jaguars aren't always in the jungle: downtown San Pedro.

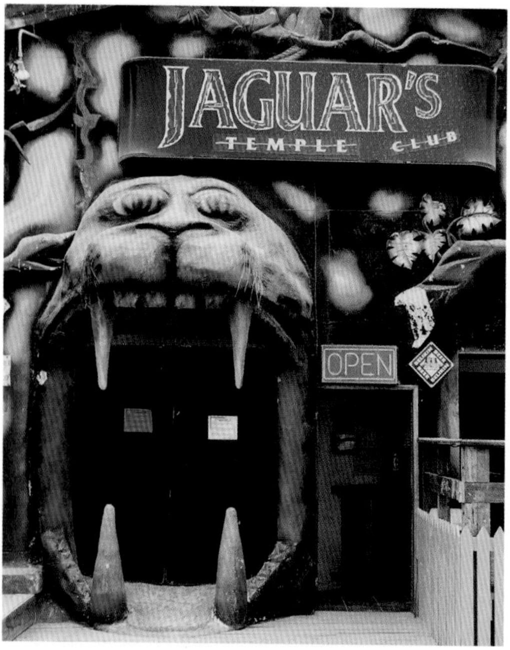

Thirty-three miles north of town is the **Crooked Tree Wildlife Sanctuary**. Here you'll find a sleepy native village and a 3,000-acre sanctuary operated by the Belize Audubon Society. Expect to find a combination of lagoons, rivers and wetlands providing excellent habitat for wildlife.

Further north is the Mayan site of **Altun Ha**, where pyramids and other structures have been cleared in the thick forest.

But most visitors come to Belize to visit the cayes, to experience, in some fashion, the abundant marine life.

Jacques Cousteau's 1972 documentary film of the diving at Lighthouse Reef's **Blue Hole** served notice to the world of the remarkable diving and snorkeling opportunities here, and many non-cruise ship visitors come specifically for the diving.

Many goods still moves among the islands by sailing sloops like this one.

Closest to Belize City are the **Turneffe Islands**. If you're an experienced diver, the wall dive known as "The Elbow" is a major attraction, but be prepared for strong currents. Divers have also reported large numbers of big, but harmless eagle rays here. Fortunately the reefs on the western sides of these islands are generally shallow, making for excellent snorkeling.

Lighthouse Reef is 20 miles further east. The famous **Blue Hole** was created when the roof on an underwater cave collapsed, creating a steep sided hole 400 feet deep that has become one of the world's premier dive sites. Like many of the country's best reef sites, it is now a national monument.

Ambergris Caye, around 30 miles north of Belize City, is served by both ferry and small planes. Most folks live in sleepy **San Pedro**, with its sand streets and more golf carts than cars. The nearby **Hol Chan Marine Reserve** is the destination of many divers and snorkelers. One of the more popular spots is **Shark and Stingray Alley**. Here generations of Belize fishermen cleaned their catches, attracting hungry sea life. A hurricane washed the island totally away, but the sharks and rays still come here. A visit here is quite an experience–you'll be snorkeling in slightly deeper water than Stingray City in Grand Cayman, but the rays will be just as friendly. When I was there in spring of 2003, the big rays would swim close enough to be easily touched. Their skin is delicate, so please remove any sharp jewelry before you go into the water here.

Stingray is a bit of a misnomer; these big rays–up to four feet across from wingtip to wingtip–get their name from a short sharp barb located at the base of their tail. However, it is very safe to swim around them.

If you've never snorkeled, you can't find a better place to start than these crystal clear tranquil waters!

Acknowledgments

Without the help and encouragement of many people this book never would have gotten beyond the idea stage. In particular, I want to thank:

Marsha St. Hilaire of Princess Cruises, for her enthusiasm, confidence, and encouragement.

My designer, Martha Brouwer, for her skill and easy manner in creating an exciting design from a sheaf of words, maps, and photographs.

David McCullough, whose fascinating book, *The Path Between The Seas,* got me thoroughly hooked on the intense drama that went on for more than a century along a rugged strip of jungle that was to eventually become the canal.

Glenn Hartmann, for his sharp editing pencil and thoughtful observations.

My family, for encouraging me through a long project.

Bruce Van Sant, for allowing me to include selections from his excellent book, *The Gentleman's Guide to Passages South.*

And to many friends and shipmates, along The Thorny Path, for sharing their numerous tales of the southern islands.

Joe Upton
West Port Madison
Bainbridge Island, WA
June, 2003

Before turning to writing, Joe Upton worked as a commercial fisherman in Alaska for 20 years. When fish prices collapsed in the mid 1990's, he developed *The Alaska Cruise Companion* for Princess Cruises. In this best selling, unique book and illustrated map set, Upton shares much of the drama and excitement that is Alaska with cruise visitors.

Upton's most recent Alaska book is *Runaways on the Inside Passage*, a novel for teens, published in 2002.

In the fall of 1998, Joe and his wife Mary Lou took their children, Matt, 15, and Kate, 13, out of school for a six-month sailing trip among some of the less visited islands of the Caribbean and then up the east coast of the US. Combining his children's writing–journals, letters, and e-mails–with his own writing, along with port descriptions and the riveting history of the Panama Canal, Upton has created a fascinating reader for Caribbean cruise travelers.

The Uptons live on Bainbridge Island, in Puget Sound, Washington.